Essays on the Modern Wind Band

Books by David Whitwell

Philosophic Foundations of Education
Foundations of Music Education
Music Education of the Future
The Sousa Oral History Project
The Art of Musical Conducting
The Longy Club: 1900–1917
A Concise History of the Wind Band
Wagner on Bands
Berlioz on Bands
Chopin: A Self-Portrait
Liszt: A Self-Portrait
Schumann: A Self-Portrait in His Own Words
Mendelssohn: A Self-Portrait in His Own Words
La Téléphonie and the Universal Musical Language
Extraordinary Women

Aesthetics of Music

Aesthetics of Music in Ancient Civilizations
Aesthetics of Music in the Middle Ages
Aesthetics of Music in the Early Renaissance
Aesthetics of Music in Sixteenth-Century Italy, France and Spain
Aesthetics of Music in Sixteenth-Century Germany, the Low Countries and England
Aesthetics of Baroque Music in Italy, Spain, the German-Speaking Countries and the Low Countries
Aesthetics of Baroque Music in France
Aesthetics of Baroque Music in England

The History and Literature of the Wind Band and Wind Ensemble Series

Volume 1 The Wind Band and Wind Ensemble Before 1500
Volume 2 The Renaissance Wind Band and Wind Ensemble
Volume 3 The Baroque Wind Band and Wind Ensemble
Volume 4 The Wind Band and Wind Ensemble of the Classical Period (1750–1800)
Volume 5 The Nineteenth-Century Wind Band and Wind Ensemble
Volume 6 A Catalog of Multi-Part Repertoire for Wind Instruments or for Undesignated Instrumentation before 1600
Volume 7 Baroque Wind Band and Wind Ensemble Repertoire
Volume 8 Classical Period Wind Band and Wind Ensemble Repertoire
Volume 9 Nineteenth-Century Wind Band and Wind Ensemble Repertoire
Volume 10 A Supplementary Catalog of Wind Band and Wind Ensemble Repertoire
Volume 11 A Catalog of Wind Repertoire before the Twentieth Century for One to Five Players
Volume 12 A Second Supplementary Catalog of Early Wind Band and Wind Ensemble Repertoire
Volume 13 Name Index, Volumes 1–12, The History and Literature of the Wind Band and Wind Ensemble

www.whitwellbooks.com

David Whitwell

Essays on the Modern Wind Band

EDITED BY CRAIG DABELSTEIN

WHITWELL PUBLISHING • AUSTIN, TEXAS, USA

Whitwell Publishing, Austin 78701
www.whitwellbooks.com

© 2013 by David Whitwell
All rights reserved.

Printed in the United States of America

This book includes essays originally written between 2000 and 2011.

PAPERBACK
ISBN-13: 978-1-936512-68-3
ISBN-10: 1936512688

Composed in Bembo Book

Contents

	Acknowledgement	vii

PART I: ON THE REPERTOIRE OF THE WIND BAND

Chapter 1	The Roots of the Modern Wind Band	3
	The Roots of the Wind Band (1992)	3
	Views of Distinguished Composers (1967)	8
Chapter 2	On the Lack of a Standard Repertoire	15
	On the State of the Profession (1977)	16
	On Forgotten Band Repertoire (2010)	19
	On our Fatal Error in Commissioning (2010)	23
Chapter 3	On My Attempts to Broaden the Repertoire	27
	Forgotten Wind Music (1966)	29
	Band Music from a Historical Perspective (1967)	37
	Vaclav Nelhybel	40
	Karel Husa	45
	Frank Erickson	50
	Ernst Krenek	52

PART II: THE MEDIUM IS THE MESSAGE

Chapter 4	On Commercial Driven Education	59
	James Neilson on the Ethical Responsibilities of the Band Director (1974)	61
	James Neilson on 'The Changing Scene' (1974)	64
	James Neilson on Ethics in Performance (1974)	68
Chapter 5	On the Futility of Band Organizations	71
	The CBDNA in the Future (1975)	77
	CBDNA and the Bicentennial (1976)	79
	On the Direction of WASBE (1999)	81
	On the Future of WASBE (2000)	83
	International Gesellschaft zur Erforschung und Förderung der Blasmusik (IGEB)	85
	Recommendations for the ABA (1993)	86

Part III: On Bands in the Educational World

Chapter 6	On University Education being based on a Sixth-Century Philosophy	93
	The Forgotten Man in the Music Department	94
	On the Nature of the Present Tense In Music	100
	Where is the Value in Conducting Clinics?	103
	Some Band Conductors Remembered	106
	Observing the Great Ones	111
	On University Life	125
Chapter 7	On High School Band Activities	131
	On Adjudicating Music Competition	137
	A Proposal for a New Festival Format	140
	A Letter to California High School Band Directors (1991)	142
	On Honor Bands and Orchestras	145

Part IV: In Memory of Frederick Fennell

Chapter 8	Fennell as I knew him	157
	About the Author	173
	About the Editor	175

Acknowledgments

I am indebted to my friend and colleague, Craig Dabelstein, for his help in preparing this book for publication.

                David Whitwell
                Austin, 2013

PART I
On the Repertoire of the Wind Band

The Roots Of The Modern Wind Band

As an artistic principle, I believe all cultured persons would agree with this statement: 'The Orchestra is not important; it is the Music the Orchestra performs before its listeners which is important.' From this it follows that the artistic value to society of any orchestra, indeed the very definition of what 'orchestra' means to a given community, is based on the nature of the music it performs. Historically this has remained true; what the word 'orchestra' has meant to eighteenth-century London or nineteenth-century Vienna has been defined by its repertoire.

In the case of the wind band, whose history is far more ancient than the orchestra, one can more clearly see that its definition and subsequent repertoire has also been shaped by its sponsors: the church, the court and the military. At every moment, however, its purpose, value to society and its repertoire have been inseparable parts of its definition.

An overview of the wind band's evolutionary changes was the subject of an essay I wrote for a 1992 meeting in Rochester, NY, celebrating the fortieth anniversary of the Eastman Wind Ensemble.

On the Roots of the Modern Wind Band

Those conductors who today make music with wind ensembles and wind bands are contemporary participants in an art form which can be documented in an unbroken tradition reaching back to the very earliest records of man. Individual wind instruments are still extant in specimens of actual instruments and cave paintings from the Upper Paleolithic Period (30,000 to 10,000 BC) and performances by ensembles of wind instruments are clearly documented as a part of the daily life in the civilizations of Ancient Greece and Rome, and even before among the peoples of Ancient Egypt, the Near East and China.

The traditions established by these ancient ensembles continued into the period of modern history we associate with Western Europe and the Christian Era. During the Medieval and Renaissance Periods there were independent wind bands maintained by the members of the aristocracy, civic governments and the Church. By the fifteenth century there were regular outdoor concerts performed by wind bands and from the sixteenth century a substantial repertoire of music played by these bands is extant.

Wind Bands during the Baroque Period

The Baroque Period is one of the most interesting chapters in the history of the wind band. The wind band entered the Baroque with the old shawms, bombards and trombones and exited the Baroque in a new instrumentation—the modern oboes, bassoons and horns.

The first band to use the new French oboes and bassoons was the twelve-member private wind band of Louis XIV, known as the *Les Grands Hautbois*. All of Europe was influenced by the court of Louis XIV, the 'Sun King,' as can be seen in the imitation of French taste in architecture, food, clothes and in the use of French as the diplomatic language for all of Europe. It is no surprise, therefore, that this wind band was also widely imitated and similar ensembles rapidly appeared in the major courts of Germany under the half-French and half-German name, *Hautboisten*. This name was used in Germany for both the independent military bands and for the court wind bands which functioned in imitation of the *Les Grands Hautbois*.

This latter ensemble, the German court *Hautboisten*, imitated the French model in its instrumentation, but not in its repertoire. The repertoire of these German bands developed from the sixteenth-century Italian church forms which had spread North during the seventeenth century: the intrada, aria, canzona, sinfonia, sonata, overture and concerto da camera.

The original overtures (a multi-movement form) and concerti for oboes, bassoons and horns by late Baroque composers in Germany, such as Telemann, Molter, Venturini, Muller and many more, are the immediate predecessors of the music for the same instrumentation which in the following generation is called *Harmoniemusik*. The Baroque overture became the Classical Period divertimento and the Baroque concerto became in the Classical Period the partita for wind ensembles and the sinfonia for string ensembles.

Although they are thus distinguished by their literature, the late Baroque *Hautboisten* and the Classical *Harmoniemusik* were the same medium: they were indeed 'oboe bands,' in so far as the principal melodic instrument was the oboe and they functioned as performance media for the aristocracy. These two characteristics, as we shall see below, form an important background for understanding the aesthetic and sociological development of the modern wind band.

Wind Bands during the Classical Period

The aristocratic *Harmoniemusik* of pairs of oboes, bassoons, horns and later clarinets was the most important wind band of the Classical Period, especially in the German-speaking countries. On the basis of scant information available to former scholars, the activities of this ensemble have for years been misrepresented as functional music, in particular, 'table music.' Thanks to research carried out during the past decade by a large number of scholars, one can now see that this wind ensemble consisted of the finest artists available and functioned in the court environment as fully as any other kind of musical medium then present. On the basis of actual music I have examined in libraries throughout Europe, together with other court documentation from the period which has become available, I believe that between 1750 and 1790 the *Harmoniemusik* performed as a 'concert' ensemble or in a 'functional' role in about the same ratio as any other medium. Anyone who proposes that this wind medium was considered during the time as being anyway less aesthetic than any other medium is making a judgment which cannot be supported by the extant music and documentation.

There were also military bands, however, even when they had the same instrumentation as the *Harmoniemusik* they tended to go under different names—*Feldmusik*, *Türkischemusik*, etc. But it was the indoor, concert *Harmoniemusik* for which there is so rich an extant repertoire, for it was these bands, and not the military ones, for whom virtually all the leading composers composed. The four-movement form 'partita' was considered at the time to be a synonym for 'symphony,' the terms being a designation of instrumentation and not a distinction in aesthetic aim.

The *Harmoniemusik* stood at the heart of musical activity in Central Europe during the Classical Period, but it was short lived for the same reason it surged into prominence—its relationship with the aristocracy. With the economic retrenchments necessary to support the military campaigns which occupied Europe from the beginning of the French Revolution to the end of the Napoleonic period, the *Harmoniemusik* became too expensive a luxury. The players who made up these ensembles did not lose their jobs, however, for it was the *Harmoniemusik* which became the basic wind section of the classical orchestra—another private, aristocratic medium.

A new kind of *Harmoniemusik* appeared during the late Classical Period, born, as the 'oboe band' had been earlier, in France. This new *Harmoniemusik* was identified by two characteristics which clearly set it apart from the long established *Hautboisten* tradition. First, the clarinet displaced the oboe as the principal melodic vehicle. Second, the 'clarinet band,' with a few exceptions admitted, tended to perform not for the aristocracy, but for the public.

The first of these 'clarinet bands' was an ensemble of clarinets, bassoons and horns which existed among the employees of a wealthy citizen of Paris, known as La Poplinière (1693–1762). I believe the choice of clarinets over oboes had some relationship to the royal *Les Grands Hautbois* which still existed. Perhaps, at first, Le Pouplinière and those who followed in forming 'clarinet bands,' among whom were the Duke d'Orléans, the Prince de Condé, the Prince of Monaco, and others, were only observing some protocol in not imitating too closely the king. Later, however, during 1789–1796, I believe one can say the clarinet sound was more directly anti-monarchical. Even though the 'clarinet band' can be documented in the courts of some French aristocrats before the revolution, it did appear first in the employ of a non-aristocrat and, in any case, rapidly became a public medium in its role as the French military band. Furthermore, one sees for the first time the doubling of clarinets in the typical military instrumentation of four clarinets, with pairs of bassoons and horns. This doubling of the melodic vehicle, the clarinet, was for the purpose of the augmentation of the sound in the out-of-doors. In the case of the principal military band in Paris during the revolutionary years, one finds the doubling of all instruments as that band had on occasion to perform in stadiums seating up to 400,000 members of the public!

The Wind Band during the Nineteenth Century

During the period of the Napoleonic Wars, 1790–1815, yet another new kind of band appears. This was the band of the civilian militia, which was called 'Volunteers' in England and *Schützencorps* in Germany. These were troops of civilians who, eager to join in the consuming public interest in all things military at the time, formed their own small military organizations in each town. These civic militia bands were modeled generally after the 'clarinet bands' and not after the aristocratic 'oboe band,' although as they were military bands one is not surprised to see the addition of at least one trumpet, together with percussion to the nucleus of the four clarinets and pairs of horns and bassoons of the French model. Here we can clearly see not only the modern band instrumentation in its initial stage of development, but the fundamental characteristics which would remain descriptive of bands in many part of the world today: [1] a woodwind–brass–percussion ensemble in which the doubled clarinet is the principal melodic vehicle, [2] an ensemble of civilians who dress in military-style uniforms, and [3] an identification with the broad public, rather than with the aristocrats.

For serious musicians who had spent their lives performing before a small handful of listeners in the palace, the new opportunity to perform before the general public must have been an exhilarating experience. In Germany and Austria large military bands, often composed of engaged civilians together with a smaller number of career military musicians, were soon performing concerts before enthusiastic audiences numbering in the thousands. At first these concerts were nearly always exclusively aesthetic in aim and repertoire. The description of one of Europe's leading critics, Hans von Bülow, of a band concert conducted by Piefke in 1858,

> The technical perfection, the painstaking nuance of every detail, the majestic power of the mass impression and finally the fresh full vibrating spirit of the noble performances …

was by no means an isolated reaction. The response of the public can be measured in part by the demand for the appearance of military bands in opera and in the attempts by composers and publishers to use the band to 'prepare' the public for the publication of orchestral music in its original version.

Unfortunately, conductors being insatiable as they are by nature, this was not enough. Nearly everywhere band directors during the final decades of the nineteenth century sought to further widen their audiences by successively lowering the quality of their repertoire. They succeeded in enlarging their numbers of listeners, but at the expense of losing their identification with aesthetic music. Thus there was once seen a sign before the Crystal Palace in London, 'There is no concert today, the band is going to play.' But, as I said, this happened nearly everywhere, thus for many average citizens in Germany and Austria today, 'wind music' (*Blasmusik*) is a synonym for 'folk music.' It was this environment which set the stage for Sousa, by the way, who thought of himself as entertaining the public, in contrast to the role of orchestras in 'educating' the public.

Unfortunately, early in the twentieth century the horrors of World War I brought an end to the public's fascination with the adventures of the military and at the same time there arrived an onslaught of new entertainment media, in particular movies, radio and TV. The result has been a full-scale retreat by the broad public which the band had for fifty years so energetically courted. Ironically, the orchestra, which had never courted the broad public during the nineteenth century (having been a private aristocratic institution in most places until rather late) has seen its audience grow to the point that today it is clearly larger than that of the band. And it has done this without losing its aesthetic image, even though it too became a civic institution with the fall of the monarchies in 1917.

It is quite incorrect to say, as one often hears, that the difference is one of literature. Anyone who spends a little time in European libraries will discover that the orchestra, like the band, has a vast repertoire of entertainment music as well as aesthetic music. The real difference is that twentieth-century orchestral conductors have, for the most part, refused to perform anything but aesthetic music. And make no mistake about it, the conductor of the Berlin Philharmonic still has that choice today—it would be very easy to turn the Berlin Philharmonic into a vehicle aimed at a broader public.

Band directors have had a very difficult time in giving up their late nineteenth-century heritage of entertaining the public. But the fact remains, in every art form there is a freedom of choice; each conductor can make of his medium what he will.

☙❧

THE ABOVE FATE of the European wind bands was mirrored in America. The great touring bands of Sousa, Prior, Conway and others, provided musical entertainment to very large audiences until the advent of the 5¢ movie, an even more broadly entertaining medium which rapidly closed out the touring band era. Those who heard the final concerts of the famous Sousa Band recall very small audiences in high school auditoriums, with Sousa desperately instituting saxophone ensembles and a variety of comedy acts in a sad attempt to regain his audience.

It was during this same period that the growth of public school bands began. Since they had imitated the famous touring professional bands in dress, instrumentation and repertoire, the relatively sudden disappearance of the professional bands left the school band directors rather disconnected with society. But this disconnect only occurred because these band directors had not identified with the real society of music lovers, but rather only with a handful of 'hero' professional band directors who were now gone.

The school band directors tried to hang on to what was left of the past by continuing to perform the role of entertaining the public, even though as the century progressed numerous new and more exciting forms of entertainment were continually being born. Nevertheless the model of the band director as entertainer of the public has been very hard to change. As a result, for most of the twentieth century the band held a less respected place among the public interested in aesthetic music.

The irony is that while this disconnect between band directors and the artistic public continued, there was at all times a large number of serious composers who held no prejudice against wind instruments and on their own wrote numerous solo works, music for small and large wind ensembles and for band on their own. This particular body of band music was unknown, and is still unknown, to nearly all band directors because of the disconnect between educational institutions and the public which supports aesthetic music.

In general, during the first half of the twentieth century, music critics ignored bands and when they mentioned them their comments were often negative toward wind instruments in general. In the 1960s I read such a comment by a London critic and, as a serious young conductor, was disturbed by it. On an impulse I wrote to a number of distinguished composers to see if they held such prejudice. I publish their answers below and the reader will see that none held such prejudice towards winds or bands and the reason is worthy of reflection. You see, for them, the real musicians and composers, it was not the medium that mattered, only the music.

Views of Distinguished Composers (1967)

1) Henk Badings (1907–1987) was a well-known Dutch composer.

Henk Badings to David Whitwell
Dettenhausen, Germany, March 8, 1967

The artistic value, aesthetic potential and information content of a musical composition are in my opinion only indirectly related to the used sound sources.

The philharmonic orchestra, with a kernel of strings, is a product of music history, it has developed organically as languages grow, but like the development of English in England, USA, Australia, Scotland or in a not yet realized direction does not result in one good and for the rest basically unsatisfying languages. There is no reason why another instrumental combination—like wind ensembles—would be excluded as a vehicle of the highest art.

2) Aram Kachaturian (1903–1978) was one of the great Russian/Armenian composers of the twentieth century.

Aram Kachaturian to David Whitwell
Moscow, Russia, July 10, 1967, written in Russian

Esteemed Mr. Whitwell!

First of all wind instruments must be divided into woodwind and brass instruments. It seems to me that woodwind instruments are more expressive than the brass instruments, and certainly, technically, are more mobile and volatile.

But to get along without wind instruments, and especially, without brass, for strong, patriotic expressions and big dramatic events, is impossible. In our time it seems to me it is necessary to treat horns like trumpets, trumpets almost like clarinets, and clarinets like violins, except for the double stops. It is wrong to consider that any one group of instruments in a symphony orchestra is better than another. Yet it is true that one can listen longer to strings than to the wind instruments.

[The London critic has written]: 'Wind instruments fatigue listeners very much.' I would say, not fatigue, but bore, or tire, it., one gets sooner used to the timber of wind than strings. If we are to take neither wind nor string instruments, for instance, but such instruments as vibraphone, xylophone and celesta, they begin to fatigue or tire one sooner. I think it is due to the bright, clear timbre which our memory retains better.

Of all these groups, string instruments are the richest, and one can listen to them for a long time. String instruments have four strings, each one of which has its own timbre and this enriches beauty of color shading.

It seems to be that the most interesting idea is mixing or connecting of different colors. This is one of the principles of instrumentation for a symphony orchestra.

In closing, I want to say that I love wind instruments very much. I feel that they have great possibilities technically, and for expression.

For the past one hundred years, the development of the orchestra moved principally along the lines of wind instruments.

3) Benjamin Britten (1913–1976) was one of the leading English composers of the twentieth century.

Benjamin Britten to David Whitwell
Aldeburgh, England, March 6, 1967, dictated to his secretary, J. W. Cullum

[That anyone would question the importance of wind music] seems rather curious in view of the most remarkable Serenade for 13 wind instruments by Mozart. [I have just had] the first performance of a new work—*Hanken Booby*, folk-song tune arranged for ten wind instruments and drums; it is very short.

4) Ingolf Dahl (1912–1979) was also a very distinguished professor for many years at the University of Southern California.

Ingolf Dahl to David Whitwell
Altussee, Austria, August 23, 1967

Since I am trying to finish a composition before my imminent departure this little note will perforce be short, sketchy and strictly 'off-the-cuff.'

Wind instrument combinations certainly have been made into 'vehicles of the highest art,' and I don't have to enumerate them. Also, whose concerts of wind music *can* be 'wearisome,' but they certainly *need* not be so. It all depends, as in any concert, on the skill and imagination of programming (variety of styles, periods, combinations) as well as the artistry of the performers. Besides, I myself have found a whole evening of unrelieved string quartet playing just as 'wearisome.'

The aesthetic potential of wind instrument combinations is great! It is probably not quite as great as the aesthetic potential of mixed instrumental groups for one simple reason, of which every composer and orchestrator (particularly in the films) is quite aware: wind instruments have a hard time, or are sometimes even incapable, of being a neutral, self-effacing, colorless background. And the absence of this neutral 'no-color' color is what mitigates against the all-wind programs and against the expressive range of wind instrument combinations. Flutes and clarinets in certain registers and with skilled players can do it, but even that is no substitute for the kind of 'all-purpose gray' of which the strings are capable *for miles on end* and which they can do without strain. The absence of the potential of this neutrality of sound is what can make a whole evening of wind ensemble music a problem. But with skillful programming, the occasional addition of a piano (Mozart, Beethoven and Herzogenberg Quintets, Riegger and Weiss Sextets, etc.) or percussion this can be easily solved.

Frankly, the most 'wearisome' thing I know is a Lieder recital (two hours! worth of soulful three-minute tidbits). I find some of my best concert memories are wind concerts (Danzi Quintet, New York Wind Quintet, Los Angeles Wind Ensemble in a Mozart-Toch program under Steinberg, etc., etc.) So, after having demolished [the London critic's] somewhat silly, supercilious, pontifical and unfounded statements, let's go back to making the best music we can!

Cordially yours,
Ingolf Dahl

5) David Diamond (1915–2005), American composer and long time professor at the Juilliard School of Music in New York.

David Diamond to David Whitwell
New York, NY, April 11, 1967

A whole evening of woodwind music is not 'wearisome'—only the programming can be. But that can be so at a symphony or string quartet concert. Three Beethoven or three Bartok quartets are too many for me in one evening; and yet the ideas are first-rate. So it is a matter of contrast in individual composers' works for one medium that is important. In general the composers chosen for an evening of woodwind music are third-raters.

Here is my idea of a not wearisome evening: A Hindemith woodwind quintet, the Carter or Barber works for that medium, my woodwind Quintet. Or: Strauss, Hindemith, Carter. Or: David Diamond Quintet, Reicha, Schonberg (very long) but works well with mine and Reicha. Forget authorities of any kind who write on 'Chamber Music.' Just play good music programmed well.

6) Alan Hovhaness (1911–2000), an Armenian composer, was one of the most prolific composers of the twentieth century. His more than 400 works included 67 symphonies.

Alan Hovhaness to David Whitwell
Seattle, WA, early March, 1967

Thank you for your good letter—I also love wind instruments and my whole purpose is to bring every ensemble into the realm of highest art ... Much should be written to contradict [the London critic's] chapter on wind music.

    He may be right if one considers the European development of strings, especially the string quartet, and the classical symphonic style of central Europe 1700–1830 roughly—but extending in both past and future—However that period is only one great musical period—earlier European music was vocal and since 1900 wind music has improved.

    True, the greatest European masters have not succeeded or not even tried to write their greatest music for winds alone, but let us remember that European culture is only a small part of the civilizations of past and future. It is quite different with the great orchestral music of Tang China about 700 which is equal and superior to European music in many respects—that music developed subtleties in wind instruments unknown today—the art of 'Embai' or darkening and covering of tones created a wind style even more subtle than our present highly evolved string style.

    Now my Symphony Nr. 17 for 6 flutes, 3 trombones and 5 percussion (no strings) is my highest contribution to music for winds so far—so also are my operas 'Pilate,' 'Burning House,' 'Trauguers' using no strings.

    Symphonies Nr. 4, 7, 14, 17 as well as 'Return and Rebuild the Desolate Places' are wind symphonies without strings—of course many chamber combinations such as 'Koku no Niwa' (Moss Garden), 'Flowering Peach' (excuse harp), 'World Beneath the Sea,' Nr. 1 and Nr. 2, as well as choral works, 'Glory to God,' 'Look Toward the Sea,' use no strings, only wind and percussion.

    There is much to be done by both composers and wind players and conductors, but I believe a new Art is being created now which will compare favorably with the string quartet and symphony of Europe 1750–1890—please excuse those poorly written ideas—I am busy working and am doing very poorly in answering your important and thoughtful letter—of course we are doing much to develop subtlety in percussion and combinations of subtle percussion and winds is a now highly imaginative art of music. We must create poetic percussion or a poetry of percussion and a poetry of winds. It is our crudely military use of percussion and winds that justify negative remarks ...

    But composers and players must both learn and improve this art. I find few percussion players understand subtle musical problems, also in most European countries. Brass playing is still on a comparative unsubtle low level of development. The performance of my Symphony Nr. 17 is an example—if good flute players who can produce mikro tonal slides by turning the instrument etc., then we often find crude or toneless trombones who play fast smears and fail to give majestic grandeur or slow mikro tonal glissandi—also a certain stiffness inhibits the grand effects and inaccuracies in mallet instruments prevent the bells, also marimba and xylophones from achieving high art. The poor unsubtle rhythmic training in percussion does much to destroy our attempts at higher art ... We need more conductors, also players, with your idealism and with the power to inspire, not follow, audiences.

Best wishes, sincerely
Alan Hovhaness

PS: Possible ways to create new ideals:
   Study in Japan: Shakuhachi, Music of Gagaku, study of rhythm and non-rhythm.
   Study in Korea (National Institute): Piri, Teikueum, Music of Ah-ak, Music of Kagok.
   Study in India: Ngagswaram (South India), Shanoi (in North India). Study of music theory in South India—Raga—melodic systems—Tala—rhythm systems.
   We must add these other dimensions to the dying European systems.

7) Walter Piston (1894–1976) was recognized as one of the most important American composers of the twentieth century.

Walter Piston to David Whitwell
Belmont, MA, May 4, 1967

I had been hoping to get time to write at length on the subject of wind instruments, but, alas, I can do no more than comment five or six words! It goes without saying that I completely disagree with the observations of [the London critic]. Of course it depends on the background and culture of the one who is listening, but at the same time I have found many uneducated persons very receptive and pleased with a wind program. The problem is to find enough pieces, since it is a difficult medium for the composer as well as for the performer. You certainly know all this, but I can only say I agree with you.

8) Ross Lee Finney (1906–1997) was a distinguished composer at the University of Michigan for many years. Among his teachers was Alban Berg in Vienna.

Ross Lee Finney to David Whitwell
Ann Arbor, MI, April 14, 1967

Winds always embarrass me as a composer. Part of it is that wind players in ensembles don't know how to rehearse; they play a work over and over but they don't seem to have the ability that a string quartet has of understanding the MUSIC and creatively projecting it. They read much better than string players; in fact they are remarkable readers but that seems as far as they go. Is it that they expect a conductor to do the creative musical job for them? Let me illustrate: in a premiere the composer hopes to have the details of articulation and tempi crystallized. He has undoubtedly been very careful in his notation, but it is the first performance that clarifies his doubts and makes it possible for him to properly edit the score. Performers vary, of course, in the help they give. Menuhin was enormously contributive to me in the work I did for him. The Stanley Quartet gives endless help. John Kirkpatrick, the pianist, wrote me hundreds of letters as he worked out my piano sonatas. My experience has been that woodwind quintets give nothing. It never dawns on them in a premiere that they have a creative job. (There are, I feel sure, exceptions, but I have not been so fortunate as to meet them.) So the performance sounds OK in a kind of blah way but it doesn't sound as you thought it might and you don't know for sure whether it ever could.

Interest in wind writing seems to me to do largely with articulation in its relationship to breath. Trouble is that wind players are so conditioned to a 19th century articulation, except in the orchestra if there is a good conductor. Performers can play all sorts of interval leaps etc., but they don't always make it add up to a musical continuity. It is true, of course, that the musical fabric for winds is more fragile and less cohesive than strings, and this forces the composer to find a simple statement that is meaningful—not easy in any art. To add strings makes the problem less.

Mannerisms of winds have been too much stressed with the result that the instrument becomes sterile in its growth. Things are changing! Thank God! Look at the flute. It used to play nothing but pastoral music: now it is in the manure heap and a lot more interesting for being there. The clarinet led the way because of jazz; it never was entirely respectable. But the bassoon and oboe are frustrating. Perhaps they just haven't got what it takes; perhaps they can only be color in the orchestra. Seems a pity. No problem with the trumpet (except orchestral trumpets aren't usually as good as jazz trumpets and ditto for trombones.) The horn has a natural aristocracy and so much variety that one doesn't worry. But all wind players should take a fresh look at the sound possibilities that lay outside of what they think is 'beautiful' tone.

I'm doing a concerto for orchestra and six wind instruments—flute, oboe, clarinet, horn, trumpet, trombone. It's fun but hard. I love the tuba!

Pardon this careless letter.

9) **William Schuman (1910–1992)** was a distinguished American composer.

I had an occasion to visit with Schuman in 1967 in New York City and he told me he was so busy with his duties as head of Lincoln Center that the only time he had for composition was in driving in to the city in the morning. For this purpose he kept a sketch pad on the passenger seat and he told me he had timed his window shield wipers, which he used as a metronome.

William Schuman to David Whitwell
New York, NY, June 7, 1967

Clearly, you and I are in agreement. We both are very fond of wind music. I would say that a wind ensemble is capable of certain kinds of expressions which strings alone cannot achieve. But I am afraid it is true that if I had to choose between one or the other as a steady diet, I would have to admit that strings are better—in the sense that they form a more general tonal palette than the more precise and unrelieved sounds of winds alone. However there is no question of an argument here, because to my mind there is no doubt that the highest art can be achieved in composing for winds alone. The only point to be made is that the medium is not as varied as strings alone, or strings and winds in combination.

But, let us not permit any academician to talk us out of our love of wind music—even [the London critic], whoever he is.

With every good wish to you, I am
Faithfully,
William Schuman

On the Lack of a Standard Repertoire

ONE OF THE GREAT STRENGTHS OF THE ORCHESTRA is a standard repertoire of fifty or so masterpieces which are performed in enough repetition to allow long-term audience members to become familiar with this repertoire and to look forward to it. It helps give the orchestra an enduring purpose generation after generation.

The band lacks this great advantage even though it has numerous first-rate masterpieces from five centuries in its repertoire. This very abundance is one problem as it tends to entice a conductor to want to always do something new, for his own musical growth perhaps. But in a university environment, where the members of the ensemble change every three or four years, surely there must be some masterpieces which the conductor believes every student must come to know during his life. I think many of us feel this way, but most of us fail to repeat these works in our eagerness to learn a new score. In retrospect, I can certainly think of great compositions, the mysterious and other-worldly *Hammersmith* by Holst comes to mind for example, which I did not perform frequently enough.

But the most important distraction in building a standard repertoire of great compositions has been the tendency toward wanting to entertain the public. Music must be fun! New is fun! But if the purpose is to entertain then one comes under a universal law of aesthetics: entertainment books no competition. That is, you cannot successfully program one great, serious aesthetic composition on an otherwise entertainment program, because in this event the entertainment program absorbs the one aesthetic work and it is lost in the mind of the audience. The reverse is also true, you cannot have a complete program of aesthetic music with one entertainment work because this one work will send the listener home believing he was entertained. Every important philosopher for the past 2,000 years has affirmed this truth. You must elect to give the listener either an entertainment experience or the catharsis of an aesthetic program. There is no middle ground.

For much of the twentieth century band conductors believed that one of the most important principles in constructing a concert program was variety. It is certainly possible to have variety in an otherwise very serious orchestral concert. But in the band world, variety too often became entertainment, in an almost vaudeville formula. If one studies band programs over almost any decade of the twentieth century one immediately encounters this extraordinary variety driven by the need for variety or the need to entertain the audience. One can see this clearly in a study of the profession which the president of the MENC asked me to undertake in 1976–1977. Here were some of the findings.

On the State of the Profession (1977)

The minutes of the first meeting of the CBDNA in 1941 indicate that the only time given to the concert band and its music was a presentation entitled, 'The Concert Band's Place in the Curriculum,' by Harold Bachman of the University of Chicago. The need for more and better literature was seen primarily from the perspective of helping maintain course credits.

By 1949 considerably more attention had been drawn to the common problem of locating literature. The proceedings of that year's convention published extensive lists and sources of band music in print, manuscript band music (388 titles, of which 179 were original compositions), woodwind ensemble music and brass ensemble music. This activity has continued, in one form or another, until the present day.

In 1950 CBDNA president Bernard Fitzgerald of the University of Texas began to shift the focus to the conductor's responsibility toward concert band literature, the necessity for his becoming more selective as well as reaching for higher musical standards of performance. The *1950 Book of Proceedings* included a 'Bibliography of Recorded Band Music,' compiled by Bryce Jordan (who later became president of the University of Texas). It listed 603 items, summarized as follows:

Quickstep marches	61%
Serious music[1]	16%
Patriotic music	6%
Concert marches	5%
Folk music	4%
Novelties	3%
Waltzes, ensembles, solos, fanfares	5%

The composer represented the largest number of times was John Philip Sousa, whose name appeared eighty times.

As college band directors began to concern themselves more with the quality of their literature, there was a natural tendency to look to the publishers as the agents responsible for so much music of doubtful value. As a result, publishers' representatives were invited to address the membership. In addition to presenting the economic realities of their business, they tended to pass the responsibility back to the conductor for the quality of published music. For example, Arthur Hauser of Theodore Presser Company, speaking in December, 1960, noted,

> Some years ago, when addressing CBDNA on a similar subject, I stated that while publishers must accept responsibility for printing much so-called 'poor' music, educators must accept the greater responsibility, because if they would not buy it, the publishers would not publish it. This situation exists principally because many educators have not had sufficient experience with good music to take the lead in insisting on its use in

---

[1] No distinction was made between original works and transcriptions.

their schools. We can expect that in time this might be rectified with a stronger emphasis on quality repertoire in the curricula of music education. I believe one would agree that this situation must be corrected if bands are ever to improve their repertoire. Without a deep-seated understanding of good music, whether it is contemporary or from another period, by many more band directors than represented by your fine organization, I fear that your efforts to improve the literature for bands will take more years than any of us have remaining in this short life.

In 1966 the proceedings of the Southwest Division convention included the findings of a 1963–1964 survey by Ray Tross of more than one hundred university conductors throughout the United States (this survey became the basis for Tross's doctoral dissertation, 'The Present Status of Band and Band Department Ensembles in Higher Education,' at Colorado State College). Tross found a majority of the conductors said they were striving to program original and contemporary works. Major works by such composers as Hindemith, Creston, Persichetti, Nixon and Giannini were beginning to be programmed regularly.

Two hundred and sixty-four concert programs were returned with the questionnaire. Some of the programs lacked a proper balance of literature from different periods. Contemporary and Romantic periods were well represented, the Baroque and Classical Periods less so. Gustav Holst and Ralph Vaughn Williams, two pillars of English band music, still remained perennial favorites for a majority of the college band directors.

One hundred and four conductors were asked, 'Of the compositions in the past five years you have programmed, which do you consider to be the finest and best original band works?' Among the total of 416 compositions listed, the most frequently mentioned were the Hindemith *Symphony for Band*, Giannini's *Symphony for Band*, the Persichetti *Symphony for Band*, both Holst Suites and the Milhaud *Suite Francaise*.

A CBDNA conference in 1960 included some remarks on the band's repertoire by the distinguished composer, Paul Creston, who offered important aesthetic observations. One must program music of 'lasting value' and it must be performed before a 'musically intelligent audience gathered to listen to significant music.' As a serious composer himself, he emphasized the quality of the compositions, concluding,

> The cause of concert band music is not helped in the least by inflicting inept, insignificant and dull tripe upon an audience.

Finally, Creston recalled that his first commission for a band work included two rules: it must be no longer than six minutes in length and must end loud. He argues that what the band needs now (1960) is major works such as 12-minute overtures, 20-minute suites and 30-minute symphonies. There was a time beginning in the late 1970s when bands were indeed beginning to play major works, including lengthy symphonies. Today, unfortunately, college band programs are once again retreating to many works of small duration. Is this because the conductor lacks faith in the intelligence of his listeners or is this the undertow of the entertainment lure once again pulling us down?

The national CBDNA conference held in Ann Arbor, Michgian, in 1967 included a very interesting panel discussion on the band's repertoire. The first speaker was Harold Bachman, born in 1892, who grew up in the last period of the touring professional bands. His basic argument reflected that world, that concerts must have 'audience appeal, geared to the music tastes of their time.' This, of course, is only a disguised argument for entertainment music.

The next speaker was Paul R. Bryan of Duke University, a serious musician who was also a recognized scholar of the works of Johann Wanhal. Paul reviewed the commissioning efforts of the various band organizations and also found a prejudice in favor of playing new works. How, he asked, can we have a repertoire when we give repeat performances of so few of our works?

Robert Vagner, of the University of Oregon, focused on avant-garde music and the efforts in this direction in the band's repertoire. He believed we are limited by the labels we give various kinds of music, quoting Charles Ives who commented, 'Nature builds the mountain and the meadows and man puts in the fences and labels.'

The next speaker was William A. Schaefer, of the University of Southern California. His assignment was to discuss the relevance of transcribed orchestral works for band. He concluded with two points he felt very important. First, commercial music has no place in a university band concert, and second, the students before the conductor are more important than the audience behind him.

I followed these colleagues with a survey of historical band music. I mentioned that the then new concept of the Wind Ensemble was finding a hostile reception within the CBDNA, whose older members did not consider it a 'band.' In fact, as a member of the national board of directors at this time, I urged a new national committee on the wind ensemble. This was rejected by the board, which instead created a new jazz committee. In fact, until 1977 no ensemble calling itself a 'wind ensemble' was ever invited to perform at a national CBDNA conference. As the national president in 1977 I broke that barrier by inviting the Eastman Wind Ensemble to present a concert in celebration of their twenty-fifth anniversary.

Another principle obstacle to developing a standard repertoire of great works is the abovementioned tendency among band conductors to always put the emphasis on performing the latest new composition. While from one perspective this may be considered a worthy objective, at the same time the result is that the great majority of compositions are performed only once by a particular conductor. I have a friend who refers to the band repertoire as 'paper plate' music—you use it once and throw it away. Aside from the aesthetic questions in this practice it is also very uneconomical in terms of the conductor's time. I mentioned above the fact that an orchestral conductor can have a perfectly good career if he knows perhaps fifty works of the standard repertoire. But the band conductor is constantly having to learn new scores, hundreds of them over the course of his career.

Another adverse result in the philosophy of always seeking the new work one hears about, is that it discourages the desire to look among the older important compositions which remain very worthy of performance at any time. To demonstrate this, in 2010 I published an essay in which I listed a number of compositions I had performed and which I regarded as important compositions. I published this list because I was certain most of the conductors who looked at the list would not even recognize most of the works on the list and would perhaps be inspired to look at these scores. I am sure it remains true today, for almost any wind conductor who glances down this list. The source of this list, by the way, is taken from a collection of live recordings made by my California State University, Northridge Wind Ensemble which I donated upon my retirement to the State Academy of Music Library in Trossingen, Germany, where they have established a 'Whitwell Archiv.'

ON FORGOTTEN BAND REPERTOIRE (2010)

Alleppo, Giancarlo.	*Prima Lux*
_____,	*Cogitationes*
Van Ammelsvoort, Jos.	*French Overture*
Bach, J.S.	*Capriccio on the Departure of his Brother*
Badings, Henk.	*Armageddon*
_____,	*Sinfonietta Nr. II*
Batiste, Edouard (19th c.)	*Sinfonie*
Beglarian, Grant.	*Sinfonia*
Beethoven.	*Siegessinfonie*
Benson, Warren.	*Dawn's Early Light*
Berlioz.	*Symphony for Band*
Brahms.	*Begräbnisgesang*, for chorus and band
Broege, Timothy.	*Sinfonia XVI, Transcendental Vienna*
Carafa, Michele (19th c.).	*Allegretto* for solo clarinet and winds
_____,	*Andante* for solo horn and winds
Casella, Alfredo.	*Introduzione Corale e Marcia*
Connor, Bill.	*Tails of the Vienna Woods*
Copland, Aaron.	*Emblems*, composer conducting
Cushing, Charles.	*Angel Camp*
Ellerby, Martin.	*Venetian Spells*
Erickson, Frank.	*Time and the Winds*
Fasch, Johann (Baroque).	*Concerto for Three Bands*
Fauchet, Paul.	*Symphony in Bb*
Fletcher, Grant.	*Concerto for Winds*
Flippa, Giuseppe (19th c.).	*Marcia funebre*
Francaix, Jean.	*Sept danses apres 'Les malheurs de Sophie'*
Franck, Cesar.	*Choral Nr. 2*
Gallo, Vincenzo (19th c.).	*Piccola Sinfonia*
Gossec, Francois (18th c.).	*Hymn to Liberty*, for chorus and band
_____,	*Le Triomphe de la Loi*, for chorus and band

———,	*Marche lugubre*
———,	*Te Deum*, for chorus and band
Gotkovsky, Ida.	*Symphonie pour Orchestre d'Harmonie*
———,	*Poem du Feu*
Gould, Morton.	*Concertette for Viola and Band*
Gulda, Friedrich.	*Concerto for Cello and Wind Orchestra*
Halevy, Jacques (19th c.)	*Marche Heroïque*
Hidas, Frigyes,	*Save the Sea Symphony*
———,	*Coriolanus*
Hindemith.	*Symphony for Band*
Holst, Gustav.	*Suite in F*, Karel Husa conducting
———,	*Music for a London Pageant*
———,	*Hammersmith*
Hovhaness, Alan.	*Symphony Nr. 4*
Husa, Karel.	*Apotheosis of this Earth*
———,	*Concerto for Wind Ensemble*
———,	*Concerto for Trumpet*, Mike Ewald, trumpet
———,	*Concerto for Saxophone*
———,	*Les Couleurs Fauves*
———,	*Music for Prague, 1968*
Hutcheson, Jere.	*Caricatures*
Ito, Yasuhide.	*Glorioso*
Jadin, Hyacinthe (18th c.).	*Ouverture*
von Karajan, Herbert.	*The European Anthem*
Kling, Henri (19th c.).	*Hommage a Haydn*
Lancen, Serge.	*Aunis et Saintonge en Fête*
———,	*Symphonie de L'Eau*
Larsen, Libby.	*Grand Rondo, Napoleon dances the Cancan*
Lefevre, Xavier (18th c.).	*Marche militaire*
Loechlin, Charles.	*Chant Louis XIII*
Linn, Robert.	*Propagula*
Lukas, Zdenek.	*Musica Boehma*
Mahler.	*Um Mitternacht*
Mascagni, arr. Carl Ruggles.	*Introduction and Siciliana from Cavalleria Rusticana*
Maschek, Paul (19th c.)	*The Battle of Leipzig*
———,	*The Occupation of Paris*
———,	*Austria's Triumph*
Maslanka, David.	*Symphony Nr. 2*
Maw, Nicholas.	*American Games*
McCoy, David.	*A Symphony for Salem, 1692*
Mehul, Etienne (18th c.).	*Ouverture*

On The Lack Of A Standard Repertoire

Mejo, Guillaume (19th c.).	*Variations on 'Gaudeamus igitur'*
Mendelssohn, Felix.	*Festgesang*, TTBB and brass
———,	*Overture for Band*
Mertens, Hardy.	*U Mundu Drentu A Ti*
Messiaen.	*Et Exspecto Resurrectionem Mortuorum*
Meyerbeer.	*Torch Dance Nr. 2*
Miaskovsky, Nikolai.	*Symphony Nr. 19*
Milhaud, Darius.	*Suite Francaise*
Munchs, C. (19th c.)	*Overture à Grande Harmonie*
Naylor, Craig.	*Convivial Tides*
Nielsen, Carl.	*Paraphrase on 'Nearer My God to Thee'*
Ochs, Siegfried.	*Variations on 'Kommt a Vogel geflogen'*
Orrego-Salas, Juan.	*Concerto for Wind Orchestra*
Penderecki, Krzysztof.	*Pittsburgh Overture*
Pierne, Gabriel (19th c.)	*Marche Solennelle*
Ponchielli, Amilcare (19th c.)	*Elegia on the Death of Garibaldi*
———,	*Sinfonia in F minor*
———,	*Sinfonia in Bb minor*
———,	*Variations on Carnevale di Venezia*
———,	*Trumpet Concerto*
Poole, Geoff.	*Sailing with Archangels*
Reicha, Anton (19th c.)	*Commemoration Symphony*
Respighi, Ottorino.	*Feste Romane*
Rimsky-Korsakov.	*Variations on a Theme of Glinka*
Saint-Saens.	*Orient et Occident*
Sallinen, Aulis.	*Chorali*
Schmidt-Wunstorf, Rudolf.	*Symphony Ardennaise*
Schmitt, Florent.	*Marche in Eb*
———,	*Dionysiaques*
Schönberg.	*Theme and Variations*
Schubert.	*Hymne*, Op. 154
Schumann, Robert.	*Beim Abschied zu Singen*, for chorus and band
Sibelius.	*Suite for Band*
Sorcsek, Jerome.	*Variations for Band*
———,	*Symphony Nr. 1*
———,	*Symphony Nr. 2*
———,	*Two Chorale Preludes*
Stokes, Eric.	*The 'Continental Harp and Band Report*
Strauss, Richard.	*Ein Heldenleben*
———,	*Rosenkavalier Waltzes*
———,	*Suite in Bb*, Op. 4

———,	*Feierlicher Einzug*
———,	*Also Sprach Zarathustra*
———,	*Till Eulenspiegel*
———,	*Don Juan*
Stravinsky, Igor.	*Le Sacre du Printemps*
Surinach, Carlos.	*Paens and Dances of Heathern Iberia*
Verdi.	*Excerpts from the Manzoni Requiem*
Villa-Lobos,	*Fantasy in the form of a Choros*
Vitaliti, Sebastiano (19th c.)	*Sinfonia, La Corona d'Italia*
Von Weber.	*Concertino for Oboe*
Wagner.	*Rienzi Overture*
———,	*Ring excerpts*
Whitwell.	Symphony Nr. 1, *The Viennese Legacy*
———,	Symphony Nr. 2, *Sinfonia da Requiem*
———,	Symphony Nr. 3, *Meditations on Hamlet*
———,	Symphony Nr. 4, *Symphony of Songs*
———,	Symphony Nr. 5, *Sinfonia Italia*
Widmer, Ernst.	*Variations on 'l'homme arme'*
Williams, John T.	*Sinfonia*

Finally, a remaining question regarding the band's repertoire has to do with the practice of commissioning composer's for new compositions. I have no objection to this practice and there are some non-musical benefits from doing this. Certainly one can imagine, for example, that the numerous commissions which Frank Battisti engaged in while at Ithaca High School must have resulted in significant educational benefits regardless of the quality of the actual resulting compositions (which is not to say, in this case, they were not good).

But there is something questionable about the fundamental idea of commissioning aesthetic music; the practice never seems to produce great music. Think of all the orchestral commissions of the twentieth century. Can you count even on one hand the compositions still in the repertoire? Do we imagine a composer has some great expression within him and that he waits until someone comes along and pays him in advance before he puts pen to paper? Do we imagine our money inspires great expressive ideas within the composer? Stravinsky once addressed this fundamental problem, cautioning that many composers use a commission to merely 'unload' some work that they have on the shelf, or worse yet, perhaps some work they were not previously inspired to finish.

> In the main, however, the need for new cantatas, string quartets, symphonies, is wholly imaginary, and commissioning organizations, like the Ford and Rockefeller, are really only buying up surplus symphonies as the government buys up surplus corn.

We should digress and mention that Mozart appears to be such an example, in his last period in Vienna. It appears that Mozart would sometimes write, let's say a quartet, from his own interest and from his heart and then place the score on the shelf. Sometime later someone might express the desire to commission Mozart to write a quartet and he would say come back in two weeks. Mozart would then take the score off the shelf, sign his name (and sometimes his title) with today's date and hand it to the customer. It is impossible to pin this down because Mozart sometime used manuscript paper which had been purchased at an earlier period. But the fact does remain that the majority of extant Mozart autograph scores have no name or date and can be identified mainly because we know what his calligraphy looks like. And for the most part those which are signed represent cases where he wrote the work for, or gifted, a specific person. Therefore it is possible that he did not sign his autograph scores in the final period at least in the hope he would sell them at a later date.[2] But, let us hasten to add that Mozart is a very unique case. In his case nearly everything he wrote in his mature period is of such high quality that whether or not the work was commissioned seems beside the point.

To return to the subject of finding great repertoire, history clearly suggests that we must be prepared for the possibility of disappointment if we choose to commission a serious composition. But there is something we can do to increase the odds of getting a composer's best work, and in 2010 I wrote an essay on this subject.

On our Fatal Error in Commissioning (2010)

The tradition of commissioning compositions from composers is laudable in many ways, particularly in the cases of interesting composers who have not written for some medium or in helping young composers become better known. However, when one looks at the history of commissioning one cannot help but notice that very few resultant compositions ever enter the repertoire. An objective critic would conclude that this is a form of benevolence but not one that produces great music.

Why is this? The reason is that great music comes from the composer having within him something which he *must* communicate to the world. This comes within the composer and is not for sale.

> The human brain is not a saleable commodity.[3]
> Beethoven

Nevertheless we could greatly increase the odds of getting a great composition for our money if we did not make one fatal error: we fail to tell the composer what we want. We have every right, since it is our money, to tell the composer what we want in terms of the

---

[2] For composers attached to a court, as was not the case in Mozart's final period, their scores frequently have no name simply because everyone in the court knew who wrote the music and no one was yet thinking of posterity.

[3] Draft for a complete edition of his works, Vienna, 1822.

emotional content of the proposed work. This has to be subject number one since the communication of feeling is the only real purpose of music. If words fail, then offer analogy: do we want Mahler's 9th or Salome's Dance of the Seven Veils? At the very least we should make it clear to the potential recipient that the goal is catharsis.

What we cannot accept in our correspondence with the potential composer is any reference to grammar. In recent requests of the past year for conductors to join in consortiums to pay some composer the only reference to what kind of music we are to receive for our money has been descriptions of grammar. A recent proposal read,

> The proposed wind ensemble work will explore poly-modal possibilities using various Indian ragas and shifting tonal centers to affect the perception of modal context. In this way it will blend a rich melodic structure in the Indian tradition with Western harmonic concepts.

This tells us absolutely nothing about the proposed music. Grammar, including everything quoted here, is the composer's business, but it is not the business of the performer or listener. A very simple example: the first chord of Beethoven's Third Symphony is an E♭ chord. Which chord tone the third horn has is grammar and was of particular importance to the composer, who was constructing a chord according to the requirements of the overtone series and his ear. But which tone the 3rd horn has is the composer's business. Changing this tone to a different note of the chord certainly will not affect how this great chord is conducted, nor is it of significance to the listener who does not listen to grammar. A wonderful composer just recently wrote me putting this in the correct perspective:

> Let me, the composer, handle the details of line, series, counterpoint, etc; and let the audience listen to the result that is the aim of all my application of technique and imagination.

So why do conductors keep talking about grammar? Imagine this: every philosopher for 3,000 years has agreed that the purpose of music is to communicate feeling. It is simply uncontested. Conductors are in the business of communicating the composer's feelings to the audience. Why then, instead of trying to talk about this, do they fall back to discussions about grammar?

Music is the only intellectual field where this happens. The critic, teacher or ordinary person who chooses to discuss Shakespeare's *Hamlet* discusses the great themes and ideas found in this work. They do not discuss grammar. Deryck Cooke mentions this in his outstanding book, *The Language of Music*.

We musicians, instead of trying to understand this language [of music], preach the virtues of refusing to consider it a language at all; when we should be attempting, as literary critics do, to expound and interpret the great masterpieces of our art for the benefit of humanity at large, we concern ourselves more and more with parochial affairs—technical analyses and musicological *minutiae*—and pride ourselves on our detached, de-humanized approach.[4]

The purpose of music is to communicate feeling, and yet we don't even try to talk about it with our students. Are we shy? Are we too introverted? Are we afraid to talk about feeling? Are we just teaching the way we were taught? Certainly we are cowards when we don't even try to talk about what is important in music and instead take refuge in the left hemisphere of the brain and lecture on grammar. Like those late medieval Christian flagellants we march along scourging ourselves with switches made of Roman numerals.

Let's be honest about the limits of harmonic analysis. When I was a student at the University of Michigan in the first two years of theory we used a book written by a professor at Eastman which turned the chord progressions of the Bach chorales into statistics. If Bach used a first inversion sub-dominant chord, he followed it 47% of the time by such and such, etc. The book even has a discussion of what the author called the 'Neapolitan second.' But it turns out there is only one instance of this in the entire chorales of Bach—it might have been a printing error! Four semesters, four times through this book. They withheld from us the knowledge that this theory was only valid for the last 15 years of Bach's music in terms of meaningful analysis. This became apparent in my third year when a professor of Form and Analysis gave us a passage from *Tristan* to turn into Roman numerals, etc. It was one of those Wagnerian passages where, using diminished 7ths, he modulates every bar, if not faster. To my horror, having successfully passed the first two years, I could not even figure out what key the music was in—prerequisite to drawing Roman numerals. So I did the most reasonable thing I could think of which was to date a young lady with perfect pitch. I took a score, pencil and portable record player to the lobby of her dorm (in those days that was as far as you could get). I told her I would play the recording and when she felt the music was in some key to shout it out. So we began and soon she said 'E-flat' then 'F minor.' I, with pencil at hand, would quickly mark this on the score. Then I returned to my abode and taking the score I would find whatever chord was mid-point between the marked spots and then write, 'on this chord Wagner modulates from …' What I had learned the first two years did not work, the Roman numerals I created made no sense, my paper made no sense, but I got an A! The object of higher education was accomplished.

Then in graduate school I was required to take another form class. Now we were required to take a pencil and draw Roman numerals for each chord of the entire 3rd symphony of Beethoven. This took some time and I vividly recall today that when I drew that final Roman numeral one under the final beat of the final bar of the fourth movement, my immediate thought was that I had learned absolutely nothing. Whatever the word

---

4 Deryck Cooke, *The Language of Music* (Oxford: Oxford University Press, 1990), x.

'Beethoven' or 'Third Symphony' had meant to me previously had not changed in the slightest degree. Of course, now I was capable, if anyone asked me, of writing an academic book on *Beethoven's Use of the Sub-Dominant Chord in the Third Symphony*.

Finally, responding to that little voice in my head which kept saying 'you don't know anything about theory,' I asked a distinguished composer and theorist to give me private lessons—a very expensive sacrifice for an enlisted man in the military who was also taking graduate work. This man told me that for the first lesson I should bring in the volume of the complete piano sonatas by Beethoven. In that first lesson, he opened the volume at random and we sat together on the piano bench while we looked at whatever page it was and discussed what we saw there. The next week he said bring in any music by Scriabin. The following week, Debussy, etc.

After about seven lessons it suddenly occurred to me that in a broader sense there is no such thing as theory. There is no such thing as the Theory of Mozart. The only place 'theory' exists is in what you see before you. There you can clearly see the theoretical principles at work—why this note has a flat sign and where that note goes next, and why. In other words, if a conductor can understand the music before him, that is all he needs to know about 'theory.' Drawing Roman symbols below each beat will not contribute to his knowledge in any meaningful way. In the time spent doing this he could probably memorize the composition.

And even if a teacher tells you that drawing those Roman symbols will teach you something important, you may rest assured that those symbols will NOT tell you anything about what this composer is communicating to the listener.

To return to commissioning new compositions, if we feel for some reason we cannot demand that the composer tell us what he or she intends to communicate, or we feel for some reason that we are not entitled to tell the prospective composer what WE want and expect for our sometimes vast sums of money, let us at least find some way to remind the composer what the purpose of music is. Cooke puts it this way,

> Music is … the supreme expression of universal emotions, in an entirely personal way, by great composers.[5]

---

5   Ibid., 33.

On My Attempts to Broaden the Repertoire

I WAS REARED IN A SMALL TOWN IN OKLAHOMA where bands and church music existed, but not orchestras. In my public school days I gave no thought to the repertoire for the band, although I do recall on one occasion being somewhat confused why a composition should have the title, *The One-Armed Paper Hanger*.

As a student at the University of Michigan I was first introduced to the world of great orchestral music and wondered why the band only played primarily marches, trumpet trios, suites of Broadway music, comedy works (players jumping up and down, etc.) and an occasional transcription of some orchestral overture. The fact is that the University of Michigan Symphony Band of the 1950s was still living in the shadow of the old touring professional bands whose aim was popular entertainment. Now there will be someone reading this who cries in alarm, 'But what about our performance of the Bach *Prelude and Fugue in D minor*,' etc. Rather than getting into some such argument let me just say that years later Dr. Revelli, after reading some of my articles on the need for better repertoire, approached me and confided that he had taken out his scrapbooks from the years I was at Michigan, had looked at his repertoire and said to me of his repertoire as it appeared to him now, 'and it made me sick!' So think what you will, ex-members out there, but this was the judgment of your conductor.

In retrospect I find it difficult to judge Dr. Revelli in this regard because his education in music history was limited and he was performing the repertoire of nearly all of his colleagues. In fact, those who were playing better repertoire in the 1950s, such as Walter Welke at the University of Washington and Fred Fennell at Eastman, were looked down upon by their contemporaries as being snobs. Fred Fennell was still hurting thirty years later when he confided to me his feelings as a young conductor on being ostracized by these older band directors.

While a student at the University of Michigan I was fortunate to live in an old rooming-house on campus which was populated by horn players, among them H. Robert Reynolds, Howard Howard (later Principal horn in the Metropolitan Opera) and Karl Glenn. This old house was adjacent to a bell tower which at that time housed the library of the School of Music. Being an aspiring young conductor it became my habit to go next door, as time allowed, obtain a score and a recording and return to my room to practice conducting great orchestral compositions. One day, for some reason, I decided to study and conduct one of the major works by Richard Strauss. Upon reaching the appropriate place on a library shelf I was disappointed to find the score I wanted missing. But next to the empty space was a score which read, on the cover, *Symphony for Winds*, by Richard Strauss! I was astounded to find such a score, which was so much more important musically than the repertoire being performed by the university band in which I was a member. I checked this score out and took it to Dr. William D. Revelli to inquire more about this work. Considering the fact that Strauss was one of the most famous composers living during his own lifetime, I was quite bewildered to discover that Revelli knew nothing about this score and, indeed, had never heard of it. The immediate implication for me was, of course, that the library may be filled with such scores which lay outside the knowledge of most band conductors. And so when I had a free hour I ran next door and gradually made my way through the collections of 'complete works' in that library.

My interest in expanding my knowledge of original, early wind band repertoire took a great step forward in excitement during the summer of 1958 when I was a member of the American Wind Symphony of Pittsburgh, conducted by Robert Boudreau. He performed *only* original wind music and as a player I found a real thrill in performing for the first time wind ensemble music by Strauss, Gounod, Villa-Lobos, Mozart and Bruckner. After playing the E minor Mass of Bruckner for chorus and wind band you really cannot ever go back to the *One-Armed Paper Hanger*. You have become a changed person, and that is the purpose of great literature.

When I began my first university position in 1969 I was 25-years-old, had finished a PhD in musicology and had completed four years of full time service in the Air Force band and orchestra in Washington, DC. I was eager to begin sharing some of the information I had been finding about early band repertoire and so I published my first articles in 1964. In 1965 I began a very long series of articles on the wind music of individual composers in the *Instrumentalist* magazine. This was followed in 1966 by my first personal appearance speaking on this topic, before a meeting in Portland, OR, of the Northwest College Band Directors Association. In these early activities I was moving toward presenting a kind of history of music based on wind music, to balance the fact that it had been left out of the traditional music history texts. Today, forty-five years later, many readers, myself included, will see many gaps here which in the future decades would be filled but at the time I am confident there was much here which was new to many band directors.

My comments on Sousa here, and in early articles, caused a great deal of animosity. Since the man and his music are little mentioned today, it is difficult to communicate to the modern reader how strongly the man's memory dominated the university band scene in the 1950s. A university band conductor's conference I attended at this time had, as the first order of business, the request that we all stand for a moment of silence in memory of Sousa. It had the character of a morning prayer to God.

With a strong graduate background in Aristotelian philosophy, it was my purpose at this time to make conductor's understand that they had to make a choice between an aesthetic medium or an entertainment medium. Either we think of the wind music of Beethoven, Brahms, Wagner, etc., as central to our band history, with Sousa and the military lying on the periphery or we make Sousa and the military central to our history, with Beethoven, Brahms and Wagner on the periphery. You cannot have it both ways, for it is going to influence everything in the profession. I am happy to say today that in the subsequent decades the profession made the right artistic choice. But at the time I had threats of violence from a member of the ABA if I ever crossed his path and a number of similar hostile reactions.

Forgotten Wind Music (1966)

The title, 'Forgotten Wind Music,' might perhaps suggest that my intention is to discuss some isolated compositions which I feel have been unjustly forgotten in the course of time. On the contrary, I wish to suggest that to most musicians *all* wind music, save that of our own generation, is virtually forgotten. My concern is that the wind music of this generation may also in time be forgotten, thus rendering our present efforts as teachers and conductors somewhat in vain.

It seems odd that by this date an adequate history of wind music has never been written. It is true that a handful of works regarding the history of bands has appeared. But these have only contributed to the isolation of our medium, for they fail to substantiate wind music's role in music history in general. In truth, the adequate history of wind music will not be written for some years. There are far too many important gaps that must be filled first. For example, one such gap is the role of wind music in late eighteenth-century France. For about two decades the important composers of France happened also to be band conductors. They wrote hundreds of compositions for band, although virtually nothing is known of these works today.

Even the basic music encyclopedias contain little information concerning wind music, wind bands, and wind instrument makers, in spite of their obvious importance at particular stages of music history. At the same time these encyclopedias are filled to the brim with accounts of insignificant, obscure singers and composers.

The music history courses in our undergraduate schools are equally narrow in their view of music history. It is, of course, very easy for a department to so color the history of music. I still remember vividly that in my two years of undergraduate music history I was led to believe that *all* music centered around the string quartet and opera. How surprising to learn later that these mediums were facets of music history and nothing more. Who has ever seen an undergraduate music history textbook which discussed, however briefly, wind music as even a fact of music history? As a result, we are graduating wind teachers and band directors who have absolutely no valid knowledge regarding the history or significance of their medium.

How is it possible that contemporary musicology, which has turned to some of the most minuscule of topics for student dissertations, has left our field so devoid of literature? I am afraid the answer lies in the fact that musicians today are not convinced that unaccompanied wind music was ever part of the main stream of musical endeavor. Moreover, I am afraid there is a logical argument behind this opinion, in spite of occasional masterworks composed for winds and the important supporting role military bands played in the development of the orchestra.

The reason wind music has not appeared to be in the main stream of musical activity is that it has always appeared to be functional instead of esoteric. The military wind bands of the eighteenth and nineteenth centuries were certainly functional and certainly not, in themselves, in the main stream of musical endeavor. The eighteenth-century court composer had little contact with these bands; the nineteenth-century artist–composer had even less contact. In addition, the composer in the eighteenth century worked without the advantage of instruction in orchestration or the publication of scores by other composers. This lack of communication with the peripheral military wind players left most composers with little practical knowledge of wind instruments. This in turn led to some substantial misconceptions.

Bach, for example, in writing 'cornetto' parts did not realize he was writing for an instrument that most of Europe had considered obsolete for decades. Johann Fux even continued writing for this instrument well into the Pre-Classical Period. In Bach's only cantata for voices and winds without strings, Nr. 118, *O Jesu Christ, mein's Lebens Licht*, he composed two parts for 'lituus.' No one has ever been able to figure out what on earth Bach had in mind. The true lituus had been a principal instrument of the Roman army.

This lack of communication between wind players and composers is very evident in the treatment of woodwinds in the eighteenth-century court music, or as they called it, chamber music. For example, both the flute and clarinet entered the orchestra not as individual instruments but as substitute oboes. The clarinet in fact was considered for a time as being a type of oboe. Thus the French *Encyclopadie* (1767) defined the clarinet as a 'sorte de hautbois' and Schubart's *Aesthetik* (1784) called it 'an alto-oboe.' Once composers began to understand the wind instruments the quality of music written for them improved dramatically. Had the wind players not been so removed from intellectual thought, works comparable to the Christian Bach Symphonies and the Mozart Serenades might have appeared decades sooner. The military bands of the day were the source for the unusual instruments, such as basset horns and English horns, whenever called for in an orchestra. Thus although the English horn had been used in military bands for some time, it was unknown in English concert halls when Haydn introduced it in 1795. This is reflected in an item in the *London Morning Chronicle* for May 25, 1795.

> Of the two additional Subscription Concerts, the first was distinguished by the introduction of an instrument called (we know not why) the English Horn; the power, tone and utility of which we are persuaded are highly excellent. It is a tenor instrument, new (as far as our enquiries could extend) to the musical world.

There is every evidence that eighteenth-century composers had no objection to composing for wind instruments, as compared to strings, if given the opportunity. Thus Haydn wrote a number of wind works for Count Morzin's active ensemble in Lukavec, Bohemia, between 1759 and 1761. There are implications, mainly Wagnesiel's compositions, that there was considerable activity in Vienna for a while. One of the most exciting opportunities came in 1782 when Mozart was offered a position as a full-time composer for a newly formed wind band under Prince Liechtenstein. Mozart was interested and perfectly willing to accept, but an agreement on contract details could not be reached. One cannot help but reflect what the future course of wind music might have been, had this not fallen through.

The existence of wind music on the periphery of musical activity in the eighteenth century undoubtedly cost wind literature many masterworks. This is perhaps suggested in Haydn's famous remark to Kalkbrenner, 'I have only just learned in my old age how to use the wind instruments, and now that I do understand them, I must leave the world.'

During the first half of the nineteenth century wind bands seemed to be moving toward the main stream of music culture. The increased activity of the military bands was first evident with respect to opera. It became very popular to have brass bands on stage, somewhere in the course of an opera. In Paris the number of musicians on stage often exceeded the number in the pit. It has been said that this was largely the reason the string body of the orchestra began to increase so rapidly, more than doubling between 1800 and 1850. The idea was so popular that bands were added to performances of earlier works, such as those by Mozart, and even spread as far as Russia. Glinka's *Russlan and Ludmilla* called for three military bands in its original version. It is interesting that even several of Wagner's early orchestral works call for military bands in the finale.

Secondly, and more important, military bands were very influential in the development of the wind instruments themselves. As the military bands were dependent upon wind instruments to carry the melodic line, they were always eager to try any new instrument or any new improvement in mechanics. Since the instrument makers were carrying on research independently and each was surrounded by a number of military bands (there were more than forty near Paris alone), the result was a bewildering variety of wind instruments. Even the standard instruments, such as flutes and oboes, differed radically from area to area. We are not surprised, therefore, that after Berlioz had been invited to judge musical instruments at the Great Exhibition of 1851 in London, he commented,

> It splits your head to hear these hundreds of wretched machines, each more out of tune than the next, three or four excepted.

Later, Rimsky-Korsakov encountered the same problem in Russia. After he was appointed head of Naval Bands in 1873, he thought it would be wise to write a textbook for his wind musicians which would include fingering charts for all the various varieties of instruments. In the end the very size of the task defeated him.

> The woodwinds, in particular, proved to include untold multitudes of makes; in reality each maker or each factory has an individual system. By adding an extra valve or key, the maker either adds a new trill on his instrument or makes easier some run that presents difficulties on instruments of other makes. There was absolutely no possibility of finding one's way through all this maze. In the group of brass instruments I found some with three, four and five valves; the construction of these valves is not always the same on instruments by the various firms. To describe all this was absolutely beyond my power.

The military bands provided a vital proving ground for new instruments as well as the players when these instruments were used in an orchestra.

In spite of these contributions, the wind band, as a concert organization, remained on the periphery. As concert ensembles, the bands, except for France, had almost no original repertoire. Therefore when Rimsky-Korsakov urged public performance for his naval bands it was necessary for him to make a large number of orchestral transcriptions. The lack of repertoire was due in part to the limited opportunities wind bands had to give public performance. Thus Mendelssohn had his early wind band *Overture*, Op. 24, arranged and published for two pianos, simply because he liked it and it was never performed in its original version.

Another problem that tended to keep wind performance on the periphery was that wind instruments were not taught in the conservatories. This meant that all wind instruction was based primarily on tradition. Therefore, Berlioz, on his tour of Germany in 1842–1843 found flute and oboe players still adding ornaments in the eighteenth-century style.

There is at least one instance in the nineteenth century, in which the lack of communication with wind bands seriously hampered the efforts of orchestral composers. This is in reference to the acceptance of the valve, the most important single development in wind instruments in the nineteenth century. The military bands had always lacked a brass instrument which could play a melody, their horns, trumpets and trombones being 'natural' instruments. Thus they eagerly tried such inadequate solutions as slide trumpets, slide horns and keyed trumpets, horns and trombones. The invention of the valve ca. 1815 was the long awaited answer. Due to the great demand for these instruments by military bands and the slow speed with which they could be made, it was not until the 1840s that valve horns began to appear in orchestras. The incredible aspect of this change to the valve horn was that the horn players did not understand that they could apply a 'fingering' combination to each note, in the modern tradition. Rather, they thought that the valve was a device to change the key of the horn, thus eliminating the necessity of carrying around the infamous 'bag of crooks.' In other words, they continued to play the horn as a natural horn. If a player had an F horn and the music was in D, he merely depressed the third valve and played the instrument as a natural D horn. We must not be too critical of those early horn players; we may be sure the hand horn technique was highly developed by this time. Moreover, the acoustical theory of the valve was not so similar to that of the woodwind theory of the tone holes as to suggest the possibility of 'fingering.'

It is not surprising, in view of these facts, that Berlioz, in his famous *Treatise on Instrumentation* of 1841, also failed to explain the valve properly. He stresses that the purpose of the 'new' invention is to *change the key* of the horn and even goes so far as to show, for those who may have preferred the old tradition, that on the new instrument one can play *every* note stopped! Berlioz's comments on this subject were responsible for throwing a whole generation of Russian composers off the track. As there were no opportunities for studying orchestration in nineteenth-century Russia, Balakirev recommended to his circle (the 'Five') that they base their study upon the Berlioz *Treatise*. Rimsky-Korsakov, in his autobiography, wrote,

> We followed the instructions of Berlioz's *Traite d'Instrumentation* regarding the use of the natural-scale trumpets and French horns. We selected French horns in all possible keys in order to avoid the imaginary stopped notes; calculated, contrived, and grew unimaginably confused.

In other words, after having written a melody, the composer went back and tried to figure out upon which natural horn the given note would fall as an open note, thus indicating the transposition above the staff. The amazing aspect of this situation is that apparently the military band horn layers were using fingerings in the modern tradition all along. Time and time again in his autobiography, Rimsky-Korsakov laments that all any of them would have had to do was 'ask a practical musician,' his term for a military bandsman. It was not until 1876 that the Russian composers began to understand the valve, some sixty years after its invention!

The first real opportunity for the wind and to become a meaningful part of the main stream of serious music came with the breakdown of the giant post-Romantic orchestra in the second decade of the twentieth century. With the large orchestral works of Stravinsky's Russian Period and the *Gurre-Leider* of Schönberg, the post-Wagnerian large orchestra was carried to it furthest logical extreme. Although frequently noted, but rarely admitted, it is clear that major composers at this time no longer found the large orchestra capable of expression. As Stravinsky's biographer Vlad says, 'it was as though the Wagnerian orchestra had exploded like a bomb in Stravinsky's hand when he composed the *Rite of Spring*.' The logical turn was toward the small ensemble. In fact, before Schönberg finished the orchestration of the *Gurre-Leider* he had begun the *Chamber Symphony*; before Stravinsky had finished the *Rite of Spring*, he had begun the *Three Japanese Lyrics* for voice, piano, two flutes, two clarinets and string quartet. Along with this turn to small ensembles was a marked increase in wind music among the major composers of Europe, regardless of age or place of residence. The period 1917–1928 saw a total of forty-nine compositions for wind instruments by Webern, Berg, Ives, Villa Lobos, Piston, Sibelius, Poulenc, Busoni, Milhaud, Schoenberg, Stravinsky, Hindemith, Roussel, Shostakovich, Vaughn Williams and Ibert. Stravinsky alone produced eight works for winds between 1915 and 1924, not to mention the role of winds in *L'Histoire du soldat* and *Mavra*.

In spite of this fertile interest being exhibited by the major composers of Europe, the American band movement failed to even notice, let alone take advantage of this movement. How was this possible? The answer is that the professional bands of the day, Sousa's in particular, were focused on entertainment. Sousa himself apparently knew no limits of bad taste as long as music entertained. Witness his work entitled *The International Congress* (1876) which he describes,

> It started with a short fugue on 'Yankee Doodle,' then ran a gamut of the principal national songs of the world, winding up with the 'Star-Spangled Banner' treated in imitation of the last part of the *Tannhauser* Overture.

A key factor in this period, a factor which was to influence band music for the rest of the century, was the adoption of a repertoire of transcribed music. We will not debate here the philosophy of transcribed music; in fact we will go so far as to comment that Wagner and Berlioz voiced no objections upon hearing band transcriptions of their orchestral compositions. However, when Sousa performed a transcription it was no longer an esoteric composition, but, rather, something played in the name of entertainment. In comparing himself with Theodore Thomas, conductor of the Chicago Symphony, Sousa wrote,

> He gave Wagner, Liszt and Tchaikovsky in the belief that he was educating his public; I gave Wagner, Liszt and Tchaikovsky with the hope that I was entertaining my public.

Sousa, moreover, believed this as an important calling,

> Believing ... that entertainment is of more real value to the world than technical education in music appreciation, I would not accept the symphonic orchestra as my medium.

From an intellectual standpoint, it appears that Sousa was never able to come to grips with the issue of transcriptions. While his programs, aside from his marches, consisted almost entirely of transcribed music, not to mention an article he wrote for a French newspaper in which he stated, 'But if an orchestra may play transcriptions of piano works, why should not a military band play transcriptions of works for orchestra?,' he could inexplicably write in his autobiography, *Marching Along*,

> These compositions (Mozart, Haydn, Beethoven, and the 'violin family') were created for one purpose only—to be played by the instruments the masters intended for them and never by any other combination. The efforts on the part of some misguided conductors and orchestrators to 'improve' on the original and the equally self-appointed task of some arranger to transcribe Mozart, Beethoven and Haydn to the wind instrument combination are greatly to be deplored ... either play them as they were or let them alone entirely.

Returning for a moment to the question regarding the lack of communication between the American band movement and the European movement away from the large orchestra, in Sousa's case it was undoubtedly a lack of insight in musical matters. How else could he have blissfully sailed along unaware of the currents which were tearing European music apart? He was certainly unaware of the significant composers of his day, if we are to take seriously his listing of Stillman Kelly, Homer N. Bartlett, Mrs. A. H. A. Beach, George F. Bristow, Adolph Martin Foerster and Ernest Kroeger, to name a few he considered important composers. Finally he had little to say for the new development in American music of his day, jazz. In fact, he wrote it off as something which would 'I am positive, some day disappear—when the dancer tires of it—unwept, unhonored and unsung.'

Sousa's attitude toward the band's role as entertainment is easily accounted for, if not explained. He was, after all, in the unique position of having to support his organization entirely through his paid audience, lacking the private support which belonged to orchestras. Such an attitude is more difficult to understand after the establishment of instrumental music in the public schools and colleges. A band supported by an educational institution does not live in terror of the box office. Indeed, it should be more free from restrictions than any musical medium in America. Nevertheless the old association with entertainment continued. Richard Franko Goldman, in his 1938 book for school band directors, *The Band's Music*, wrote,

> Since the primary purpose of the band is to entertain, rather than to educate or to elevate, no one will question the propriety of light music on band programs. In other words, the increased demand of band audiences for 'good music' does not mean that bands can take a sudden and definite break with their pasts.

Such an influential book, recommending as it did the continuation of the band's commitment to entertainment, helped blind band conductors again to European developments. As a result Richard Strauss's composition of two major works for wind band during this period went entirely unnoticed. The band movement still remained on the periphery!

What about the state of instrumental music in 1966? More important, what can we do to move bands toward the main stream of serious musical activity? First, let's consider the orchestra. Harold Schonberg, in an article in the *New York Times* (January 9, 1966) is concerned, as are many others, because the orchestral repertoire in New York begins with Beethoven and ends with the late Romantics. Granted, a little before and after is thrown in, most of the contemporary music being what he calls 'ephemeral fluff.' In addition to the performance repertoire, he is concerned for the direction orchestral composition is going.

> Things don't look good. Behind all the activity there is a kind of sterility. One of the major reasons could well be that the contemporary musical scene is in a mess. The avant-gardist go on contemplating their navel, or attempting to shock with their penny firecrackers. If we had a strong school of contemporary composition in the United States, it could act as a spearhead. But the fact remains that no young composer, or school of composition, has come up to interest anybody aside from a tiny group of specialists.

The problem with orchestral repertoire in this country is indeed serious. In every generation of orchestral history before our century, the orchestras played the music of their time. There was always a need for more new music; only occasionally was there a desire to revive old works. But today professional orchestras are financially dependent upon a repertoire of the dead. This is a dangerous sign in any art form. We are much more interested in what Andrew Wyeth's work will be like in 1966, than we are in what it was in 1930. We honor great art of the past—we use it to study—to teach. But there would be something seriously wrong if the art of our generation did not inspire interest among those who hold art to be a valid segment of our culture.

This brings us to one of the most ironic aspects of the band medium at present. Most bands still depend heavily upon orchestral transcriptions for repertoire. Aside from the aesthetic question of transcriptions, the playing of them seems to imply to other musicians that the band has no repertoire of its own. Paradoxically, the band is actually the only instrumental medium that could perform exclusively compositions of our generation.

In light of former band conductors failing to observe the musical trends of their day, perhaps we should consider what we are doing to secure our repertoire. To be sure, we are commissioning more works than ever before. But even this has to be approached with some care. Stravinsky has cautioned that many composers use a commission to merely 'unload' some work that they have on the shelf, or worse yet, perhaps some work they were not previously inspired to finish.

> In the main, however, the need for new cantatas, string quartets, symphonies, is wholly imaginary, and commissioning organizations, like the Ford and Rockefeller, are really only buying up surplus symphonies as the government buys up surplus corn.

All in all, bands have done rather well by this process, however, and we certainly do not wish to discourage this means of building the repertoire.

One area of real concern is that most of our commissions are going to American composers. Outstanding as these men are, I wonder if we are not making the same mistake that so many of our predecessors have made in not noticing the new currents of activity, especially in Europe. How many of us can honestly say we know any of the works of Peter Maxwell Davies of England; Ondes Martenot of France; Luis de Pablo or Carmelo Bernaola of Spain; Franco Evangelisti or Aldo Clementi of Italy; Pijper, Flothus, Baaren, Tonde Leeuw, Peter Shat, Ketting or Vlijmen of Holland; Mortensen, Hovland, Rautavaara or Norgaard of the Scandinavian countries; Keleman or Strebotnjak of Yugoslavia; Cazouleas or Kounadis of Greece; or Anatol Vieru of Rumania? And yet, these men are all writing music for various combinations of wind instruments, including at least one work which has been highly reviewed. More important, for the most part they are writing out of their own interest rather than financial persuasion. We must investigate these men and encourage the talent we find.

Another area in which we must exert pressure, if our art is to join the main stream, is our undergraduate literature and history courses. We must see that our future band conductors are given an honest perspective of the role of wind instruments and wind music in music history. In this respect we might also consider orchestration courses. Perhaps we should not teach orchestration and band scoring as separate courses, but as integrated courses. For in truth, the mechanical properties of wind instruments, or their presence or absence altogether, was not without influence on orchestral scoring in the eighteenth and nineteenth centuries.

Finally, if bands are to become a serious medium, part of the main stream of music, they must arrive at a firm commitment regarding their oldest problem—the functional as opposed to the esoteric nature of their performance. Bands are presently, and will probably continue to be, bound to certain functional duties, the marching occasions in particular. There are those who say that this dichotomy will prevent the band from ever becoming primarily a musical medium. In the present concept, perhaps so, but I believe that it is possible for bands to attain both functional and artistic ends if they are willing to define the two. We must remember that the orchestra, as we know it, also arose from a dichotomous position. In the eighteenth century the court and opera orchestras were truly functional. Orchestral concerts supported by the public were unknown for most of the century. When an orchestra, such as the one in Bonn of which Beethoven was a member, gave a concert it was done so on the musicians free time. In time, the orchestra succeeded in creating an audience that was divorced from its functional appearances. It is to be expected that there is some overlapping. An orchestra playing an occasional opera overture in concert should only be analogous to a band playing a march in concert. But the band has always had a difficult time defining *its* functional and artistic moments. It has nearly always, in this century, tried to accomplish both at once. Thus instead of creating an audience that expects entertainment at a football game and an audience that expects great music at a concert, the band has created a large audience that does not know quite *what* to expect. Whom can we blame? Is not our latest 'trend' to present excerpts from classical music, in concert formation, on the football field? Or, on the other hand, how many times have we heard conductors say, 'My audience won't let me play a whole program of serious music.' Obviously the band has not yet made its role clear to the public, not to mention other musicians. Even if band concerts contained no transcriptions, even if music history texts gave a more realistic view of instrumental music in general, even if we had closer ties with the musical developments of a given generation, the confusion which this problem presents would tend to make the band's acceptance as a serious medium questioned. I feel the vital step bands must take is to offer fellow musicians and audience alike a concert medium free from mundane entertainment commitments and, on the field, an entertainment medium free from artistic pretension.

A SIMILAR PAPER I delivered the following year at the national conference of the CBDNA held on the campus of the University of Michigan. If the paper was more brief, it had the advantage of reaching an audience of the most influential university band conductors of 1967.

Band Music from an Historical Perspective

There is a vast body of eighteenth- and nineteenth-century literature that exists for large wind ensemble or wind band. Only a few random specimens from this body of literature are now available. No one has been able to study enough of the unpublished music to be able to judge the relative worth of what we do have. For example, I published a short work for chorus and band by the late eighteenth-century Frenchman, Charles Catel. It was simply a manuscript I found that seemed to be worth performing. I do know that works for chorus and band exist in great numbers from the French period, not the least of which is Gossec's *Te Deum* for voices and 300 wind instruments. Until we can see most of these works we shall never know if the little piece I published is representative of the best or the worst of them.

The reasons we do not know this body of music today, and the reasons we should, are all related to the social position of the band itself. In the eighteenth and nineteenth centuries the wind band was primarily functional and not a medium for artistic expression. The non-functional artistic works we have were written sometimes on commission, such as Gounod's *Symphony*, but more often simply out of the composer's own interest.

The first basic change in the traditionally functional role of the wind band was personified in Sousa. With Sousa the band became a vehicle for entertainment, and vastly popular at that. Entertainment as a goal was very important to Sousa, and not only from a financial standpoint. He once wrote that he believed entertainment was 'of more real value to the world than technical education in music appreciation.' By 'technical education in music appreciation' he meant the appreciation of orchestral music. More to the point, in comparing himself with Theodore Thomas, conductor of the Chicago Symphony, Sousa wrote in his autobiography, 'He performed Wagner, Liszt and Tchaikowsky in the belief he was educating his public; I performed Wagner, Liszt and Tchaikowsky with the hope that I was entertaining my public.' Whatever Sousa's contribution to bands, or however popular he made them, he did not succeed in moving bands into the mainstream of music culture.

Twentieth-century bands in the United States, Europe and South America are best characterized by their adoption of orchestral repertoire in transcribed form. The long period during which we primarily performed transcriptions produced one far-reaching detriment. It placed us in an artistic competition that we can never win—the band versus the orchestra. This curious association has led to a situation in which a public school will tend to support either a band or an orchestra, rather than both as it should. It even has extended our vocabulary with such ludicrous terms as 'bandestration' to fill a gap seemingly created by the term 'orchestration.' More important, we have been sidetracked to a position where neither the public nor scholars view us in relation to our own history. In this century books dealing with music history, orchestration and aesthetics have virtually left us out. I challenge anyone to find a standard undergraduate music history text that deals with the history of wind instruments or their music, however briefly. I challenge anyone to find a music encyclopedia that does justice to such a man as Sax, a figure of considerable influence on music of the nineteenth century. And yet, are not the same encyclopedias filled to overflowing with accounts of insignificant singers and court musicians of the past centuries?

We can begin to reestablish our heritage by performing some of the music written for wind band and wind ensembles during the past two centuries. Perhaps it should be stated more emphatically. Perhaps it is vital that we give our future band conductors, who I assume are among the ranks of our college bands, the historical background they will not otherwise receive in college.

There is a body of eighteenth- and nineteenth-century wind music that I believe should form a part of our repertoire. But before such an addition to the repertoire of a large number of conductors is possible, some important problems must be studied.

First, what role shall this music play in the traditional university band program? The very need for collective thought in this area is implicit in the titles we see on programs. We have wind symphonies, wind orchestras, wind sinfoniettas, chamber bands, chamber winds, in addition to regimental bands, concert bands and symphonic bands. Why cannot the word 'band' include all the wind band music from Johann Christian Bach to Nelhybel? Why cannot the band be a flexible medium, changing according to the requirements of the composition? I realize I am suggesting a death blow to any future attempts at creating a so-called standardized instrumentation, but this concept has never worked and there are fundamental artistic and nationalistic reasons why it never will work. Since composers have primarily been the object of our search for a standard instrumentation, I might suggest that the best way to give confidence to prospective composers of wind music is to demonstrate our confidence in past composers of wind music.

Second, we must locate this body of music. In what museums does it exist? Who in this country has copies—and of what? Who will lend them out for performance? Who is interested in publishing the best of them?

Third, what are the best solutions regarding obsolete wind instruments? In addition, what solutions are best in balancing modern horns and clarinets in the performance of music written for eighteenth-century horns and clarinets?

Fourth, we must make information available on eighteenth- and early nineteenth-century rhythm and ornamentation traditions as well as editorial practices.

These obstacles and more stand in our way. Fortunately, some are studying these very problems, but duplication and waste of valuable time occurs. Considering the decade or so that the wind ensemble movement has been in progress and considering the large number of colleges that maintain some sort of smaller wind group, I find it curious that the CBDNA has not done more in this area. In order to facilitate the performance of this body of eighteenth- and nineteenth-century music, in order to bring into clearer focus the relationship of current bands and music history itself, I call upon our next president to appoint a standing committee on the wind ensemble.

Such a committee would face an enormous task—a task requiring, in time, the help of all wind conductors. But let us begin. We have nothing further to gain in performing a borrowed repertoire; we have everything to gain in redefining our position in light of a two-century-old tradition. Let us give old works new performances and let us describe new works according to how they reflect or break old tradition.

THE NEXT PRESIDENT, and his board, rejected my call for a committee on the wind ensemble and instead created a new standing committee on jazz.

I learned from this and similar experiences that one cannot look for change or for artistic progress from the band organizations. They are really social gatherings and that has its place. If there is to be artistic change in any medium it has to be the work of individuals, individuals who in their own work set the highest example they can. Consequently I encouraged composers whenever possible and performed more than forty premieres during my career, but also brought important composers to my campus to work with my students and me. In the memory of four of these men I should like here to present here some essays I wrote recalling some of my experiences and impressions of these men.

I begin with the first European whose music was the first known to many band directors. His music took the educators of America by storm and I am sure he broadened the musical views of them.

Vaclav Nelhybel

Following his formal education at the Conservatory of Prague, Nelhybel was off to a fast start as a composer and as conductor of the second most important orchestra in Prague, that of the Smetana Theater. In order to understand Nelhybel's sudden departure from his native land one must recall the significance of the formal and familiar forms of some European languages, a distinction quite missing in English. In German, for example, one only uses the familiar form with small children, immediate family members and pets. The etiquette of this is rigidly observed, as one can see in the case of a sixteenth-century university student who somehow forgot himself and addressed a university administrator in the familiar German and was immediately thrown into prison! Then there is the example of Robert and Clara Schumann who were *engaged* for more than a year before she proposed that perhaps they should stop addressing each other in formal German and begin to use the familiar form. This kind of formality between two persons is still found in the German-speaking countries. I recall an occasion during a visit to make a recording with my friend Albert Benz, the conductor of the Luzern Wind Orchestra, and his wife, Claire, when she decided that we should begin to use the familiar form of German. When I agreed, she immediately arranged a dinner in an elegant restaurant for us to commemorate this event.

Needless to say, an orchestra member would never, under any circumstances, address the conductor in the familiar form. The Communist Party took control over night in Czechoslovakia one day in 1948 and Nelhybel had a rehearsal with the Smetana orchestra the following morning. Before he could begin, one of the horn players came up to the podium and informed Nelhybel that he, the horn player, was now the new Party representative of the orchestra. While it would have been disconcerting enough for a European conductor to have to deal with political inference with the orchestra, what really shocked Nelhybel was the fact that this horn player addressed him, the conductor, in the *familiar* form of the language. Nelhybel left Czechoslovakia the next morning for, as he told me, he did not want to work in a society where an orchestral member addressed the conductor in the familiar form of the language. Again, for the reader's information, it would be like speaking to a conductor as one would speak to a dog or a child.

Another aspect of the new Communist Party control was a rigid control of aesthetic values. It worked like this: if one composed a symphony one had to first submit the score to a party committee for them to affirm that the music reflected party values (i.e., the music should be understood by the masses). If the committee gave its stamp of approval, the party would publish and distribute (free to foreign conductors) the score and pay for a premiere performance and often a recording. On the other hand, if the party failed to give its stamp of approval, the composer was not allowed to either publish the score or, even at his own cost, arrange a public performance. It represented a strong stimulus to follow the party values and resulted in a lot of worthless popular music.

In Nelhybel's case, leaving the country because of the party's takeover, the officials confiscated all his music, including an opera, and these works disappeared forever. I suggested to Nelhybel that it must be devastating to loose all these original scores, but he replied, no, they were youthful works and he was glad no one could see them now. When I was living in Vienna in 1968–1969 I had a couple of recording engagements in Czechoslovakia and on one trip there, it may have been at the Prague Radio station, I played for some officials there a recording by my University of Montana band of a dazzling performance of Nelhybel's *Prelude and Fugue*, which I knew would have surpassed any band recording known to them at that time. I think they must have remembered his name, and the fact that he was no doubt on some party list of deserters, because when the performance was over their faces showed no emotion whatsoever and one person complained in a way that could have several meanings, that the music sounded 'commercial.' They repaid me by making me listen to a twenty-minute long recently made tape by one of their staff composers, of very loud, noisy and completely uninteresting aleatoric music. With all three or four of them staring at my face they demanded to know what I thought of this music. The reader will understand that while the music was playing I ignored it and used the entire time to think of what I would say when it concluded.

After fleeing to the West, Nelhybel told me he was fortunate to obtain a full-time position as the first music director of Radio Free Europe. One of his published works, the wonderful set of pieces for woodwinds (2 flutes, oboe, 2 clarinets and bassoon), *Impromptus*, is a product from those radio days, used on a program for children.

Moving to New York City in 1957 with his wife, Dorothea, a direct descendant of Heinrich Schütz, of whom she owned some original personal artifacts, and a scholar in her own right, Nelhybel obtained a position as organist at a Czech Catholic church on the upper East side of New York City. Like many large city churches during this period, this church had been experiencing significant decline in membership. As a result, nearly all the nuns had been reassigned and two floors of their adjacent residence were made available to Nelhybel. While the position paid little money, having a large free apartment (with stain glass windows!) in New York City was equivalent to a significant amount of money. It was at this apartment that my wife and I first visited with him, in perhaps the Winter of 1965–1966. Having warned us to ignore the sign over the door-bell, which was not his name, we found the residence charming, with its door in the living room which opened into the choir loft and the organ console, where he often practiced. On the walls were paintings, as well as tapestries. All of which had also been created by Nelhybel. I recall we had lunch at a European café where I saw for the first time a type of juke box which showed videos while the (European) pop music was playing. We had nothing in this country like this, but it wasn't long before it came and resulted finally in MTV.

During these frugal years in New York City Nelhybel had one very interesting engagement, composing the incidental music for the famous CBS Television program in which Jackie Kennedy ushered Charles Collingswood on a tour of the White House. The program producers reached the contemptible decision that 'Nelhybel,' in those cold war years, was too 'un-American' sounding and so they used a pseudonym. It was very interesting to hear, as Vaclav described these days of filming in the White House, that he found JFK very pleasant and cordial but that he had 'bad vibrations' all three days he was in contact with Jackie. He was the very first person I had ever heard who spoke poorly of Jackie, who was then at the very height of her world-wide reputation.

During this period, Nelhybel told me he had a conversation with a woman in New York who found that, like most artists in Europe, he knew nothing about America's peculiar brand of music education. She offered to pay his expenses to attend a MENC conference in Virginia to observe the music-making there and Nelhybel returned interested in writing for young musicians. He first spent a number of months visiting a local high school, passing out brief excerpts he had composed. These fragments featured various kinds of harmony and rhythms which he used to observe the student reaction. He told me he did this because, while he knew the French, German and Czech child, he had no confidence that he understood the American teenager.

The compositions which emerged from this experimentation, first the *Chorale for Band* and then the *Prelude and Fugue*, certainly rewarded his efforts and also capitulated his career in this country. I vividly recall looking at the (manuscript) score of the *Prelude and Fugue*, the first of his compositions I came to know. Its Eastern European sound, its linear style then unfamiliar in band compositions and the general excitement of the music made me an instant and enthusiastic supporter. I immediately invited him to come to Missoula to guest conduct my University of Montana Band, but he wrote saying he was not free.

> Vaclav Nelhybel to David Whitwell
> New York City, March 9, 1966
>
> I am extremely pleased that you plan to play my music in your concert on May 22. Unfortunately I am *not free* that day. Beginning May 15 I have a series of live radio programs in New York on Sunday mornings; the series ends June 26. I am very unhappy that I shall not be able to be with you on May 22. I have heard from many people very much good about you and your musical activities. From what I heard you must be one of the (not so many) well equipped technically and completely devoted to your work.

Something in his schedule changed and he did, in fact, come to Missoula to conduct. He found the rolling hills and mountains of Western Montana reminded him of Czechoslovakia and I think enjoyed his visit.

> Vaclav Nelhybel to David Whitwell
> New York City, June 5, 1966
>
> Thank you for having me invited to make music with your ensemble. I was enchanted with the reaction of your musicians. It was a pleasure to work with them. Your band is a sensitive musical instrument with an enormous range of communicative power …

Please tell Hello to *all* the members of the band and tell them that I loved to work with them and that I was very happy with the results. I was touched by their friendliness—despite my tough rehearsing. I knew that they were able to give me all the subtle details—thus I tried to get them.

Thank you for everything. Best regards to everybody and especially your lovely wife. I wish you a successful tour in South America.

He *was* tough, very professional, in rehearsal and one saw him working as one would work with professionals. This was before his period of American fame had begun and later I noticed his many subsequent experiences conducting American high school students had moderated his demands, and musical expectations as well.

I had him return in January 1967 to conduct a large number of his chamber works As his name was rapidly gaining recognition as a composer I also arranged for him to give a public lecture before the faculty and students of my school, the University of Montana. He gave a very interesting talk but, as will be no surprise to anyone familiar with American Academia, the composition faculty was noticeably absent. Being young and new to the business, I was quite shocked at this as no composer on our faculty had a reputation at all.

I also wanted Nelhybel to observe my preparation of the band for our forthcoming Midwest tour and performance in Ann Arbor, Michigan, before the national CBDNA Conference. Returning to New York, he wrote,

Your band is really in excellent shape and I am convinced that your trip to the CBDNA will be very successful. I know it will be a great and exciting experience for all your players to participate in this unique national band festival.

Nelhybel visited me in Los Angeles four months after I had returned from Europe to accept a position with the California State University, Northridge.

Vaclav Nelhybel to David Whitwell
New York City, January 20, 1970

It was so nice to see you and Giselle back in the States. Your home has a wonderful Old World atmosphere, and I so enjoyed your hospitality.

Among the California music educators you have already won a very high reputation. All to whom I have been talking about you were very happy to have you in the Los Angeles area. They all said: 'Now something is going to happen! Great!'

During the following years our paths crossed many times and of course I performed and recorded much of his music. Whenever I sent him a tape he was always the perfect European gentleman.

Vaclav Nelhybel to David Whitwell
New York, December, 1971

Thank you for the recording of *Symphonic Movement*. A *Perfect* job!

Vaclav Nelhybel to David Whitwell
Newtown, CT, November 18, 1985

THANK YOU. The last recording is very good. I am *very* pleased.

This last recording may have been one he asked me to make of a composition he wanted to enter in a composition contest somewhere. There was another occasion I was able to be of service to him, this at a large MENC convention being held in Los Angeles. He had written a work for band with six or eight antiphonal brass instruments and he was scheduled to perform it at this convention. Due to some scheduling problem the high school band who was to contribute the antiphonal players did not arrive. I was in a rehearsal room with my wind ensemble preparing for a concert later that day, when suddenly Nelhybel burst into the room and begged if he could borrow the players needed for the performance which was scheduled in five minutes, or something like that. I gave him the players, of course, and the concert went without a problem. He was most thankful and in almost disbelief that my students could, without rehearsal, read and perform their parts from manuscript. But I had very strong players at that time, most of whom had considerable experience jobbing in Los Angeles, so really there was nothing to be surprised at.

One of the things I admired about Nelhybel was that he was determined to make it in life as a composer. He had always turned down teaching positions, which would have been most welcome for many composers, and when I first knew him he was living on a very meager scale. Finally, from about 1970 on, Nelhybel's music became the 'rage' among school bands and orchestras and a great deal of it was published. His increased good fortune allowed him to buy a home in suburban Newtown, CT, and finally resign from his church job. I called him to congratulate him on his move from New York City and he told me that on the first Sunday in the new home his wife made him fall on his knees and pray, 'Dear God! Thank you that I don't have to go to church today!'

His reputation finally was such that he began receiving performances and various honors back in Europe, as he mentions in one of the last letters I have from him, some four years before his death. I had written to him asking where I could obtain a copy of a long out of print brass fanfare he had written based on the old Czech hymn later used by Karl Husa in his *Music for Prague, 1968*. I used to like to perform it before performing the Husa work, since this hymn is unknown to Americans and is not really in a recognizable form until the end of the first movement of the Husa. I thought it helped the listener to understand even the three timpani notes which begin Husa's work.

Vaclav Nelhybel to David Whitwell
Newtown, CT, February 21, 1992

Dear David,
Enclosed is the chorale. Dorothea sends her greetings. Our children Jana is 23 years old and Chris is 21 years. Jana plays violin, studies political science and Chris is some kind of engineering in Boston …

I live the same life as 29 years ago—only I travel less. In March I'll be conducting a very official concert of the American–German friendship in Germany.

Best regards from me and Dorothea to Giselle. Your boys must be by now two men. Well—C'est la vie!
Cordially,
Vaclav

෴

Karel Husa

I suppose everyone can remember the first time they heard Husa's *Music for Prague, 1968*. I first heard it when Ken Snapp played me a tape of his recent premiere performance. I was immediately eager to perform each of his works as they became available. I think I gave the third performance of the *Prague* and the second of the *Apotheosis of this Earth*.

The *Music for Prague, 1968* had a special impact on me because I was in Prague in 1968 when the Russians invaded. I had an appointment at the radio station to discuss a possible conducting engagement and I remember the difficulty in finding the station, for although I had a map, the citizens of Prague had taken down all the street signs to make it difficult for the Russians to find whatever they were looking for. I also recall that the Russians had issued an order that no citizen was allowed to carry on the street a transistor radio, which in those days were inevitably small black radios. So everyone was walking around Prague holding a square lump of coal to their ear, thereby driving the Russians crazy as they had to stop everyone only to find a piece of coal.

Karel Husa was always impressed that I always rehearsed his major works without scores. I used to tease him about this, saying since he composed the work he should already know the notes. In a letter of July 18, 1997 he wrote, 'I am back and practicing "Prague" in front of my mirror, trying to learn this darn piece from memory, as you ordered it.' Five years earlier he had mentioned that even his wife was teasing him about this.

Karel Husa to David Whitwell
Ithaca, NY, May 21, 1992

Many thanks for performing my Music for Prague 1968—*from memory too!*—it makes me jealous, for I never did it myself! Simone has the greatest respect for you (and says why can't *I* conduct from memory)!

I was also very taken by the *Apotheosis of this Earth*, which I first saw when Karel sent me a photocopy of the autograph score. I remember vividly turning the pages at my kitchen table, with the score pushed back so my tears would not fall on the score. One early performance I gave of the *Apotheosis* was before a conference of the CBDNA meeting in Tempe, AZ, where many conductors heard this masterpiece for the first time.

Karel Husa to David Whitwell
Ithaca, NY, February 21, 1972

Dear Dr. Whitwell:

I have received a letter from our mutual friend, Dr. Kenneth Snapp. He told me about the great success of your concert during the CBDNA conference in Tempe, Arizona. He also told me how excellently you and your ensemble performed my *Apotheosis*. I am sure that your idea of projecting the color picture of the earth must have been effective and I would have like to have seen it. As a matter of fact, last spring we played the tape of the *Apotheosis* at the house of Professor Carl Sagan—working now on the Mars exploration in Pasadena—and he also projected a picture of the earth.

I know that you have performed this composition several times before. My friend, Mr. Charles Bay, has written to me about your performance in Los Angeles.

I am most grateful to you for making my music known and hope I will be able to thank you personally sometime in the future.

Yours most sincerely,
Karel Husa

A few months later I sent him a tape recording of this performance.

Karel Husa to David Whitwell
Interlaken, NY, June 5, 1972

Dear David,
Before leaving home [for his vacation cabin on Lake Cayuga where he wrote the *Apotheosis*] I listened to your tape, you so kindly sent to me, and I understand that people were pleased and amazed, for your performance is very exciting. I am also glad to know that the music is playable and your excellent performance proves it. Dr. Revelli thought last year that this piece will not be played often because of its difficulty; fortunately it is not so. I think there must have been about 80 performances this season (at least) thanks to young conductors such as you, Bob Reynolds and others.

I sincerely hope you will kindly keep it in your repertory, as you communicate the excitement so powerfully (second movement). I also liked your ensemble, which sounds very sensitive, for instance in the first movement. And above all, I was most impressed by your tremendous conducting technique when I saw you rehearse at Eastman … I was looking at your very economical gestures, simple and exact way of explaining problems to the band; I thought it was most effective.

Contrary to the hope of Husa, no one is performing this work today. Of course I understand the desire of most band directors to do only new works, but in a time when the world climate is the subject of discussion everywhere it is amazing to me that this most appropriate of all music is not on everyone's program.

The *Apotheosis of this Earth* had been commissioned by Revelli and I am sure that at that time it was the most difficult score he had ever conducted. I asked him, shortly after the premiere, what he thought about the *Apotheosis* and he answered, 'How can I understand the music when I can't even understand the title?'

I performed the *Apotheosis* with a number of All-State Honor Bands and he mentioned a performance with the Wisconsin All-State Band in 1973, 'I heard about your *great success* in Wisconsin.' After a performance with the Southern California All-State Band in 1977 I sent Husa a recording and he responded,

Karel Husa to David Whitwell
Ithaca, NY, January 26, 1977

First to let you know that the record of the Southern California High School Honor Band arrived and I have listened to it with amazement again! How can you make young people play the way they do, as it is impossible they can be able to project a piece like this at 14–15–16–17 years of age!

I know it is you who can do it, yet I do not know how you do it. It's amazing!

Because I had conducted the *Apotheosis of this Earth* so many times Husa often asked my advice, such as the possibility of making a choral version. One of his concerns was about the spoken words at the end of the work.

Karel Husa to David Whitwell
Ithaca, NY, May 14, 1973

Can you tell me your sincere opinion on the following: do you think that the sentence *This beautiful Earth* should not be said in the last movement? This was the opinion of two or three people, among them Irv Lowens of the Washington Star (I have the impression they thought it perhaps a little naive). As the chorus-orchestra version will go into print, I would be grateful for your view. Please be completely free in giving this opinion, as I do not want to have anything 'corny' in this piece. (Personally, I do not think it is out of place, but composers sometimes stick to their first ideas and are 'stubborn' to correct or change). However, I would change if this is a rather general feeling.

It was my advice to Husa not to change a thing. He also mentioned a concern that due to the rather somber ending the audience sometimes felt it inappropriate to applaud.

It was in this year, 1973, when I first met Karel in person as I was performing this work with a summer high school band at the Idyllwild Summer Music Camp, run by the University of Southern California. Husa heard I was doing the *Apotheosis* and he drove up the mountain to observe the rehearsals. Once he appeared I organized a camp session where students could ask him questions and I recall someone asked him what he thought when he looked at a score of, say, Haydn. Husa responded, 'Why I am always amazed at the technique.' This reflects one of the basic characteristics of the man, a genuine modest evaluation of his own abilities. One day he went for a walk with my colleague Ron Johnson, who was also in residence. While walking Husa suddenly stopped and Ron asked, 'What's wrong?' 'I am just listening to the music,' replied Husa, meaning the sounds of the wind in the tall trees and the birds. This reflects another great characteristic of his, an intense interest in everything.

Once when telling me of Revelli's comment that the *Apotheosis* was too difficult to play, Husa was reminded of a similar story. Apparently Lukas Foss, conductor of the Buffalo Symphony, had programmed Husa's *Concerto for Brass Quintet and String Orchestra*. Three weeks before the concert when his brass players declared the piece impossible to play, Foss invited five players from the New England Conservatory to substitute and they had no problems! This reminds me that one year when Lukas Foss was the director of the Ojai Festival in Southern California he asked me to conduct an off-stage band in a performance of a very interesting (and little known!) cantata by Hindemith and Bertolt Brecht, written just after Charles Lindbergh's famous flight in 1927. All the world was talking about how this was going to change the future and this cantata takes the opposite viewpoint. Maybe airplanes will not be so good for mankind! I think about this in airports today.

Another composition by Husa which I really like is the *Saxophone Concerto*, a work I consider the finest concerto of the twentieth century for any instrument, including piano. I performed this composition in 1973 with Arthur Hegvik, a member of the faculty at Westchester College of PA, at that time, and a guest with the Philadelphia Orchestra when a saxophone was required.

> My wife listened with me and we both were amazed! It is a tremendous and powerful performance.
> Mr. Hegvik plays beautifully, and at all times musically. And what a rhythm and technique. I have never heard the fast slow movement so fast, but of course this is the tempo I like and had in mind. It is incredibly virtuoso playing in all three movements!
> At the same time you and your wind orchestra are on the same level technically; it is nearly unbelievable to hear all the difficult passages in the II and III movements played so well at that speed. Naturally to put the orchestra together and be at all times with the soloists depends on the conductor and you did a magnificent job.
> I am so excited about this performance that I would like to suggest it to Colombo-Belwin-Mills Educational series, if you consent. [1973]

He wrote a separate note to the soloist, observing 'I must confess that you and Dave have achieved something that does not happen to me every day: that I was even impressed by my music!

Every performance, it seems, was followed by an enthusiastic letter from Husa. Here are a few regarding other compositions.

The Trumpet Concerto

> Would it be possible to get 2 more records? There are radios over the country who play concerts of my music and are asking me for good performances. Yours and Mike's [Ewald] *certainly is* an extraordinary one. [1974]

The Piano Concerto

> You and the members have prepared my music—not always easy—so carefully and musically, so it was not difficult for me to conduct!
> It was a pleasure to see you again, also conducting—and with an amazing *maitrise*. The world of music has an exemplary champion not only of old, but also of new music in you. [1993]

Les coulers fauves

Your tape just arrived and I played it immediately. What an exciting performance. What a drive and power! I am most grateful to you and all the members of your wind orchestra for such a spectacular reading! The bravos are a wonderful recognition of an extraordinary performance! And your 'driving' tempo toward the end is absolutely perfect. [1998]

Let me acknowledge that these comments are more reflective of Husa's generous personality than of my performances and I am sure he must have written letters like this to many conductors. In the same way, while I think of him as a perfect friend, so does, I am sure, everyone who knows him. That is perhaps the real measure of this great man.

Husa followed my activities with interest and enjoyed it whenever I sent a recording, even if not his own music.

Karel Husa to David Whitwell
Ithaca, NY, May 27, 1977
Dear David,
The recording of the *Rite of Spring* and the *Don Juan* arrived last week and I am listening to it with amazement. It is so *excellent* and powerful! I know the Strauss transcription (which you do beautifully *too*) but I do not know who did the Stravinsky. In any case, Bravo to you for making your ensemble a first class one!
 Best wishes to Giselle, your sons and to you from Simone and me!
 Karel

In 1979 Don Hunsberger took a sabbatical and Husa, Fennell and myself were invited for residencies and concerts in Rochester. Husa's visit followed mine and he kindly wrote,

The Eastman wind players enjoyed you very much, as I spoke with them. Please give regards to Giselle from Simone—she was reading with great interest about her, your sons and life in Europe.

In 1989 it took all the courage I could gather together to send a tape recording to Husa of the premiere of my first composition, a Symphony. Needless to say, he was too generous.

Many thanks for the tape of your Symphony; I enjoyed listening to it, even so you say it sounds like old music; but it is written so perfectly well for a combination of wind instruments, so it really sounds!

We shared some funny occasions, such as once when we were adjudicating in Hawaii and a swarm of local bugs entered the hall forcing us both to flee the hall. Once in Kansas City we were among a number of conductors participating in a concert before the CBDNA. After I conducted and returned to the dressing room I shared with Husa I found him in a state of concern for he had failed to pack his tux shirt. Of course I immediately took mine off and Husa put it on in time to make his entrance. He was the final conductor and all the conductors were supposed to appear together at the end for a bow. I had to wear a turtle-neck sweater, since I lacked a shirt, and of course I was criticized by a couple of men for not wearing my tails like everyone else.

Husa also shared many personal thoughts with me, his difficulty in getting a visa to visit his father in Czechoslovakia in 1978, his pleasure in 1988 when after not playing his music for twenty years the Prague Concert bureau had asked for some of his music and, of course, his eventual great honors by the government and public in Prague after the fall of the Communist regime.

I used to faithfully send him notices about him that I read in Europe. Once, in 1991 for example, I saw a copy of the *Music News of Prague* which had his picture on the cover. He was very grateful and observed, 'I didn't think I would see myself on the cover either.'

Similarly, in 1990 I had been in Paris and noticed in a shop that sells autograph letters and documents that autograph notes and letters by Husa were now selling on the market at from $50 to $150.00. I sent him a page from an auction catalog which documented this and he wrote back,

> Thank you for the Lubrano Catalog … It has completely changed our family life at home: Simone now keeps all my notes such as: 'I will be back at 5:00 PM' or 'the dog got his food at noon and I took him out.' 'I am at the Dentist,' etc.

Of all the happy moments I associated with Karel Husa I think the happiest were the moments late in his life when he began to receive, especially in his native country, the international acclaim he so richly deserved. He once told me that at the Prague Conservatory when he was a beginning student, Vaclav Nelhybel was an upper classman and generally considered the man to succeed. I don't believe they were close during the several decades they both lived in the United States, but it must have also been a satisfaction to Husa to have had the greater career.

ଽଡ଼ଽ

Frank Erickson

Frank Erickson was a very nice, unassuming, honest and friendly man. His career began as a student, arranging for the USC marching band. I would describe him as a practical musician. He had certainly guidelines he followed in arranging and he was able to produce a great amount of useful educational materials. His composition, *Toccata for Band*, must have had more performances during the 1960s and 1970s than any other work.

When I came to know Frank well he had just discovered Mahler. Apparently he had not had much exposure to orchestral music during his working life and only when he retired did he begin listening to records. He called me on the telephone one day crying, 'Have you ever heard any music by Mahler!?' He was very excited. It is too bad this catharsis did not occur earlier in his life. The one new composition of his which he produced at this time was the *Time and the Winds*, a work he wrote on his own out of his respect for Frederick Fennell. This composition did not sound like Mahler, but it sure was a 'new' Erickson. I performed this work at my university and then invited Frank to tour with us as a guest conductor. It did not appear to me that Frank had had much conducting experience, but I am sure he enjoyed himself, as he later wrote to someone,

> During this past month the California State University, Northridge Wind Ensemble premiered a new composition of mine, *Time and the Winds*. The work is very challenging and I had the opportunity of rehearsing this number and conducting it on four different concerts. I can't remember ever conducting a band that was as responsive and that played as musically as did this fine group.
>
> I also had the opportunity of closely observing Dr. Whitwell at work. Not only does he have the ability to conduct an entire concert of difficult works from memory, but he is truly one of our finest conductors, and there are very few with his depth of musical understanding.
>
> As you might be aware, the Los Angeles City School System has deteriorated to a very discouraging level. This is the area from which Cal State Northridge draws the majority of its students. But despite this obstacle, David Whitwell has been able to maintain a program of the highest standards.

This letter, written in April 1992, also documents the great disappearance of band programs in the Los Angeles school systems following a series of tax revision.

During this period I asked him about his *First Symphony for Band*, a work I remembered playing in manuscript while a student at the University of Michigan during the 1950s. I remember it as a serious and moving composition. Frank told me that Revelli told him it was too long and made him chop it up to make a much smaller work. Then, of course, the work made no sense and no one was interested in it. Revelli's was a common viewpoint in the 1950s. I recall an occasion when his assistant, George Cavender, was guest conducting a transcription of the first movement of the César Franck *D minor Symphony*. While this work has an almost monothematic exposition section, Cavendar, deciding the piece was too long cut out the development section, thus rendering an even longer monothematic experience. Anyway, Erickson apparently took Revelli's lesson to heart and prepared his second symphony in such a way that it was published in three separate movements—the ultimate in a chopped up composition.

Sometime in 1996 Frank called me again. He had run out of projects and wondered if I would recommend an orchestral work which needed a good band arrangement. Instead I recommended an American edition of the great Miaskovsky *Symphony for Band*. I sent him my copy of the score, which was valuable to me as it had a number of markings from my performances. After some time Frank called me to tell me he had reduced the entire symphony to a five line, concert pitch score. He said he always did this first as the only way he could really understand the harmonic movement of a composition. He was then preparing to make from this a new band edition. And then, suddenly, he was dead. After a respectful interval, I wrote his widow in hopes that I could retrieve my personal score. I never had a response from her and so I must regard the score as lost. But what could I say, her loss being so much greater than mine.

This also brought to mind a similar occurrence from the 1970s. I received a call one day from Carmine Copolla, the father of the famous film director Francis Ford Copolla. The father, a former flautist in the Detroit and NBC Symphonies, was also an amateur composer. He called me to tell me that he had finished a band composition that he had been working on for thirty years, a massive score based on the history of China, and wondered if I were interested in doing the world premiere. I told him I would be happy to study the score but could make no promises regarding a performance until I had studied the work. When the work arrived in the mail, I studied it a bit but found no interest in performing it. My colleague, assistant conductor Morrill Pfeifle, however, wanted to study the work with the thought of doing the premiere with our second band. He was mindful, as was I, of the unusual potential for publicity in Los Angeles due to the Copolla family. Morrill took this huge score with him and his family on a flight to Northern California to visit his parents. On the return flight, Morrill apparently misread his map and flew his plane into a mountain. The entire family was killed and the score burned in the subsequent fire. I had the difficult obligation of calling Carmine to tell him the score to which he had devoted thirty years of his life was lost. But, again, what could he say in view of the fact that an entire family had been lost as well?

༄༅

Ernst Krenek

Southern California has long been a magnet for older artists from colder Europe. A friend once described a private dinner which included among the guests Stravinsky, Schönberg and Milhaud. Unfortunately, in this case, the lack of previous communication among these three carried over throughout the dinner.

One of these great refugees from Europe was Ernst Krenek, who was probably the most decorated living composer when I came to know him in the 1970s. He had been widely celebrated in Europe at the time of the performances of his opera, *Jonny spielt auf* (1926), but his music was in disfavor with the Nazi and was banned by them. This led to Krenek's move to America in 1938. His opera, *Charles V*, had been commissioned by the Vienna State Opera in 1938, but the opera was forced by the Nazi to drop plans for the premiere. Forty years later a revival of interest in Europe began with a production of this same opera and this led, as I was delighted to see, to Krenek becoming once again, at the end of his life, a very famous person. While I appreciated his great career and his many European decorations, what always gave me a cold chill when I was in his presence was the fact that here before me was a man who had been the son-in-law of Mahler! He had been briefly married to Anna Mahler in 1924.

Krenek was also a very highly literate person. Visiting his home in Palm Springs, one would see lying everywhere on tables and desks books he was currently reading. They would cover a dozen topics other than music and would be in six or eight languages. One wall of his bathroom contained one of his frescos. One of my fond memories is of taking an octet of my students down to his home in Palm Springs, CA, and performing the great Mozart C minor *Partita*, K. 388/384a, as a little birthday present on the occasion of his seventy-fifth birthday. We set up in his back yard with two chairs for our only audience, Krenek and his wife. When we finished, I turned around to see Krenek sitting there crying over this beautiful music which he had never heard before.

The occasion of his seventy-fifth birthday was also celebrated by a concert of his works at California State University Northridge. The Wind Ensemble and I did his famous marches, but also his two masterpieces for winds from the 1920s, the *Symphony for Winds*, Op. 34 (1924–1925) and the *Kleine Blasmusik*. My goal was to do all his wind ensemble compositions, but unfortunately I found that one of them had been lost during World War II. Krenek also referred to this work in response to my invitation for him to conduct one of his compositions with us.

Ernst Krenek to David Whitwell
Vienna, October 2, 1975
Dear Mr. Whitwell,
Many thanks for your letter of September 5, which reached me here yesterday during my tour in Europe.

I am happy to hear that you have decided to put several works of mine onto your program of May 16. In the meantime you have probably learned from Bonnin that my *Intrada* does not exist any longer. It was a small, incidental work, to be sure, so that not too much was lost.

Of the other works, the *Symphony*, Op. 34 is the most substantial and requires more rehearsing than the other pieces. If you would like me to conduct something, I think the *Kleine Blasmussik* would be the best choice, because it could probably be managed in one rehearsal if it was prepared a little beforehand. We can discuss these and other details at leisure when I return to Palm Springs in two weeks from now. I'll call you then.

Looking forward to this pleasant occasion with best wishes and thanks for your interest.
Cordially yours,
Ernst Krenek

Frederick Fennell was passing through town at the time and so I had him conduct the marches, which he did famously with only one run-through on the afternoon of the concert. I asked Krenek, by the way, about the origin of the marches and he said they were requested by the contemporary music festival then held in Donaueschingen, Germany. At this point he had a good laugh, recalling that he was once, shortly afterward, walking down the Ringstrasse in Vienna and heard his marches 'blaring down at me from speakers on the light posts.'

Earlier I had written to Fred asking if he would like to conduct, instead, the *Symphony*, a wonderful composition, but a very difficult work which I was hoping I could avoid memorizing. His wife responded for him,

Well, when Fred called I told him about your idea of having him conduct the Krenek Symphony. Well he was very excited about that, but he said he hadn't conducted it in many years and would have to study the score again. But he thought that would be a great idea ... So it's all settled—you don't have to worry about conducting that piece—he'll do it.

I no longer recall the sequence of events, I think Fred's schedule became a problem, but in the end I conducted the *Symphony*. I recall the performance vividly, particularly in glancing from time to time at Krenek who was seated on stage just behind the curtain. He was seated with his head in one hand, with a pronounced scowl on his face. I, of course, began to worry that perhaps I was making some great mistake—performing the work too fast, or too slow. Indeed, it became a contest in my mind between the competing worry over Krenek and trying to remember the *Symphony*. When I asked him after the concert if there was a problem with the performance of the *Symphony*, he replied, 'Oh no, I was just trying to remember it. I have not heard it in fifty years!' The following week he wrote,

Please accept my sincere thanks for arranging the excellent performances of my wind pieces and the spirited rendition of my *Symphony*. It was an exhilarating experience. I also enjoyed especially conducting your fine ensemble in the *Kleine Blasmusik*.

Fred also sent a nice note after the concert,

Frederick Fennell to David Whitwell
Miami, FL, May 26, 1976

Dear David:
I was genuinely impressed with the rapid strides which have been made on all sides at Northridge, beginning with recruiting and the inevitable final evidence of that in the extremely high standard of performance which is emerging there. I was impressed with their handling of styles, and pleased with their reaction to Krenek. It was great to see him again and to find him not missing a thing at age 76, in spite of the absence of vision in one eye and hearing in one ear. His pieces stand as positive contributions, not alone to the neo-classic inspiration of the Stravinsky time—which of course they are, but as positive reflections of a musical conviction that is still present in what he's doing today. Your simply masterful memorization of the symphony was a plus in its performance.
    I urged his wife to urge Boonin to make *Kleine Blasmusik* available for sale, and I hope you will urge Boonin to do the same.
    My brief opportunities to peruse *Dream Sequence* convinces me, as it does you, that this is a very successful commission; perhaps we can get into more of this in August.
    FF

On this concert Krenek conducted the several movements of the *Kleine Blasmusik*. Krenek told me he wrote this work, as well as the *Symphony*, during the 1920s when all the young composers were fascinated with Stravinsky's surprising turn to his neo-Classic style. Krenek told me he was also excited about the Stravinsky works at this time and wanted to see what he could do in a similar style. While the *Kleine Blasmusik* therefore must be called neo-Classical, to me it was something more specific. I hear in this work the moods and feelings of nineteenth-century Vienna and Krenek communicated this vividly. He was, by the way, in spite of his age and physical disabilities a first-rate conductor, due to his vast experience. On the podium and off, he was always friendly, patient and helpful to the students.

The composition which Fennell mentioned above, the *Dream Sequence*, was a work commissioned by the CBDNA while I was president. I was determined to get another major work from him while he was still alive and he produced a major work which is very advanced in style. That being the case, it has thus far had very few performances, but someday it will be regarded as standing side-by-side with the contributions of Stravinsky and Hindemith as great works for band of the twentieth century.

A note from Krenek demonstrates his careful participation in the details of his appearance at the forthcoming conference at the University of Maryland.

Ernst Krenek to David Whitwell
Palm Springs, CA, January 13, 1977

Dear David,
Many thanks for your detailed information on the convention strategy. Everything sounds fine. Your suggestions re: speck, etc. are congenial.
 Will there be any program notes on the works presented? Also I'd like to know how to dress for the concert …
 I am very sorry this convention causes you such headaches, but I am not surprised. These things are very laborious.
 Incidently, is my date at CSUN definite (May 14, I believe)? When do I rehearse there?
 All good wishes until soon,
 Ernst

As I was busy with organizing the rest of the convention, held in 1977 on the campus of the University of Maryland, I asked Bob Reynolds to take over the details of the commission. Bob did a great job and I am sure he must have enjoyed his visits with Krenek. Bob and I had previously agreed beforehand not to impose on Krenek a required list of instrumentation, but rather to leave him the flexibility to accommodate his inspiration, yet we needed to be sure he knew basically what an American band was. Bob decided it was best to solve this problem by taking down to Palm Springs, and leaving with him for a while, a dozen or so scores of fine earlier compositions for band, Schönberg, Milhaud, Hindemith, etc. Bob further thought it would be helpful to take a stack of fine recordings of these works for Krenek to listen to. On the day when Bob visited Krenek in Palm Springs, Krenek looked confused and asked what the recordings were for. Bob answered along he lines that he thought it might save time in Krenek's perusal of the scores. Krenek, still with a confused look on his face, looked at Bob and replied, 'I can read music!'

I had inherited a CBDNA which was completely broke and so Bob also had to come to the rescue with his personal funds to pay Krenek for the commission until such time as the CBDNA could repay him. The premiere, at the University of Maryland, was conducted by Richard Floyd, who did a fine job.

I also had Krenek come to Northridge again that spring and conduct the *Dream Sequence* with my own wind ensemble. Krenek wrote later,

> Ernst Krenek to David Whitwell
> Palm Springs, CA, May 16, 1977
>
> Dear David,
> This is to tell you how much I enjoyed conducting your excellent band in my *Dream Sequence*. Please be good enough to let these fine young people know how much I appreciate their attitudes and accomplishments and with them for me the best of luck …
>
> Thank you again for putting the work on the program after you had been so instrumental in causing it to be created.
>
> All the best, and greetings from both of us,
> Ernst

The following fall I was living in Salzburg and Krenek wrote to me wondering why I did not conduct the *Dream Sequence* in Austria. This suggested to me that he had not had much recent experience with European bands, for whom at this time the *Dream Sequence* would have been quite above their technical level.

> Ernst Krenek to David Whitwell
> Palm Springs, CA, July 29, 1978
>
> Dear Dave,
> It was good to hear from you that you are enjoying your time in Salzburg. Sorry you did not do the *Dream Sequence* at the Mozarteum—it would have been a European first!
>
> The premiere of *Charles V* is schedule for October 26 in Darmstdt. Perhaps we shall see you there? In the meantime, all the best.
> Ernest

PART II
The Medium is the Message

On Commercial Driven Education

THE FAMOUS PHRASE BY MARSHALL MCLUHAN, 1911–1980, a Canadian philosopher of communication, in 1964 'The Medium is the Message,' was intended to point out that aspects of the medium are always imbedded in the message. In more recent times, particularly in political and business advertising, one hears fears that the phrase has become more literal. I believe this phrase might very well be the most accurate five words available to describe the twentieth-century history of the American school band movement.

From the days early in the twentieth century when the school band movement began to flourish in America, it was an industry driven movement. Manufacturers of instruments, uniforms and music have more than anything else influenced the history of the movement. These manufacturers are in the business of making money and while they may donate money from time to time for conferences, etc., the history of the century has clearly demonstrated that they are not really concerned with the philosophy, values and practices of music education. Let me give a personal illustration. In the 1960s the CBDNA became interested in the poor tone quality of saxophone playing and instituted a committee to study this. The work of the committee, including travel and hotel expenses, was contributed by a major band instrument company. After nearly two years of study, which included making professional tapes which were listened to by conductors, we found that in fact there was one mouthpiece which noticeably improved the quality of sound. But at this point our manufacturer host stepped in and killed the entire study, for fear that the findings might make other manufacturers angry. A specific scientific piece of knowledge which would have been of help to bands and private teachers all over the country was buried. The medium, the industry, was the message.

In an ideal world we should have a national body of music educators, dedicated to the highest musical values, to the highest ethical values of the teaching profession and to the primary aesthetic values of music education. If we had such a teaching corps then the art of music and music education would dictate to the industry what was needed. And the industry would respond, so long as they make their money. If there is not such a strong teaching corps demanding the quality of music they need, for example, then the industry fills the gap and publishes what will sell on a broad basis, that is the lowest common denominator. Arthur Hauser of Theodore Presser Company made this very clear in a speech to the CBDNA in 1960.

> Some years ago, when addressing CBDNA on a similar subject, I stated that while publishers must accept responsibility for printing much so-called 'poor' music, educators must accept the greater responsibility, because if they would not buy it, the publishers would not publish it. This situation exists principally because many educators have not had sufficient experience with good music to take the lead in insisting on its use in their schools.

But, as Mr Hauser admits above, the publishers do not have entirely clean hands. This subject was addressed to me in 1970 by a major European conductor.

> Recently I obtained from Norway a version for 10 brass and percussion, or rather a microfilm of Grieg's manuscript [of his Funeral March] … Based on this I have done a version for British type brass band, and another for orchestral brass (4 horns, 3 trumpets, 3 trombones and tuba). I don't know whether this manuscript dated 1878 is the original—I rather doubt it. However there is no doubt in my mind that it is a masterpiece of its kind. It was performed by the British Youth Wind Orchestra last year in Gloucester Cathedral and was enthusiastically received by the players—the best sort of compliment I think. I should add that a shamefully simplified and mutilated version is published in your country as 'Solemn Procession' or 'Trauermarsch' (sic) and I fear the arranger or publisher haven't realized—or bothered to find out that this is an original wind piece, and before being grotesquely mangled, a masterpiece.
>
> I cannot understand why American arrangers are so arrogant as to believe that they can or ought to 'improve' on other peoples' compositions by wholesale alterations and/or omissions and why publishers are either too dishonest or ignorant or both to acknowledge such goings-on. I have wasted a good deal of money in the past on things purporting to be, for example Mendelssohn, which turned out to be mainly the work of Chester Z. Philistine, Jr.
>
> These things harm the cause of wind music and the reputation of American music and musicians.

Leaving aside for a moment the 'reputation of American music and musicians,' not to mention the impact of our repertoire on the field of music education, what is the impact of this industry on promising, serious young composers? During the 1970s I tried, through performances and introductions, to encourage a young composer, whom I still believe is one of the greatest talents I have ever met. An early work of his won a prize in a band competition, but then the associations he had with the publishers greatly discouraged him. He no longer writes band music, but here are some excerpts of his letters from this period.

> I refuse to compromise when I should be composing! I despise all those phony Celebratory, Dedicatory, Jubilant, etc., Statements, etc., etc., consisting of nothing but falsely noble gestures and bloaty scoring, slam-band marching band drums—but no music! …
>
> Years ago, while I was still a student, I often pondered with delight the foundation of a national organization to purge the band repertoire of all the junk; elevate the best literature to a level comparable to that of the listings of orchestral music; encourage new composers to challenge their imaginations in the pursuit of the creation of new works for the band; and carefully screen all new entities, based on the criteria for the initial purge mentioned above. What I am asking is Utopian and even tyrannical, since I am asking people to forget while we expunge the schlock element from the band's history …
>
> ……
>
> The educators are in the business of educating others to prepare them to educate others, who will educate others, etc., all according to the dictates of the publishers.

When I became president of the CBDNA in 1975, one of my goals was to attempt to raise the general question of ethics in the profession. After all, other professional organizations, including those in medicine and law, do make some attempt to frame this question for its members. My first effort was to appoint a national task force on this subject consisting of a small number of the most famous names within the profession. To lead this effort I chose Dr. James Neilson, Educational Director of Leblanc Instrument Company and previously Director of Bands at Oklahoma City University. He was better educated than most members of the profession and was a very musical conductor and educator. Having come from the English Salvation Army Band tradition, he possessed a firm moral foundation.

Unfortunately, Neilson was not able to persuade his other distinguished committee members to take part in a study of ethics in the profession, but he did provide me with the following three essays on the subject.

JAMES NEILSON ON THE ETHICAL RESPONSIBILITIES OF THE BAND DIRECTOR

James Neilson to William D. Revelli
cc: David Whitwell, president-elect, CBDNA
Kenosha, WI, October 11, 1974

Dear Bill:

Your letter has been face up on my desk for days, a constant reminder that you have requested my assistance in providing a *raison d'etre* for the deliberations of the CBDNA Ethics Committee. There are so many things one might say, of course, but how to say them correctly eludes me. Before I say anything, however, I must set forth a premise that is basic to my argument. *While the school band movement is an important factor on the American educational scene, it has only a secondary position in American cultural life.* You are aware of this fact and so am I, and a very few among the more visionary of our colleagues also. I must also tell you that the paragraphs to follow will not make sense unless this fact is borne in mind.

Are school band directors so engrossed in peripheral and often nonmusical activities they have forgotten that the inscription carved on the cornerstone of music education's towering edifice reads, *'Music for the child'* and not *'The child for music'*? It seems to me that a list of important benefits accruing to the school band program might best read like this.

First, *it is for the spirit*. Unless it makes the students kinder in heart, more gentle and honorable, more compassionate and generous and easily moved to good works, it fails to achieve its basic purpose, that of expanding the spirit.

Second, *it is for the mind*. Unless it makes students more aware of beauty and eager to comprehend its sources, and better able to understand its intellectual substance because of their strict obedience to music's artistic and intellectual disciplines, it fails to achieve its second important purpose, that of ennobling the mind.

Third, *it is for the body*. Unless it assists students toward developing sounder bodies and a heightened sensitivity and increased alertness toward fulfilling the demands made upon the body by the intellect, it fails to achieve its third important purpose, that of coordinating the body's physical activities in a way that enables students to take part in all the creative processes involved in making music. Good music in excellent performance is not possible until the spirit moves, the mind perceives, the intellect commands, and the body obeys.

The foregoing represents the permanent values of the good school band program. School band directors must begin to understand that all other benefits are temporal in nature. The impact these lasting values have on students' lives should be discussed more openly at band director association meetings and, hopefully, with the general public at the proper time. When the school band program really works, it is because conductor and students have submitted themselves to a never-ending discipline of spirit, mind and body. This is why a majority of students in good bands belong to that small group of the academically elect whose honor and integrity compels them to disassociate themselves from anything that is sordid, in school or out. It is about this the general public should be made aware, while much less emphasis is placed on the fringe benefits.

The duties of school band directors, both high school and college, can be set forth succinctly.

1. To guide students to the achievement of musical literacy. Parenthetically speaking, this is a rare accomplishment if major emphasis is placed on the acquisition of repertory either for contest purposes or to glorify a conductor's ego.
2. To enable students to understand and enjoy hearing and playing good music of all kinds, 'folk' and 'popular' music no less than 'serious' music.
3. To integrate the students' possession of musical skills and knowledge with life values.
4. To send students into the world determined to seek out and participate in music-making activities of some kind.

Since music truly exists only when it is heard, it needs performers and listeners no less than composers. The silent notes and symbols the composer places on paper represent only the face form of this art. When the performer recreates these notes and symbols, he must do so only through the dignity of ordered sound. Only then may he reveal whatever beauty he has found in the composer's original creation. Thus, it is the further duty of school band directors to make certain that performances by school bands are of genuine artistic merit. An inept translation of a composer's silent notes and symbols robs even great music of its right to existence. When they are performed ineptly, even the greatest works of Beethoven, master composer, become bad music at that time and in that place. One often wonders how many thousands of band students over the past fifty years have been 'turned off' permanently from enjoying good music because a 'bad' band director persisted in doing all the 'wrong' things. School band conductors must insist on lofty standards of performance. To do less is a disservice to the art of music.

Is it not right, then, to expect the personal character of the school band conductor to be based on integrity in all things, music included? Some place or other I read the concomitant characteristics of musical integrity given in this order: essential goodness, inner serenity and, following that, musical talent and musical knowledge. If a disciplined spirit must be added to the complete control of intellectual and bodily disciplines in order to make a musical performance convincingly sincere, why then do not band directors discuss the spiritual values inherent in good music with students more often than they do at present? What makes this subject taboo at rehearsals, band director meetings, and the like? Unless they are discussed, how else can band directors make certain that students understand the spiritual values of good music in a way that will cause performances by their bands to elevate the entire fellowship of musicians?

A fellowship that includes not just the conductor and students of the moment, but all musicians there present as well, together with all musicians who make or have made music anywhere, anytime, any place. A most notable fellowship, I hasten to add, and one in which the school band directors must prove themselves constantly as worthy 'fellows.'

The high level of musicianship that school band directors must attain cannot be achieved through a blinding flash of revelation. There is no royal road to success when pursuing this endeavor. The way to consummate musicianship is long and the road thereto rough and filled with pitfalls. To succeed, constant study and diligence must be coupled to an unswerving devotion to integrity. Moreover, true musicianship becomes valid only as spiritual understanding expands in equal measure to intellectual comprehension. Heaven save students from band directors who are stimulated only intellectually by music. Intellectual dogma has little place in the constantly growing experience of mind and spirit that bespeaks superior musicianship. Since it evades the spirit of the law to conform to its letter, intellectual dogma is far too confining in the rehearsal room. Its presence there negates music's spiritual values, values best expressed by words like these: *love—majesty—warmth—joy—aspiration—righteousness—contemplation*—and yea, at times—*sorrow—contrition—tears—lamentation—forgiveness*.

The thoughtful school band director does not place himself at the center of his musical experience to ask: 'What can the school band program do for me?' Rather, he inquires: 'How may I serve students best through the school band program?' It is his belief in the permanent values of what he does that impels him toward righteous and positive action, and will enable him to teach and respond to student needs in ways that will enrich their lives and bring peace and inner serenity to them. The extent to which a good band director acts on this rightly held belief marks the boundaries of his influence for good on students' lives, and enables him to go on, and on, and on, undaunted even when faced by bitter adversity and keen disappointment that causes lesser men to give up the battle and fall by the wayside.

The beautiful 'sounds of music,' is the language by whose use we are able to bring the grace, peace, joy and beauty of heaven down to earth. A language not confined by bonds of race, color or creed, that speaks its message of infinite good will to men and women everywhere. An universal language that mankind soon may use to bring about a day the peoples of the wide world desire so fervently to see, the day that will usher in 'the dawn of peace and brotherhood of man under the fatherhood of God.' There are some 1,500 school band directors in America at the college/university level. What will they do, what will be their commitment to the world-wide fellowship of musicians as together we work to hasten the coming of that glorious day?

The second essay by Neilson, a wonderful contribution by the way, has its focus on an ethical expectations for education in the public schools.

James Neilson on 'the Changing Scene'

James Neilson to Dr. William D. Revelli
cc: David Whitwell, president-elect, CBDNA
Kenosha, WI, Oct. 30, 1974

Were I to give this long epistle a title, the one most apt might be—THE CHANGING SCENE.

The educational scene was in constant change and ferment during the 1960s. Educational philosophies, procedures and practices that had been sacrosanct for decades were subjected to fierce scrutiny and criticism. Educational priorities were reordered and redefined over and over again. New teaching philosophies were propounded. Hundreds of revolutionary teaching practices and procedures were tried and often discarded quickly as valueless. Even although the decade of the 1970s is now well under way, the fervor of educational revolutionaries continues unabated and the education scene remains in ferment.

In the late 1960s and somewhat belatedly, music educators became alert to the facts of the 'changing times.' Strange voices were heard in the world of music education, voices that repeated this dogma with rising confidence and most noble sentiment: 'This is the way, the only way. Walk ye in it.' The more strident among these voices often suggested that all that had gone on in music education during the past decades, both good and bad, was suspect, and not relevant to today's world and its needs. Many among these voices said and continue in this plaint, that music of the great masters should be relegated to minor status in education, and that American symphony halls and opera houses are indeed 'museum places' unfit for the needs of a modern day world. Many music education revolutionaries still seek to cancel the major music-making activities of school choirs, bands and orchestras and displace these with music-making activities centered on ethnic musics and 'now' music, both serious and popular. Music education revolutionaries are often adamant in upholding their belief that ethnic and 'now' music are the only musics today's young people can and should study, assimilate, appreciate and perform.

While the truth concerning the best possible future for music education certainly lies between the polarities of the good that has been accomplished in the past versus the good that may yet be done in part by proposed revolutionary activities, music educators must, nevertheless, prepare themselves for problems that will result because of inevitable changes bound to occur if present day programs of music education are to survive the twentieth century. Radical or not, these changes can usher in a bright, new day. A day when music education becomes a joy unspeakable for those who give, the teachers; and music learning an experience full of glory for those who receive, the students.

Band director associations continue to fail in recognizing the permanent nature of changes now taking place in the world of music education, sad to say. I have often heard the period from the late 1940s to the mid-1960s described as the 'glory days' of the school band movement. 'Glory days' or not, they will never return. Believe me, they will never return in that specific way. The time is here for all persons in music education, band directors included, to share a common concern in the matter of formulating educational philosophies whose implementation will make it possible to establish meaningful goals for the musical education of American youth, goals that are discrete, concrete, concise and measurable. Since a large concern of its individual members is the training of school band directors, should not the CBDNA assume a leadership role in this matter? Perhaps, and in an effort to outline CBDNA responsibility, the ETHICS COMMITTEE should prepare a paragraph on this subject for possible inclusion in the Declaration of Principles.

Tentative agreement has been reached in some states concerning future goals for the total program of music education in the public schools, grades K through 12, goals that define the forward thrust of music education, what it is about, how it should operate and the results it should achieve. A state-wide committee of Wisconsin music educators has just completed the task of preparing a document—*Musical Goals Grades K Through 12*—a copy of which follows, a document far and away the most important of its kind I have ever read ...

Youth is much more aware of today's educational problems than are we of an older generation. Unlike us, 'Youth' dares to face today's problems unafraid as it considers what must be done to get out of the dilemma that music education and music educators face. Perhaps the ETHICS COMMITTEE should propose a similar, youthful IDEA COMMITTEE for the CBDNA to assist this organization in chartering its course for the remainder of the 1970s. A committee whose membership would be limited to persons in the 30–40 age group. I can think of a half dozen likely candidates, young intellectuals of perspicacity who have ability to bring form and substance to their dreaming.

Musical Goals Grades K Through 12
Skills

Students will have skill in listening to music.
1.1 They will recognize the broad melodic and rhythmic structure of musical composition.
1.2 They will be familiar with the sounds of musical instruments and the types of human voices.
1.3 They can hear and identify more than one melody at a time.
1.4 They can recognize patterns of melody and rhythm when repeated in identical or altered form.
1.5 They can respond through music to the basic meter, tempo and rhythm of music.

Students will be able to sing.
2.1 They will use their voices confidently in speech and song.
2.2 They will sing in a way that is satisfying to themselves.

2.3 They can carry an independent part in group singing.
2.4 Their singing will be expressive.

Students will attain some skill on a musical instrument, if only at an elementary level with a percussion instrument, recorder, guitar, autoharp or some other type of social instrument.
3.1 They will be able to express themselves on a musical instrument.
3.2 They will be able to provide an accompaniment for singing or rhythmic activities.
3.3 They will be familiar with the standard keyboard.

Students will be able to use musical notation in performance.
4.1 They can identify musical symbols and terms.
4.2 They are able to respond to the musical notation of unison and part songs.
4.3 They can follow a part in instrumental compositions.
4.4 They can use musical notation to confirm and reinforce their aural perceptions.

Students will be able to create musically.
5.1 They can improvise melodic and rhythmic patterns.
5.2 They can compose simple songs.
5.3 They can notate their original ideas.

Understandings
Students will understand the importance of design in music.
6.1 They will know the component parts of music and the interrelationships that exist between rhythm, melody, harmony and form.
6.2 They are able to recognize design elements aurally.
6.3 They realize that the active listener can, in a sense, share in a composer's act of creation or the performer's act of recreation.
6.4 By understanding how some music communicates, they will have an insight into what it communicates.

Students will relate music to man's historical development.
7.1 They will recognize that music has long been an important part of man's life.
7.2 They will understand that music's development in civilization is one of the unique elements of their own heritage.
7.3 They are familiar with the styles of music produced throughout history.
7.4 They will have some acquaintance with the music of the past and the persons who composed it.
7.5 They will be able to relate this musical knowledge to their understanding of man's social and political development.

Students will understand the relationships existing between music and areas of intellectual endeavor.
8.1 They will understand and can relate the aesthetic concepts common to all the arts.

8.2 They will understand how music and literature enhance one another and together illuminate history.
8.3 The mathematical and physical aspects of music will be known to them.
8.4 They will understand the physics of musical instruments and sound production.

Students will understand the place of music in contemporary society.
9.1 They will understand the function of music in the life of their community.
9.2 They will accept some responsibility for the quality of the music they choose.
9.3 They are able to relate music to contemporary issues.
9.4 They are aware of contemporary developments in sound production and musical styles.
9.5 They will recognize the ways in which social and political issues are reflected through music.

Attitudes

Students will value music as a means of self-realization.
10.1 They will recognize the unique way music can express feelings.
10.2 They will recognize the potential for emotional renewal and release through music.

Students will desire to continue their musical experiences.
11.1 They are aware of the position of the musician in today's society.
11.2 They will understand the opportunities open to them to engage in musical activities both as a vocation and an avocation.
11.3 They will listen to music on radio, television and through concerts.
11.4 They will look for community musical activities in which they can participate.
11.5 They will keep informed concerning happenings in the world of music.
11.6 They will seek for additional music experiences in areas in which they have found satisfaction.

Students will discriminate with respect to music.
12.1 They will learn to make personal choices based on musical knowledge and skill in listening.
12.2 They will be able to evaluate musical performances and exercise judgment in this area.
12.3 They are aware o the functional uses of music in society.

✼

James Neilson on Ethics in Performance

James Neilson to David Whitwell
Kenosha, WI, Sept. 28, 1978

Dear David,
Thank you for sending the cassette tape which I listened to yesterday evening. The performances of music by R. Strauss were totally admirable … That was a 'virtuoso' wind orchestra, my friend, in every way, conducted by a 'virtuoso' conductor. Bravo!

As you requested, I am mailing the cassette to Dr. Revelli together with a letter containing your Salzburg address.

Segments from the same transcription of *Zarathustra* were played at our last ABA meeting by a very famous university band, conducted by an equally famous band conductor. Since it was the last number on the program the conductor chose not to include the famous last measures in which, however softly, opposing tonalities represent nature in conflict. Rather, and I presume to bring about a rousing close, there was a return to tutti measures that appear early on in the work. About a dozen of us in the hall sat on our hands, despite the inevitable standing ovation going on round about us. When queried by the transcriber about the evident lack of enthusiasm on the part of a few colleagues, I could only reply that 'the conductor had missed the point.' As indeed he had. One either plays all of *Zarathustra* or none of it. There is no middle ground. Indeed, all Strauss' Zoroaster's poem is not complete until its last tragic sentences. Ah me! Our little world of band conductors is filled with mediocrities.

༜

THE ETHICS TASK FORCE failed to produce any results to present at the national conference in 1977. However I had one more plan to addresses ethics at this conference. I scheduled a one-hour session with no agenda, only the title 'Ethics for Band Directors,' or something like that. By having no agenda I had hoped to promote members to stand up and offer situations which bothered them, or situations in which they would like advice from others, etc. No one was willing to begin, but I had come prepared with some sample topics. For example, are their ethical concerns associated with a high school band raising money for trips to entertainment centers, Disneyland or Six Flags parks. No one spoke. I tried a few more general questionable areas (in my mind) with the same results. It was the most silent hour in the history of national conferences! It was quite clear that either no one wanted to publicly position themselves or that they believed these subjects were none of the profession's business.

I believe the latter is the root of the problem. There are university band directors who look upon all band activities, whether a summer camp, guest conducting and adjudication or sponsored travel, etc., as an opportunity for outside income. Obviously the education of children should be at the center of all the activities just mentioned and I believe that most university conductors believe that is true. However once money for services is attached to educational activities it seems to suddenly become a private affair. This is exactly why many states now make the salaries of educators a matter of public knowledge.

An interesting illustration of this situation manifested itself while I was president of CBDNA. As the year of the American Bicentennial was approaching in 1976 during my presidency, my attention was drawn to a great advertising campaign sponsored by a private entity which offered a high school band march from coast to coast. A particular band would march a mile and give a concert thus allowing the student to feel a vicarious participation in the great national celebration. A number of my famous colleagues had their pictures printed in this advertising in support, with the promise that the students would get to play under these men. What bothered me was a small print enticement to high school band directors everywhere which promised that for each student the teacher persuaded to pay and join the great parade, he, the band director, would get a cash rebate from each student's payment. In other words, money was going, under the table, from the parents of the child to the pocket of the high school conductor.

Any form of teacher enriching himself at the expense of his student seemed to me to raise an ethical question. I wrote a letter to each of the famous university conductors who were participating outlining my concern and proposing to call a meeting of the national board of directors to discuss this question. I indicated that if the board was as concerned as I was, I would call for a motion for the CBDNA to publicly disassociate itself from this activity.

I did not hear from any of my colleagues, but I soon had a phone call from a lawyer somewhere in the Northwest representing the organizers of this national cross-country march. The lawyer said, 'I don't think you understand! This law firm has 200 members!' He then went on to make threats against me and the CBDNA, to which I answered, 'Take your best shot!'

I never heard further from the lawyer and the parade was called-off even before I could call a meeting of the board to discuss it. But I do recall receiving a phone call from Bill Revelli, who was very angry with me. He actually screamed at me, 'How dare you involve yourself in my personal commercial opportunities!!'

Ethics for band directors, it seems, stops at the bank.

On the Futility of Band Organizations

THERE IS SOMETHING ABOUT MODERN MAN which impels him to join groups of men with similar interests. In some fields, such as in labor, these organizations can help bring about actual laws which help its members. Some organizations, as in medicine and law, exist for punitive purposes, among others. But in the arts, where the views of the individual are given wide latitude, these kinds of organizations rarely amount to more than offering social opportunities for members to meet old friends.

If one looks at wind bands in the United States from almost any perspective one can find serious problems in the conduct of these ensembles. Typically a young man of talent is attracted by the opportunity to improve some facet of the band field only to find that the band organizations he belongs to are generally incapable of taking any action other than planning the next meeting. The reason for this lies in the very wide latitude of views found in the organization; they are members of the same organization but they have little in common in their views. Consequently it is my view that in matters of art, aesthetics and philosophy one cannot count on any accomplishment by organizations. The individual who wishes to see change or improvement must attempt to contribute as an individual for he will find little support from organizations in the arts. Indeed, he is likely to be opposed by the very organizations who have the most to profit because their strongest motive is to just remain as they are.

This chapter offers historical insights into some of the band organizations and recounts my own activities in trying to lift the sights of my colleagues. First, to establish my credentials for speaking on the subject of band organizations, here is a summary of my participation in a few of them.

College Band Directors National Association
 Life Member
 National President (1975–1977)
 A. A. Harding Award (1977)
 National Conducting Clinician (Greeley, CO.), (1983)
National Conferences, Guest Conductor
 Ann Arbor, MI (1967)
 Tempe, AZ (1972)
 Kansas City, MO (1990)
National Conferences, Speaker
 Ann Arbor, MI (1967)
 Berkeley, CA (1975)
 Kansas City, MO (1991)
 Boulder, CO (1995)
 Denton, TX (2001)

Regional Conferences, Conductor, Clinician or Speaker
    Pullman, WA (1966)
    Rochester, NY (1972)
    Reno, NV (1974, 1992, 1994, 2000)
    Philadelphia, PA (1774)
    Greensville, SC (1976)
    Houston, TX (1976)
    San Luis Obispo, CA (1980)
    Long Beach, CA (1982)
    Hayward, CA (1982)
    Santa Barbara, CA (1988)
    Washington, DC (1994)
    Kansas City, MO (1998)
    San Antonio, TX (2012)

World Association for Symphonic Bands and Ensembles
    Life Member
    Member, Founding Board of Directors (1980–1981)
    Board of Directors (1997–2001)
    Editor, *WASBE Journal*, 1997
    Chair, Conductor Development and Training Committee (1999–2000)
    Co-Chair, History Committee (1989–1999)
    Planning Committee for World Conference (1997–1999)
    World Conferences, Guest Conductor
        Manchester, England (1981)
        Kerkrade, The Netherlands (1989)
        San Luis Obispo, CA (1999)
    World Conferences, Speaker
        Kortrijk, Belgium (1985)
        Manchester, England (1991)
        Schladming, Austria (1997)
        San Luis Obispo, CA (1999)

National Wind Ensemble Conference
    Guest Conductor, Madison, WI (1973)
    Host, California State University, Northridge (1975)

National Band Association
    Elected, Fellow, Academy of Wind and Percussion Arts (2007)
    Honorary Life Member (2007)
    National Mentor for Conducting (2010)

International Gesellschaft zur Erforschung und Förderung der Blasmusik
    Board of Advisors (1977–2012)
World Conferences, Clinician
    Graz, Austria (1977, 1985)
    Uster, Switzerland (1978)
    Trossingen, Germany (1979)
    Toblach, Italy (1990)
    Abony, Hungary (1994)

Music Educators National Conference
    Life Member
National Planning Committee (1973)
National Chairman, Committee on Bands (1775–1776; 1990–1992)
Member, Special Research Interest Group
National Conferences, Conductor
    Atlantic City, NJ (1976)
    Anaheim, CA (1986)
Regional Conferences, Guest Conductor, Clinician or Speaker
    Portland, OR (1965)
    Missoula, MT (1967)
    San Francisco, CA (1975)
    Honolulu, HI (1976)
    Orange, CA (1976)
    Los Angeles, CA (1976)
    Fresno, CA (1976)
    Seattle, WA (1977)
    Salt Lake City, UT (1977)
    San Jose, CA (1977)
    Sacramento, CA (1980)
    Long Beach, CA (1984)
    Oakland, CA (1990)
    San Diego, CA (1994)
    San Bernadino, CA (1995)
    Pomona, CA (1997)
    Santa Clara, CA (1998)
    Pomona, CA (1999)

California Music Educators Association
    Member, 1969 until present
    Hall of Fame Award (2009)

Texas Music Education Association
    Keynote Speaker, Austin, TX (1977)

Tyrolian (Austria) Conductors Conference
    Clinician, Graz, Austria (1981)

American Bandmasters Association
    Member, Research Center Committee
    Advisor, Research Center
    Member, Oswald Composition Contest Jury
    Member, Philosophy and Purpose Committee (1993–1994)
    Conductor, National Conferences
        Tokyo, Japan (1984)
        Ashland, OR (1988)
        Washington, D.C., (1992)
        Honolulu, HI (1994)
        San Antonio, TX (1996)
        Williamsburg, VA (2004)
        Gainsville, FL (2005)
        San Luis Obispo (2007)

Austrian National Band Association
    Gold Medal for Service, 1994

Kappa Kappa Psi
    Honorary Life Member, 1964

John Philip Sousa Foundation
Member, Board of Directors
Sudler Composition Competition Committee
    Director, Oral History Project

P. S. Gilmore Society
    Member, Board of Directors

Frederick Fennell International Young Conductors Competition
    Member, The International Jury

North American Band Directors Coordinating Council
    Member (1971)

Center for Wind Band Repertoire, Indianapolis, IN
    Board of Directors (1994–1996)

The Instrumentalist Magazine
    Board of Advisors (1967–1988)

The Journal of Band Research
   Editorial Board

The CBDNA Journal
   Editorial Board

The College Band Directors National Association (CBDNA)

The CBDNA was founded in 1941 by William D. Revelli of the University of Michigan for the purpose of discussing common interests. In 1941 many university bands were sponsored by the military and were officially part of the campus R.O.T.C. program. The obvious goal of Revelli and his colleagues was to find a place for these bands within the music department. This took longer than most readers can imagine. In 1975 we had a national conference of the CBDNA on the campus of the University of California, Berkeley, at which time neither the university band, nor the orchestra, nor their conductors were members of the music department. I was once offered a position at Columbia University in New York City, but the phone call came from a student, for the band was run by an organization of students, not the regular faculty. I believe examples such as this still exist at some universities. When I hear of these situations I feel we are back in the sixth century trying to argue for a place for music in the curriculum.

The CBDNA as I came to know it in the early 1960s had little sign of life, usually meeting for only one day in Chicago before the Mid-West Band Conference. My election as president-elect in 1973, at age 35, was a surprise to me and almost everyone else. The election occurred during an afternoon business session and the results were announced at an evening banquet. Youth must have frightened some of the men for Mark Hindsley, Director of Bands at the University of Illinois, came up to me after this banquet, in tears, pleading with me not to destroy the CBDNA. As the man who had been elected president was suffering from serious physical problems I had to assume much of his duties as well, which gave me more time to try to make some changes.

My first goal was to try to breathe some life into the organization. The standing committees had the same persons in charge for many years and had accomplished almost nothing. I thanked them for their contributions, explained that I wanted to bring in some new faces and let them all go and replaced them. Then I organized twenty-four task force groups, each with a member from every division whom I picked for the most part from among young men who had never had leadership opportunity. Altogether this resulted in well over one hundred new, young workers for CBDNA which brought an immediate new enthusiasm felt by everyone in the organization.

The most serious problem I had to solve was that I inherited a bankrupt organization. Previously the entire board of directors received free room and board, plus their flights, in Chicago for the Mid-West board meeting. I had to explain to these gentlemen that since the only agenda item was the fact that we were broke that I was canceling the meeting. I did point out that I would be sitting in a certain meeting room in Chicago, at a certain time, and if enough board members just happened to be in Chicago anyway and could attend I would call a meeting to order. They were all present. Next, there had been a Book of Proceedings published and distributed free after every conference. This had to go as well, unfortunately. There were significant unpaid debts for the 1975 conference in Berkeley, including a suite of rooms for the president and his grand arrival by helicopter. We commissioned a major work by Ernst Krenek but we had no funds to pay him. Bob Reynolds loaned the profession this money and before my term ended we were able to repay him. In the end I was able to pass on to the next president a vibrant and solvent organization.

If the CBDNA were to truly be a national association I thought it imperative to move the conferences away from the Chicago area in order to make it possible for new young members to attend. Therefore the 1975 conference, which I had to design, was held on the West Coast in Berkeley, CA, on the campus of the University of California and the 1977 conference on the East Coast at the University of Maryland.

One of my goals was to begin to try to get the members to move away from thinking of themselves as band directors who provided civic entertainment and to begin to think of themselves as artistic conductors. Actually at the moment they stepped on the podium everyone of them thought of themselves as conductors, it is just that they were not accustomed to think like conductors before the concert, with respect to the kind of literature they offered their students, in their own score preparation and how they presented themselves on the podium. For the Berkeley conference, therefore, it was my desire to have some conducting clinics and to my astonishment I found that there had never been one previously in the history of this organization! So I had four, two were 'talking' clinics, one of which was by Bob Reynolds who demonstrated a level of score study which surely must have been unknown to most of the members. The second was by Revelli and I had told him I wanted him to speak about Italian expressivo performance practices. He did not stay with that topic but he obviously gave a lot of thought to his session and he gave some practical 'tricks of the trade' which I, for one, used ever after. For the other two conducting clinics I wanted to take two of the most famous 'Big Ten' conductors and give them a high school band and then, using a familiar score, demonstrate what they would normally do in the first rehearsal with a new band. As it turned out, both of these men were afraid to do this and each requested, and I supplied, secret advance rehearsals with their respective bands so they would not be embarrassed in public. Therefore the entire idea was lost.

One memorable occasion for me at the Berkeley conference was hearing the premiere of the *Angel Camp* by Charles Cushing, a work I consider to be one of the very best band compositions. I ran back stage to ask the composer how I could rent the score and parts for I wanted to perform his work immediately. I found him much distressed by the quality of the performance he had just heard and telling everyone in sight that he would never allow anyone to ever perform his music in the future. In fact, I had to wait until he died, some years later, before I could get the score and parts from his family.

For the 1977 conference at the University of Maryland I invited the Eastman Wind Ensemble to perform a concert in honor of the twenty-fifth anniversary of this famous ensemble. The 1975 Berkeley conference was the first that an ensemble calling itself a 'wind ensemble' had ever been allowed to perform at a national CBDNA conference! Only Bands were invited! This caused much discussion and angry comments during the next two years. I knew no one could object to the Eastman anniversary occasion and so I used it to confirm that 'wind ensembles' were now accepted. I never heard the subject mentioned again.

Both of these conferences contributed a great deal to bringing the CBDNA back to life, financially and spiritually. I, on the other hand, was quite exhausted and when someone asked if I would consider being the next president of the National Band Association I had to say no.

The requirements of my office in the CBDNA required me to give two formal addresses which I later reprinted as essays.

The CBDNA in the Future (1975)

I have two concerns regarding the future of the CBDNA. First, I believe the organization needs to be a forum for the most open, free and wide-ranging discussion. Some of our various philosophies tend to unite us and some divide us into separate camps. Due to the social and fellowship aspects of our organization (which are very important) there is a danger we will concentrate only on ideas that we share. I believe the CBDNA is more important as a forum for ideas we do not share.

The second fear I have is that as the organization becomes more effective there will be a tendency for the organization to become concerned primarily with its own preservation. Then its value would be lost, for its value lies in what it does for the membership. I believe this organization should exist to help each individual member achieve his highest artistic and career ambition. That is not a selfish goal, but rather a democratic one.

My personal debt to the CBDNA is great. In this organization I have found real friends, dependable advice, and unfailing support. I recommended to new and younger members that they take the initiative, be active in the organization, and use it for their own growth. That the organization is responsive to younger members is witnessed by the fact that I was elected to national office after only seven years of teaching experience.

I think the average director does his job rather well and is eager to do it better. The problem is that to do the job well he has almost no time left for the most important obligation every conductor bears: his own growth as a musician. Nothing is more critical to the long-range nature of our profession than this problem. The successful college band director who works a hundred hours a week asks, 'Where do I find the time?' The college band director who may barely find time to study scores he performs asks, 'Where do I find the time to study scores purely for my own musical growth?' The only answer is the one Erica Jong has hung in her studio: 'Art doesn't demand much; only everything you have.'

The repertoire of the college band has changed dramatically in the last decade. Ten years ago, very few college bands performed programs consisting primarily of original compositions. Today there are very few that do not.

We devote the greatest amount of rehearsal time to the quest for the technically perfect concert. In the future we must devote more time to spiritual qualities. Their discussion lends strength to the quest for technical perfection; their omission robs it of meaning.

The individual college band director is going to have to become more proficient in defining his profession. We are going to have to learn the language of the American educator and to present in that language the ancient beliefs of our profession.

The average college band director has tended to slight his relationship with the rest of music education and ignore the other professional organizations. This diffidence rather reflects the fact that he tends to be a strong, confident and highly independent musical figure, accustomed to doing things for himself. Again, in the future he will be denied the luxury of privacy. The college band director will have to learn to reach more in his relationships with other music educators—for his own sake.

The college band director could exert much greater influence on the quality of music education in the United States. In a recent interview with *The Instrumentalist*, conductor Georg Solti made the astounding statement that what he misses in America is a basic music education for each child. How can he say that? Our schools are frantic with school bands, school orchestras, and so on, of which there are virtually none in Europe! I think where our educators would disagree with Solti is not in the definition of education, but in the definition of music. If you really want to take the pulse of music education in the United States, read the new music reviews in *The Instrumentalist* and *The School Musician*! I am sure Solti would say that whatever all this activity is, it isn't music.

To put this in different words, we have taught performance and how to achieve it—and have done it very well. What we haven't really taught is taste, aesthetics, or how to judge the quality of music itself. As a result our young band directors and the quality of music education entrusted to them fall victim to a problem defined by Weingartner. He said a bad performance can ruin a good piece of music. But one cannot speak of a good performance saving a bad piece of music. A good performance of bad music only brings the weak points of the composition more clearly into focus.

The coming decades will test our profession in many ways; battles fought in the 1930s will have to be re-fought in the 1980s. It will surely demand the best in each of us. When we take our stand, when we fight those battles, I hope it will be the spiritual power of great music that is our banner and that sustains us. In more than four centuries, it has been the spirit of great music that has produced wind band conductors' finest moments.

In the 1580s Dalla Casa, filled with the spirit of great music, formed the state wind band in Venice. He desired something more than the expected accompanimental role of the Renaissance. By the way, if there are those of you who feel that the sixteenth century is a bit remote to have much relevance, there is a Venetian document of 1550 which reads, 'Those players who refuse to play *canzoni* in procession will no longer be employed in the chamber,' or, if you are not in my marching band you can't be in the concert band.

The Mozart wind serenades were written for a society of wind players and conductors who, filled with the spirit of great music, could not accept the social definitions of their time.

The band repertoire for the French Revolution came into existence because a group of conductors, filled with the spirit of great music, wrote symphonies rather than marches for the education of their military bands.

In our century this spirit has produced a number of college band directors who have risen above the didactic necessities to make great performance an accepted goal of music education.

Those of us to whom the college band movement is now entrusted owe to dedicated predecessors and to college band directors yet unborn that our era be judged as one in which the spirit of great music was central to our literature, fundamental to our aesthetic, primary in our teaching and the common bond of a dynamic society of men—the CBDNA.

CBDNA AND THE BICENTENNIAL (1976)

First, I bring you the most welcome news possible on these occasions—that is that these remarks will be very brief.

I am happy to report that the CBDNA, nationally, is healthy and growing. It continues to be *the* organization doing most for college band directors, as the reports of the twenty-odd Task Forces and various national committees will demonstrate in College Park next year. It continues to run the best conducting clinic in the United States. The CBDNA continues to be the only organization which is commissioning new works for band by internationally recognized composers. In College Park we will hear the latest of these—a major work by Ernst Krenek.

The great Bicentennial year is here! We have hardly begun the year and we have already been driven to near exhaustion by endless commercial motives and every huckster's gimmick. But that's all right, for commercial motives and huckster's gimmicks are part of our country's history too—and for that matter, part of our profession's history as well.

But every thoughtful person must at one time or another pause to reflect on the more lofty ideas which have been part of our country's experience. It strikes me that a noticeable distinction in this country's history is how much has been accomplished by ordinary people. We haven't had any Napoleons or Louis XIVs upon whom the entire country's story revolved for a generation or more. Even most of our presidents have been rather ordinary men.

In this regard my thoughts always turn to Lincoln. In many ways he was not only ordinary but typical of us all. Like most people he lacked the grace which the wealth of a Jefferson or a Washington produces. Like most people he lacked the sophistication which the world travel of a Franklin grooms. There is much in him with which his contemporaries and our contemporaries as well can identify. And yet, he seems at the same time to represent the very best in the American to a degree that makes it hard to think of another who can stand in his company.

Because our professional problems are people problems, not organizational problems, I find myself reflecting on this ageless Lincoln when pondering our profession during this year of national celebration.

One of Lincoln's most pronounced characteristics was a desire at all times to bring people together. This reminds me of the single most divisive issue among our profession today: the name we give our top concert medium. At our recent meeting in Chicago, the national officers received expression of this concern, in particular that there was a widely-shared opinion that not enough performing groups at our last convention in Berkeley were called 'bands,'—too many were called 'wind ensembles.' It seems to be irrelevant that they were all large groups, playing 'band' music—like the Hindemith *Symphony*—only that they were not *called* bands.

I cannot help but think Lincoln would respond to this concern by telling some story about two old former friends of his in Illinois who, when they were urgently needed in town and had a problem in basic transportation, stood arguing the merits of a palomino and a pinto—when of course the point was that they needed a horse. The suggestion, which I have heard, that if one calls his group a 'wind ensemble,' he is ashamed of the word, 'band,' no more follows than saying that the man who preferred the palomino was ashamed of the word 'horse!'

We don't care if a colleague prefers a different brand of trumpet in his group than we would use. We rarely object if a colleague has an entirely different concept of literature. We don't care if a colleague prefers a different style of uniform than ours. Why in the name of Heaven do we care what he calls his group? Why does it bother us that he is more comfortable with sixty players while we are more comfortable with seventy-five?

I think it is time for the profession to put name-calling behind us. The CBDNA should be an umbrella organization in which every member of the profession is welcome, regardless of his philosophy or his preferences. If we want to make value judgments of a colleague, let's do it on a really substantive basis—like the quality of his music making, or the quality of the education he gives his students. But let's no longer worry about what he calls his group.[1]

I grant that it is that which we have in common which makes it possible to have an organization like the CBDNA. But if we are going to have a CBDNA, we should not only accept but treasure our differences—for it is in those areas in which we differ that we can also learn and profit from our association together.

In one way Lincoln was an outstanding example of a basis quality of the American character. That is the quality of self-improvement—two centuries of 'pulling ourselves up by our boot-straps.' This quality is going to become critical in our profession. For years members of our profession sought to bring the quality and direction of our literature up to the standards of the rest of the musical world. Now rather suddenly, within one decade, we find we have arrived. We now have a basic repertoire of older masterworks and we are, internationally,

---

[1] I was once criticized as being pretentious for calling my top group a 'wind orchestra,' by a man who called his top group a 'wind symphony!'

rapidly becoming the leaders in contemporary composition. We are rapidly reaching the point that the Bachelor of Arts will not begin to prepare a young band director for dealing with the musical challenges of his music.

The problem is that the education of a band director in the future will continue to be oriented toward the mechanical, rather than the musical and spiritual necessities of his profession. Prominent teacher organizations, instead of helping with this problem, are instead compounding it by seeking to further broaden the mechanical competencies. Instead of studying Berlioz, they want us to be able to name three native instruments used in Borneo. We will have to find ways to instill in our young followers a desire to pursue an intense life-long study of important music. He will have to do it by himself.

A final characteristic of Lincoln which I would like to mention is his genuine love of helping others. Of course, in his time one's neighbor was a vital link in survival. Today it is the reverse—we seek privacy. It is not unusual at all to live in an apartment building and not even know your neighbor's *name*. This works against what should be the most fundamental characteristic in a teacher—the desire to help people. In our profession we have become increasingly competitive. Our profession will suffer if our personal instincts to compete overshadow our sense of fellowship. Let us this year begin to create a professional association in which our foremost pleasure, after music itself, comes from seeking to help our colleagues. We will all profit and perhaps we will come to understand what Lincoln meant when he said, 'The better part of a man's life consists of his friendships.'

World Association for Symphonic Bands and Ensembles (WASBE)

On the Direction of WASBE (1999)

When I was elected president-elect of the CBDNA I had some thoughts about holding an extra CBDNA conference in London but I soon became so busy with ordinary CBDNA work that I gave up that idea. When I became president in 1975 the vice-president was Frank Battisti who had been having similar thoughts. I set aside several hundred dollars in the budget for Frank to use in exploring his idea.

Beginning in 1978 I was living nine months a year in Salzburg and Frank visited my home there to discuss whom he might meet. I took him to visit with Wolfgang Suppan in Austria, a man active in everything and who later became a president of WASBE. I also took Frank to visit Hitler's Eagle Nest in nearby Brechtesgarten. It was a wild storming day on top of the mountain, very much like *Das Götterdämmerung*, and Frank was running around the paths yelling, 'I love it!'

I had urged Frank to have his conference in central Europe, due to the large numbers of good civic bands, but Bill Johnson, who was on sabbatical in England, convinced Frank on Manchester. When we were all back in the States the three of us had a meeting at Bill's house in San Luis Obispo where we organized on paper a four-day conference which was to occur in 1981. Our model for the Manchester conference was an earlier creation by Frank, something called the National Wind Ensemble Conference. This annual event, which lasted eight years (1970–1977) was a unique band organization as there were no officers and no agenda other than listening to concerts of new repertoire or repertoire which might not have been heard before. I, for example as the host in 1975, programmed early music including repertoire from the French Revolution with chorus.

At the request of Frank and Bill Johnson, I agreed to bring my Northridge group over to perform the final Gala concert. I programmed a very solid program which included the Florent Schmitt *Dionysiaques*, the premiere of an English Symphony and the Schönberg *Theme and Variations*. I had invited my old friend, Bob Reynolds, to conduct the Schönberg as a vehicle for introducing him to my European friends. The concert made quite an impression on the English, who had at that time a very weak tradition of the concert band as we know it, their passion running to the brass band concept. Indeed, BBC, who recorded the concert, continued to broadcast it for a number of years; every few months a royalty check would arrive. The concert paid off at home as well, for I had taken to England the president of my university and I found out later that Col. John Bourgeois, conductor of the US Marine Band, had told the president that Northridge had the best university band in the US. The president quoted that everywhere and I saw no point in ruining his fun by explaining that John was a very old friend of mine and that his comment was pure hyperbole.

This concert in Manchester in 1981 was, in everything but the name, the beginning of WASBE. As mentioned above, the model was the earlier National Wind Ensemble Conference, but now with publishers invited to display European band music. It was the members present, excited over the success of this conference, who created WASBE in order to continue this new tradition. I was asked to be on the new board of directors but had to decline due to a lack of time.

The original idea of WASBE, again, was to be an emphasis on hearing serious new repertoire. However, once there was a board of directors, with a new president every two years, the character of WASBE soon began to change. It was an attractive idea, for example, of holding the conference each time in a new country, but this soon turned into a situation where the local host, eager to show off his country, placed a great deal of emphasis on local folk music. This made nice tourist events, but the original idea of an organization for serious conductors seeking new important repertoire was soon lost.

In addition, becoming an organization not addressed to needed values in the profession, and having no enduring core of purpose, it quickly became evident that people joined when they planned to attend a conference, but did not continue their membership. Thus, the membership of WASBE for years stood at about 1,000, but it was always a different 1,000. Each incoming president, wanting to increase these numbers, began to try to think of ways to expand the outreach, by adding military bands, for example. One president wanted to add audience members as potential members, meaning the entire planet was a target. But it had the opposite effect.

Nevertheless, I served where asked, on the board of directors for four years, on various committees and speaking or conducting on four conferences. When Felix Hauswirth was elected president he asked me to take over the job of Editor of the *WASBE Journal*, something I had no desire to do. But, because he was a friend, I agreed to do one issue, which would give him time to plan for what was to happen next. I did enjoy my work on this one volume as it was entirely dedicated to the role of emotions in music. It was my effort in trying to get one of these organizations to think about music rather than the organization.

It was with this concern for the focus on music that I wrote an incoming president a letter in 1999.

On the Future of WASBE (2000)

David Whitwell to Tim Reynish
Northridge, Nov. 26, 1999

Tim, I want to urge you to keep your eye on the bottom line, with respect to WASBE. Here is the bottom line: we are all children of a mother of ill-repute, and her name is ENTERTAINMENT. But this is a relatively recent development. Wind band leader/conductors of the 16th, 17th, 18th and first-half of the 19th century thought of themselves as artists, not entertainers. Bach, Haydn, Mozart, Beethoven, Wagner never thought of the wind band as anything less than an art medium on the same level as string ensembles.

All this changed only in the late 19th century, and we must break this chain for important reasons:

[1] Society does not need us for the purpose of entertainment music. There is much genuine entertainment music already out there. Not to mention we now have 500 channels of entertainment on TV. Sports are nothing but entertainment (someone needs to remind the world that soccer is only a game and, as a game, it doesn't matter who wins!) Certainly, no one can make a case that entertainment should be part of the school curriculum. We are not needed for this purpose by society; we ARE needed for the development of man.

[2] We need to return self-dignity and respect to the conductor—even to those who are unaware. We must remodel the next generation of wind conductors so that they think of themselves as artists, not entertainers. To this end the conference must have so clear an emphasis that the young received this message—and have sessions which help them become better artists. The current crop, those interested in 'cheap beer and scenery,' must be ignored. Like educators of any age, it is the future that is our concern, not the past. It is because we do not think of ourselves as artists that the rest of the musical community doesn't—not the other way around. It is because we do not think of ourselves as artists that the repertoire is so poor—not the other way around.

Over the years various members, especially the Austrians, asked me to run for president of WASBE, but after having been president of CBDNA I never again wanted to deprive others from having this pleasure. However, with my full-time retirement from university work in 2000 and my continuing concerns for WASBE, I eventually agreed to allow my name to be considered. To this end I addressed a letter to the board of directors in which I mentioned some of the concerns I have expressed above. In addition, I was particularly concerned that WASBE always had its European conferences in small, out-of-the way villages instead of in major cities. I felt our conferences contained performances and repertoire the major music critics really should hear, especially since there was not in Europe the cultural prejudice against bands that one finds in the US. But you have to take the music to the critics and so the reader will see I stressed this in the following document which was intended to inform the board of directors of the direction I would want to go if elected.

David Whitwell to Members of the WASBE Council
Northridge, November 24, 2000

Earlier this Fall I was asked by Leon Bly to think about the possibility of being a candidate for president-elect. This was soon followed by a similar request from Wolfgang Suppan asking if I were willing to serve and indicating that on the basis of the membership ballots returned by November 2, 2000, that 'many members' had expressed a desire for my election.

Naturally, I felt very honored by the high regard reflected in these communications and as requested I promised to give thought to this prospect.

I then made the time to study in depth the various records and communications of WASBE over recent years. As a result of this study, I find that my views regarding what WASBE should be are in fundamental conflict with how WASBE has evolved in recent years …

PURPOSE

I do not see much evidence of real purpose in WASBE at the present time. We do have a great deal of activity and function, especially in the production of paper—journals, newsletters, repertoire lists, etc., but to me it all appears as function without purpose. That is, I fail to see the presence of a higher purpose which determines the kind and content of our efforts.

In my view it is this lack of a clear purpose which is the chief cause of the dramatic fall off in our membership. I believe people join to attend a particular conference, but since they find no purpose to commit them to a cause, and hence to attract their continuing financial support, they simply do not continue as members.

My sense of purpose for WASBE is one that I have devoted my entire career to, to lift the artistic understanding in band directors everywhere and to help them see a higher obligation to their players and their towns than simply entertainment. Since every citizen, save those in third world countries, now has available 500 channels of TV, surely our role in the production of entertainment is no longer what it was in the nineteenth century. Indeed, I believe that the town band director has the unique opportunity, even duty, to bring culture to a town which might otherwise not have the opportunity to hear live, artistic music. To me, everything that WASBE does, in conducting clinics, in discussions of repertoire, in involvement of composers, etc., should support this purpose …

ORGANIZATION

As I mentioned above, I (speaking now only for myself) regarded in the beginning that the great promise of WASBE was as an organization of serious, artistic conductors in search of similar minded colleagues throughout the world. Publishers and composers were welcome because of their abilities to help us.

In subsequent years I find WASBE to have become greatly expanded in its role and in the number and kinds of activities of its committees. From the various correspondence of Tim Reynish, I believe he would like to expand the organization even further, to small ensembles, to individual orchestral members, etc.

The CONSTITUENCY given in the Portsmouth document expands even more; now we are an organization of 'conductors, composers, professional & amateur performers, teachers, audiences.' It seems to me that includes all persons in the industrialized world.

My first concern is that WASBE is becoming so diffuse that it will become structurally inept. I am afraid that the organizational effort required just to keep track of all the committees, net-working, etc., will preclude any possibility of developing meaningful purpose or focus.

THE 2005 CONFERENCE
In my view it is critical to WASBE that we begin to hold our conferences in major musical centers.

I often hear members express concern that we are not recognized by the 'real musical world.' But we do not expose ourselves to the real musical world. Consider, for example, our international youth wind orchestra. If we held a conference in Berlin or Milano, such a gathering of international young musicians would certainly attract local TV and, no doubt, national TV. But if we meet in some small village, the media will never hear of it or cover it.

Further, I believe that most of our membership would be more willing to attend, and would be willing to pay more for housing costs, and registration costs, if the site were a major musical center, such as my preference for 2005—Leipzig.

If the principal conference for 2005 is Singapore, I will not agree to serve as president. I would love to visit Singapore, but I believe the average member from Europe and the US will not go. It, like the Japan conference, will turn out to be in effect a regional conference and not a world one. I have no desire to put all that personal effort into a conference poorly attended. Sorry.

For the organizational work for a Leipzig conference Leon would, of course, be the ideal person. But we could not expect him to do this without increasing the funds we pay him. This increase should come from the registration fee. We should not fear these costs. We are far below the dues and conference fees of other worldwide musical associations.

At this time the board of directors in effect held the election, choosing one name which was then submitted by mail to the membership for approval. The other candidate whose name was before the board submitted no plans for his possible term of office and, being present, said nothing whatsoever about his plans. The vote was taken and the result was Other Candidate 19 and Whitwell 1 (a member from Israel). I did not take this as a personal affront, as I might have if I were young. But it did signify to me that WASBE was dying a natural death. Indeed, the last world conference attracted very few members and the following conference was cancelled. I am afraid it is too late to restore the grand dream we all had in 1981.

International Gesellschaft zur Erforschung und Förderung der Blasmusik (IGEB)

This organization is an Austrian-based one dedicated to the development of wind music. I was present at the founding of this organization and was a member of the board of directors for more than thirty years. Attending one of their conferences one had the opportunity to meet real scholars and important European musicians. It was here that I first got to know the great Baroque trumpet authority, Ed Tarr, for example. It had a certain class, as wind conferences go, for if you read a paper you automatically had your room and board paid for. At their meeting in Trossingen in 1979 the German government even paid for the transportation of all people attending from wherever you entered Germany to Trossingen and back.

I spoke at five of their conferences and I recall that one of these, in Hungary, I spoke on 'Improvisation in Harmoniemusik repertoire.' A member told me that if I gave this talk in Vienna they would hang me from a light post.

This organization also published my first book, on the band music of the French Revolution. One of the unique benefits of this organization is that each member receives a free book every year. I allowed them to have my book to publish for this purpose when the organization was just beginning, with the understanding that I was doing this to help them build their membership. My understanding was that the book would be published only for these members and for this purpose and so I agreed to waive any royalties. Following this arrangement, the book was immediately out of print and in later years my attempts to obtain an additional copy went unanswered by the German publisher. Only a few years ago I discovered, in a European catalog, that the publisher has been selling this book for thirty years, with no offer of royalty for the author. I feel I have been taken advantage of by this organization and I have withdrawn my membership.

American Bandmasters Association (ABA)

Recommendations for the ABA (1993)

The ABA is the oldest band organization in America, going back to Sousa and the men of his era. It is an honorary association with no apparent purpose, save a composition contest. The majority of members are in retirement and thereby for me is the only value this organization has. An older, retired military officer, for example, now lives in a world where no one knows who he is or was. The same is true for those living in retirement homes. But they can appear once a year at the ABA meeting and find people their age who remember them; it is as if they briefly regain their identity. There is a place for an organization which does this.

This dormant social organization would be quite harmless were it not for one inexcusable, in my view, flaw. The ABA has a long history of membership by invitation. In the beginning the candidate also had to submit to a test of composition ability as well. This has evolved into a system whereby one is nominated for membership, and then investigated by a committee. What comes next is most objectionable. At a business meeting with all attending members, the nominee's name is the subject of an open debate. Some speak out, objecting to the nominee; others speak out in support. A great majority of the members present will have never heard the name in their life, but nevertheless they listen to, and take away with them, negative comments as may be offered. Keep in mind the nominee did not ask to join, much less to have his name and career publicly criticized!

The last of these meetings which I attended included a debate over a fine military conductor, who had been active in making recordings. Someone stood up and said, 'he is too flamboyant!' It seemed to me that this and similar objections which I heard on this occasion were actually inspired by jealousy. In any case, to me it was a disgusting scene and on this occasion the candidate was rejected. These discussions are of course supposed to be in secret, but the information always makes its way out.

I myself was a victim. I believe it was in 1967 that my name was nominated and the result of this discussion of me was that I was not accepted. I was told by insiders that since I had resigned from the University of Montana in order to study with Eugene Ormandy in Philadelphia it was taken as a sign by some that I was not interested in bands! The problem was that since I was already well-known in the profession by this time the word quickly spread around the country that I had been 'black-balled' by the ABA. Of course, I did not ask to be a member and had no interest at the time in being a member, but yet this apparently negative characterization of me was the talk of the profession.

This was followed by obsequious pleas by important leaders of the profession for me not to be offended, to please give them another chance, 'we need you more than you need us,' it has happened to a lot of men before, not to be accepted the first time, etc. I was not exactly angry at this needless and uncalled for insult, but I certainly wanted nothing further to do with the ABA. For more than ten years I refused to allow them to put my name forward and it was only because I grew exhausted with the embarrassing pleas by the leaders that in 1979 I finally said OK. At that time one had to be sponsored by a member from one's own state and California had then only two members. So they designated one of the older men to formally present my name to the membership. On the night before he was supposed to do this at the convention he, being quite drunk, called me up and said, 'I know I'm supposed to know the details of your background but could you please help me out?' I was voted in and at the convention of 1980 I was formally introduced to the membership by the three most distinguished men in the organization standing by my side as if inviting anyone to dare to criticize.

In 1993 the current president of the ABA placed me on a Philosophy and Purpose Committee, which never met. I took the occasion to send the following letter.

David Whitwell to Dr. William P. Foster
Northridge, CA, Oct. 22, 1993

Below are some of my thoughts relative to direction of the ABA and the Philosophy and Purpose Committee.

Membership
There are two problems here.
[1] The present procedure of open discussion of persons who, after all, have not even asked to be members, is undignified and reprehensible. I have witnessed misstatements and unfounded accusations go unchallenged and reputations damaged unnecessarily.

We may not be legally liable for what has gone on in these sessions, but in my opinion we are morally liable and therefore I, personally, will never again attend such sessions.

[2] If we are to be perfectly honest, we must admit that for the past forty years the following is true:
[a] At no time have all the best members of the profession been members of ABA.
[b] With regard to matters of character, etc., the ABA stands no higher than any cross section of the American public.

The current system simply does not do what we pretend it does.

> I recommend we drop all pretense to the concept of 'the best,' replacing it instead with simply 'distinguished.' I believe a small committee appointed by each President should propose prospective members on the basis of their known contributions to any facet of the band business. On the basis of that recommendation alone, the names should be presented to the membership for a pro-forma vote. No discussion! I believe the results will be just as good over time, and we will eliminate these reprehensible open discussions.

In 1984 the ABA held a joint convention with the Japanese Bandmasters Association in Tokyo. The Japanese had specifically requested to hear two American ensembles, mine and the one at Indiana University, America's largest music school. I had been in Japan for several weeks of concerts throughout the country in 1960 with the Air Force Band, so I knew it would be an unforgettable visit for my students and thus I raised the necessary funds to go.

The history of American style bands in Japan began with several men here recommending the easiest, thus most trashy, literature to the young movement there. Thus for my concerts there in 1984 I played only first-rate musical compositions, such as the Hindemith *Symphony* and the Schmitt *Dionysiaques*, works I knew would be new to them. In gratitude I still receive each year, now twenty-eight years later, notes of thanks from Japanese conductors.

As I am a life member of a number of organizations, when I retired I decided to no longer continue membership in any organization in which I had to pay dues and so I resigned from the ABA. I had belonged for thirty years and never felt like a member.

There are some additional fine organizations which I simply did not have time to participate in on a regular basis, but by whom I was honored.

- *The National Band Association* awarded me their highest honor in 2007, honorary membership in their Academy of Wind and Percussion Arts.
- *The California Music Educators Association*, in 2009 awarded me their Hall of Fame honor.
- The *Austrian National Band Association* awarded me their gold medal in 1994.
- The *Kappa Kappa Psi Band Fraternity* awarded me honorary life-membership in 1964.

This past honor, a life-membership in the Kappa Kappa Psi, came in my second year of teaching, so it was obviously not awarded on the basis of my achievement. I feel the need to write a word about the president of Kappa Kappa Psi at this time, Jack Lee, Director of Bands at the University of Arizona and one of my earliest supporters. Jack had been the man responsible for developing the outstanding reputation of the Michigan Marching Band. He left Ann Arbor, for reasons unknown to me, and moved to the Arizona job.

By the time I met him in 1963–1964, Jack was an unhappy man and, again for reasons unknown to me, was ostracized by the other university band directors. He had written a book called *The Art of the Marching Band*, in which he argued that the marching band be considered an art form and not a military representative. In retrospect, although I have no interest in marching bands, I think he was right, that the field should be considered a stage. Certainly in my view what marching bands do at half-times of football games is exceedingly boring. In fact it was during the time I was president of CBDNA that the major television networks were beginning to cut back on the time devoted to covering the bands' performances. Bands were getting only several seconds coverage. I, using my title, contacted an executive of ABC to ask about this and was told that studies of water consumption in major cities showed major increases during the band shows. People were not watching; they were going to the bathroom and missing the commercials!

Well, everyone made fun of Jack's book, but it must have been more than that which left him isolated. I found him a very interesting man. He had one of the nation's largest collections of tin soldiers from the eighteenth and nineteenth centuries, including full bands of different regiments of various countries. He even had part of the private collection of Hitler. I took a film crew over from Los Angeles to Tucson to film these for background use in a video on the band music of Beethoven for most of them were from that period.

On that visit, Jack showed me a large manuscript score he was composing, *The Last Words of Christ* for orchestra and chorus. The man, not popular on his faculty and isolated by his profession and unhappy in his marriage would go home at night and drink and compose this massive orchestral work. For me it was tragic through and through.

I don't think I ever saw Jack again. But my experience in knowing him has caused me to forever reflect on the fact that there must be out there hundreds of band directors who are nearly unknown to the profession and who yet have remarkable stories to be told. It may be that their story is more interesting than the band's story.

PART III
On Bands in the Educational World

On University Education Being Based on a Sixth-Century Philosophy

During the earliest years of the Christian Era the Church, in its attempt to create a new citizen, went to great lengths to rid the life of the citizen of all emotions, as being the first step toward Hell. St. Basil went so far as to say a good Christian should not even laugh, for laughing is a form of emotion! After the Church closed the 'pagan' schools and then reopened them, music became a problem for the curriculum because to every normal person music is above all else a special communication for expressing the emotions.

The Church solved the problem with music by making it a branch of mathematics but before long it was apparent this was not accepted as Truth. The next step was to divide music into two branches, Speculative Music and Practical Music. By Speculative Music the church meant the grammar of music, theory and mathematics, and this was accepted for the curriculum. Practical Music meant performance and this was not accepted into the curriculum. Better leave this to the musicians out on the street to teach.

This division has led to problems which are still with us in the university, beginning with a certain prejudice against performance which is said by the grammar people to not really be scholarly. I once heard a professor at the University of California at Berkeley say publicly, on this very point, 'Playing a clarinet is to Music as typing is to Literature.' It doesn't count, in other words. But this viewpoint is entirely wrong, because it is only when music is performed live that it is truly *music*. Music is for the ear. 'Music' written on paper is not music, it is a symbolic representation of music, even though we mistakenly use the word 'music' incorrectly in this regard every day in every school.

Following on the heels of this linguistic error, the grammar teachers (theory, composition, etc.) naturally focus on grammar and completely leave out discussion of the emotions in music. One reason for this is because those medieval Church theorists who invented the notation system we use today were under instructions not to include any symbols representing feelings or emotions in their newly invented systems. And so to this very day we do not have in our notational system for music a single symbol which represents any of the emotions. Since the grammar teachers then do not have these symbols to include among their description of music, they fail to teach it. What harmony teacher uses the word 'pain' in class?

At the same time, instrumental studio teachers in America are technique-oriented and they rarely talk about emotions either. What clarinet professor, after listening to a student play an etude says, 'what emotion are you feeling?'

The result is that in many university music departments the fundamental point of music is missing. In 2010 I wrote an essay on this subject.

The Forgotten Man (in the Music Department)

Here is a friendly experiment for the music major to try the next time he goes into the studio for his private lesson. After he has begun to play for his teacher the material which the latter has assigned for him, regardless what that material is, let him stop, turn to the teacher and ask, 'It is not clear to me right here what emotion I should be conveying to the listener.' What the student will experience next is something as close to absolute silence as is possible to experience in our modern urban society.

This will happen because the odds are very great that the American studio teacher will have forgotten that music makes no sense without a listener. The listener is the 'Forgotten Man' in American music education. In which harmony class does the professor address what the symbols on the blackboard mean to the emotions of the listener? Moving the emotions of the listener is the sole purpose of music. While our harmony professor will give the obligatory ear training exams, he is not teaching harmony with respect to the emotional purpose of music. He is teaching harmony as an abstract language and he and his course should be transported to the Romance Languages Department.

And his colleague, the history professor, is his teaching focused on the emotional purpose of Baroque music or is he reading data? As he assigns reading material for his students, is he teaching music for the eye or the ear? And what will his students recall of Baroque Music when the course is finished? Will they recall how this music intended to impact the emotions of the listener, a topic which the Baroque composers were so concerned about, or a few facts about various composers? Most of these professors should be transported to the History Department because they are not teaching music.

We wonder how effective university music education would be if all instruction were done by ear. No books and no blackboards allowed in the music building! This should not seem a radical thought, if one only remembers that music is for the ear and not for the eye.

How did our university music professors, who should certainly know better, lose track of the only real purpose of music—to move the emotions of the listener? Civilization for thousands of years has made it so clear that the meaning in music lies in the expression of emotions from performer to listener. In one of the very oldest examples of extant ancient Greek literature, the *Odyssey* by Homer, the poet is careful to document the power of a song by a minstrel on the emotions of the listener.

> This song the famous minstrel sang; but Ulysses grasped his great purple cloak with his stout hands, and drew it down over his head, and his comely face; for he had shame [that his guests, the Phaeacians, should see him] as he let fall tears from beneath his eyebrows. Yea, and as often as the divine minstrel ceased his singing, Ulysses would wipe away his tears and draw the cloak from off his head ... But as often as he began again, and the nobles of the Phaeacians bade him sing, because they took pleasure in his song, Ulysses would again cover his head and moan. Now from all the rest he concealed the tears that he shed.

Because of the impact Ulysses experienced from the first performance, he now begs the singer to 'change thy theme' and sing no more of the fate of the Achaeans, but rather of the 'building of the horse of wood.' This request the singer complies with, but again Ulysses was again moved to tears.

> This song the famous minstrel sang. But the heart of Ulysses was melted and tears wet his cheeks beneath his eyelids. And as a woman wails and flings herself about her dear husband, who has fallen in front of his city and his people, seeking to ward off from his city and his children the pitiless day; and as she beholds him dying and gasping for breath, she clings to him and shrieks aloud, while the foe behind her smite her back and shoulders with their spears, and lead her away to captivity to bear toil and woe, while with most pitiful grief her cheeks are wasted: even so did Ulysses let fall pitiful tears from beneath his brows. Now from all the rest he concealed the tears that he shed, but Alcinous alone marked him and took heed, for he sat by him and heard him groaning heavily.[1]

It was with the arrival of the Christian Era that the listener became the Forgotten Man, at least in so far as literature was concerned. The Church, which tried to destroy the ancient books and controlled new ones, attempted to create a philosophy of music without emotion. Only the words are important they said and even St. Augustine reports that he felt he had sinned when he paid attention to the music instead of the words while singing in Church. Aside from trying to protect the new Christian from the influence of emotion in any form, the Church also warned that the listener should not admire the composer, or any artist, but rather they should focus on God who made the artist.

In time, however, the curtain of the Dark Ages lifted and with the arrival of Humanism and the Renaissance the Forgotten Man returns. Clearly the lute virtuoso, Francesco da Milano, had the listener in mind when he gave this performance in 1555.

> He made the very strings to swoon beneath his fingers and transported all who listened into such gentle melancholy that one present buried his head in his hands, another let his entire body slump into an ungainly posture with members all awry, while another, his mouth sagged open and his eyes more than half shut, seemed, one would judge, as if transfixed upon the strings, and yet another, with chin sunk upon his chest, hiding the most sadly taciturn visage ever seen, remained abstracted in all his senses save his hearing, as if his soul had fled from all the seats of sensibility to take refuge in his ears where more easefully it could rejoice in such enchanting symphony.[2]

And we hasten to add that with most fine artists today there is no Forgotten Man; they have the listener foremost in mind. Once while I was the director of bands at California State University, Northridge, we hosted a French horn clinic by the great principal hornist of the Chicago Symphony Orchestra, Dale Clevenger. During an opportunity for the horn students to ask questions of this great artist, a student asked, 'What are you thinking while you are sitting there in the orchestra, with Solti conducting, while the orchestra is performing, let us say, Mahler's *Fifth Symphony*?' And Clevenger answered immediately, 'Why, I am looking out at

---

[1] A. T. Murray, trans., *The Odyssey* (London: Heinemann, 1960), VIII, 60ff, 470ff.

[2] Pontus de Tyard, *Solitaire second* (1555).

the audience, trying to communicate my emotions to them!' Imagine that! There in front of him is Solti energetically waving his arms, surrounding him are dozens of string players moving their bow arms and weaving back and forth in their chairs, not to mention the physical reality of the music itself. But Clevenger is distracted by none of this! He is thinking of communicating his emotions, as found in Mahler's music, to the audience! And he is doing exactly what every performing musician should do. All this motion, by the way, has long been associated with music; notice how similar are the words, motion and emotion. Do we bottle up the emotions of our students when we make, or allow, them to sit upon the stage like statues?

It is only natural, therefore, that we must return to the question: How did the educational community forget the listener? Philosophers as remote in time as Socrates (whose teaching we have in the writings of Plato) have clearly communicated that the listener was fundamental to music education. Plato, for example, writes of the several prerequisites necessary to the successful music student in his book, *Philebus*. In addition to considerations with respect to demeanor, being able to tune his instrument and loving his teacher, Plato says the music student must have a good ear and understand theory (systems compounded out of pitches). But he hastens to qualify this by observing that this is not what we mean by being a musician.

> SOCRATES. But you would not be a real musician if this was all that you knew; though if you did not know this you would know almost nothing of music.[3]

The student must understand how emotions appear and 'come to be in the movements of bodies.' In another place he makes it clear that the performer must communicate his feelings to the listener to be successful. The performer, affected by this divine power (of the composer), is also inspired, his 'soul is in ecstasy' and the audience is then similarly affected by this and emotionally respond.[4] Plato illustrates this by the brilliant analogy of a magnet. The magnet is the composer's feelings, this is passed on to the performer in the manner a piece of iron touching the magnet becomes magnetized and then once again touches and magnetizes the listener.[5]

When this last step is *not* the concern of the studio teacher and the listener is the Forgotten Man then the student plays his recital but afterward is met by his friends who say such things as 'that was very interesting' or 'you really play well!' These are not the kind of comments a recitalist wants to hear.

Nowhere is the Forgotten Man so evident as in music education studies. Music educators have forgotten that the music students, no matter how young, are and must be listeners. Since the Forgotten Man is often reflected in school rehearsals one often hears a rehearsal in which the ensemble plays a bit, then they stop and the conductor talks, then they play, then he talks, then they play, then he talks, etc. Ironically, nearly all of what we *call* music education is focused in the intervals when there is *no* music!

---

[3] *Philebus*, 17c.

[4] *Ion*, 534, c – 535e.

[5] *Ion*, 533d, 535e.

When you see a school rehearsal and none of the students are looking at the conductor, then you know you have another Forgotten Man. The fundamental problem in this case is that the conductor's facility as a listener is enormously limited by the score on his music stand. The score is addressed to the wrong hemisphere of the brain; there is not a single symbol in the score addressed to feeling! It is because the score is of the rational world, and not the experiential world, that the conductor tends to talk so much—talk also being of the rational world.[6] And when he is thinking about what to say next, while the ensemble is playing, he cannot be a listener. Our senses do not operate well simultaneously. Everyone has heard the joke about the conductor who, upon the occasion of a loud bass drum stroke, cries 'who did that!?' I actually witnessed such a scene when I was a student in the famous band of William D. Revelli. On another occasion he had just asked a horn player to play the tuning pitch when he suddenly thought of a long story to tell. This horn player was skilled in circular breathing and hence continued to play the tuning note without a break during Revelli's long story. Revelli was completely unaware that his story had this musical accompaniment, a dramatic demonstration that he who talks is a poor listener.

This conflict between the rational and the experiential leads us to propose an interesting question. Throughout evolution the ear has specialized in hearing sounds important to personal experience (hearing the tiger outside the cave). It must have been a period of millions of years before the ear was expected to take on any form of intellectual function. The eye on the other hand, as several thousand years of philosophers have argued, *is* of the realm of Reason. Music must have existed and been appreciated by listeners for a million years before the eye had anything to do with it. The ancient Egyptians had no notation system for their music and neither did the ancient Greeks,[7] yet they had flourishing and effective musical performances.

We should like, therefore, to propose a physiological question. Perhaps we have overlooked the possibility that it is not so easy for the ear to deal with rational data, such as language. How many times have we heard the professor complain that the student did not *hear* some point of his lecture? And all conductors know, or should know, that when they begin talking in rehearsal almost no one is listening.

Even speech conveys its meaning in the emotional inflections we give it. Indeed all philologists believe that music preceded language as a form of communication in early man. There may not have been language, as a structured thing, but there must have been vowel sounds of expression, much like a dog makes. So early man was a skilled listener to the emotions of musical sounds long before he had a language. It is residual knowledge of this that virtually all ancient treatises on oratory warn that it is emotion that attracts the attention of the listener. They noticed long ago that the speaker can even lie and the audience will believe him if he speaks with emotion. Notice the emphasis which Cicero (106–43 BC) gives this in his advice to the orator,

---

[6] The conductor who memorizes his score is freed to be a listener on a higher level.

[7] Excepting the last years of the final period, the 'Roman Period' of ancient Greece.

> Now there are three things in my opinion which the orator should effect: instruct his listener, give him pleasure, stir his emotions ... But whether or not the orator succeeds in conveying to his listeners the emotions which he wishes to convey, can only be judged by the assent of the multitude and the approbation of the people ...
>
> When one hears a real orator he believes what is said, thinks it true, assents and approves; the orator's words win conviction ... The listening throng is delighted, is carried along by his words, is in a sense bathed deep in delight ... They feel now joy now sorrow, are moved now to laughter now to tears; they show approbation detestation, scorn aversion; they are drawn to pity to shame to regret; are stirred to anger, wonder, hope fear; and all these come to pass just as the hearers' minds are played upon by word and thought and action.[8]
>
> ......
>
> For just as from the sound of the strings on the harp the skill with which they are struck is readily recognized, so what skill the orator has in playing on the minds of his audience is recognized *by the emotion produced*.[9]

Another important ancient Roman philosopher, Quintilian (30 –96 AD), could just as properly be speaking to music students when he explains to young orators his secret to the communication of emotion to the listener.

> The prime essential for stirring the emotions of others is, in my opinion, first to feel those emotions oneself. It is sometimes positively ridiculous to counterfeit grief, anger and indignation, if we content ourselves with accommodating our words and looks and make no attempt to adapt our own feelings to the emotions to be expressed. What other reason is there for the eloquence with which mourners express their grief, or for the fluency which anger lends even to the uneducated, save the fact that their minds are stirred to power by the depth and sincerity of their feelings? Consequently, if we wish to give our words the appearance of sincerity, we must assimilate ourselves to the emotions of those who are genuinely so affected, and our eloquence must spring from the same feeling that we desire to produce in the mind of the judge ...
>
> Accordingly, the first essential is that those feelings should prevail with us that we wish to prevail with the judge, and that we should be moved ourselves before we attempt to move others. But how are we to generate these emotions in ourselves, since emotion is not in our own power? I will try to explain as best I may. There are certain experiences which the Greeks call ¿avradias, and the Romans *visions*, whereby things absent are presented to our imagination with such extreme vividness that they seem actually to be before our very eyes. It is the man who is really sensitive to such impressions who will have the greatest power over the emotions ... It is a power which all may readily acquire if they will.[10]

Because the issue is moving the emotions of the listener, Quintilian and other early writers on oratory recommend the study of music. They advise one to observe the musicians to see how they do this. Interestingly enough, Quintilian points out that *some* things, in particular movement, can only be learned from the study of music!

> Let us discuss the advantages which our future orator may reasonably expect to derive from the study of Music.

---

[8] Cicero, *Brutus*, xlix.

[9] Ibid., liv.

[10] Quintillian, *The Education of an Orator* (Institutio Oratoria), VI, ii.

Music has two modes of expression in the voice and in the body; for both voice and body require to be controlled by appropriate rules. Aristoxenus divides music, in so far as it concerns the voice, into *rhythm* and *melody*, the one consisting in measure, the latter in sound and song. Now I ask you whether it is not absolutely necessary for the orator to be acquainted with all these methods of expression which are concerned firstly with gesture, secondly with the arrangement of words and thirdly with the inflections of the voice, of which a great variety are required for law practice. Otherwise we must assume that structure and the euphonious combination of sounds are necessary only for poetry, lyric and otherwise, but superfluous in law, or that unlike music, oratory has no interest in the variation of arrangement and sound to suit the demands of the case. But eloquence does vary both tone and rhythm, expressing sublime thoughts with elevation, pleasing thoughts with sweetness, and ordinary with gentle utterance, and in every expression of its art is in sympathy with the emotions of which it is the mouthpiece. It is by the raising, lowering or inflection of the voice that the orator stirs the emotions of his hearers, and the measure, if I may repeat the term, of voice or phrase differs according as we wish to rouse the indignation or the pity of the judge. For, as we know, different emotions are roused even by the various musical instruments, which are incapable of reproducing speech. Further the motion of the body must be suitable and becoming, or as the Greeks call it *eurythmic*, and this can only be secured by the study of music.[11]

Like the ancient orators, we too in music education also deal with 'stirring the emotions of the listeners.' Or, at least an objective outside observer might conclude that since communicating emotions is the only purpose of music that this must be at the heart of music education. But because music education is not in fact based on developing the emotional nature of the child, the listener is the Forgotten Man in music education.

The musician that Socrates interviews in Plato's book, *Ion*, tells us what he sees from the stage when he looks out at the audience.

> ION. I look down upon them from the stage, and behold the various emotions of pity, wonder, sternness, stamped upon their faces when I am performing.[12]

This may not be what we see from the stage of concerts by educational musicians. But if the listener is the Forgotten Man in music education then we cannot expect different results. You reap what you sow.

In conclusion, there is one more consequence of the Forgotten Man in music education. Although no university music faculty wants to admit it, or discuss it and certainly not feel a responsibility for it, we are nevertheless involved in the education of the audience. And we have a very large exposure here. The average university music department provides some two hundred concerts per year before, let us say an average audience of one hundred persons. Multiply that by 2,618 universities and you find we have an exposure to over fifty-two million adults per year. Of course there is some duplication, but maybe less than we think. I know from experience that in Los Angeles that one can say in general that the adults who come to hear a senior recital are never seen again.

---

[11] Ibid., I, x.

[12] *Ion*, 534, c - 535e.

Then if you include the rest of music education, in particular high school concerts, the exposure grows. There are 27,468 high schools in the US, but it would be unrealistic to assume they all had orchestras, or even choirs who sang classical music. But if we estimate that the average high school had a mere two concerts of classical music per year, with an average of one hundred adults in the audience then you have another five million adult exposure.

In sum, we may be reaching through educational classical concerts nearly one third of the adult population in the US each year. But the media tells us that the adult audience for classical music has fallen to two percent among American adults. That is a conspicuous condemnation of the effectiveness of our role in educating the public.

We in music education need to cross our fingers and hope that it never occurs to anyone to lay the responsibility for that dismal statistic at our doorstep.

✶

ANOTHER REASON why it is incorrect that the grammar teachers call what they teach 'music' is that most of what they teach is past tense, whereas true music is present tense. In 2010 I wrote an essay to expound on this idea.

ON THE NATURE OF THE PRESENT TENSE IN MUSIC

A friend of many years wrote recently that he was preparing to move into a professional home for senior citizens. This friend has an extensive collection of early music, literary works and musical instruments and so I asked him how does one cope with the idea of giving everything away prior to making such a move? To illustrate his current frame of mind, he wrote as follows:

> I don't find it a matter of coping, but rather a matter of having no choice. I have too much stuff that I no longer need, though some of it has sentimental value. For example, I saved the programs of every concert I played, and I never even looked at them for 40 to 50 years. So what value do they hold for me? None.

It is a very interesting phenomenon that he points to. We all have similar collections of old programs, not to mention pictures and recordings. And like my friend, the curious thing is that we never feel an obligation to go back and look at these things. Suppose that today I said to myself, 'I wonder what music I performed in 1982?' If I were to dig out my programs for 1982 I would no doubt find it a very interesting exercise. There would be, for example, repertoire I had completely forgotten and names of guest artists and conductors would, by the merest exposure to the eye, bring back a flood of memories. The exercise would, no doubt, repay the investment in time with a very pleasant hour or two. But, again, the interesting question is, why do none of us do this?

I have a case on the wall of my office which contains some two hundred cassette recordings of my concerts. They have a catalog number on the binding, and perhaps a date, but no information on the repertoire on the tape, which is to be found in a catalog which affords the necessary space for this information. So, sometimes when faced with a long drive across town I will grab a cassette at random and listen to it in the car as I drive.[13] Since for several decades I was one who joined the efforts at improving the image of the band by performing much very new music and dozens of premieres, there are on these tapes a great deal of music played one time and one time only. And so it often happens that I will hear, as I am driving, some composition which I do not recognize whatsoever. I cannot recall the music or the composer's name, I cannot recall ever having performed this music (which I am hearing on a recording of my own concert) and when I return home I have to consult my index to identify the composition. And yet I know that there was surely a time when I invested a great deal of time studying this score and, indeed, memorizing it for the concert.

How does one explain how such a performance, with all the personal investment it entails, can completely be deleted by the mind? I don't think the quality of my memory, in general, is to blame. I have a good memory. I have conducted all rehearsals for a performance of the *Rite of Spring* without a score and I retain extensive quantities of precise dialog from conversations held beginning with the 1940s.

All of our minds have a certain sense of discrimination when it comes to memory. For example, our minds seem to know, sometimes even in advance, whether to remember something for long periods (a phone number) or whether to let things enter and exit the mind without being retained at all (nearly all of today's newspaper).

But with music, there is another fundamental factor at play. Although the subject is never discussed in our educational formative years, the fact is that *real* music exists *only* in the present tense—it exists perfectly in step in time with us as we are hearing it. A musical score sitting on a shelf is not music. A recording of last night's performance is not music. What we pass out and is placed on the 'music' stands is not music.[14] This is why most of us do not enjoy listening to our own recordings. The recordings are not real music, they are only sounds frozen in the past tense. While we may retain in our mind the exhilaration of the concert itself, experiencing live music, now in the recording we find only a cold document of that concert. And in listening to this document we are listening outside of the actual experience and it is for this reason, as all artists know, that now as mere objective auditors we tend to notice small flaws which seemed almost beside the point in the live experience. And it is for the same reason, the transformation of the experiential into past tense documentation, that musicians have little interest in looking back at programs and recordings of prior concerts. As my friend has suggested above, we collect and store them away for almost no purpose at all.

---

[13] Talk radio, of course, being an impossible waste of time, even if thought of as entertainment.

[14] Here other languages are more helpful. In Germany it is 'die Noten' or 'die Stimmen,' which is placed on the stands and would never be referred to a 'die Musik.'

It is precisely because real music exists only in the present tense that we should not casually accept recordings as being 'music.' Music is present tense; recordings are past tense. They have only value as an aid in helping us to recall the real music, but they do not substitute for music. In this way they are analogous to photographs. A photograph can strengthen our recall of a loved one, but the photograph never becomes the loved one (for one thing, the loved one is not two inches tall).

Who Stole our Present Tense?

Nearly all of traditional education is geared to the future. Learn this or else! Practice or else! For young adults all experience seems deferred. They are focused on 'When I get,' not to mention everything about Wall Street.

Old people, of course, live in the past tense.[15] My wife, Giselle, has observed that only small children, before school age, live in the present tense, or as she says, 'in the moment!'

So who stole our present tense? How did we come to have a society in the Western world where we do not live in the present? If one wishes to pursue this question, there is perhaps no better place to begin than with the writers of the early Christian Church in Rome. Gibbon, in his famous study of Rome, gives five reasons for the remarkable rise of the early Church and one of these was 'the doctrine of a future life.'[16]

> When the promise of eternal happiness was proposed to mankind on condition of adopting the faith, and of observing the precepts, of the gospel, it is no wonder that so advantageous an offer should have been accepted by great numbers of every religion, of every rank, and of every province in the Roman empire. The ancient Christians were animated by a contempt for their present existence, and by a just confidence of immortality, of which the doubtful and imperfect faith of modern ages cannot give us any adequate notion.[17]

In other words, to the average person in fourth-century Rome the Church said, you may be poor, have inadequate clothes and shelter and be miserable, but do as we tell you and in the next life you will walk on streets of gold![18] And from that day to this both Catholic and Protestant churches emphasize the future tense more than the present tense.

We cannot help but add one more thought in this regard. As Gibbon points out in the book we have cited, before the Christian movement there was a long tradition in ancient literature dealing with various thoughts about a future life after death. It is very possible, therefore, that these ideas were more commonly known two millennia ago and if so perhaps the Roman

---

[15] I was speaking with the 85-year-old Fred Fennell once when a student reporter came up and asked him, 'Dr. Fennell, what are your plans for the future?'

[16] Edward Gibbon, *The History of the Decline and Fall of the Roman Empire* (Philadelphia,, 1845), I, 508ff.

[17] Ibid., 532.

[18] This is one reason why in the Middle Ages the aristocracy was quick to use the clergy and their promise to help control the population.

Church misunderstood one of the admonitions of Jesus. Maybe what Jesus meant was, 'if you don't take these teachings to heart *now* (in the present tense, 'in the moment' like a child), they won't be of any value in the *future*,' when he said,

> Truly, I say to you, whoever does not receive the kingdom of God like a child shall not enter it.[19]

On top of this, as we have pointed out, the schools also do not focus on the present tense. What is the affect on our civilization when we are reared in the wrong tense? It should be no surprise to us when we observe the wide-spread disorientation of youth and young adults.

Of course we are not going to be able to change religious philosophy, but one should hope that the educational world might devote more thought to the present tense of their students. Certainly only then will the educational world come to understand the potential of music, since it only exists in the present tense.

ANOTHER AREA where we omit feeling is in the teaching of conducting. We teach conducting gestures as if they were abstract communications. This is another problem on which I wrote an essay in 2010.

WHERE IS THE VALUE IN CONDUCTING CLINICS?

Why do our conducting clinics devote so much time to things which no great conductor of the past ever gave a moment's thought to?

I, for one, have become very suspect of clinic formats where one or more master teachers watch a young person conduct an ensemble and then dispense pithy and humorous comments which seem to be designed more toward entertaining those present than in actually reforming the technique of the student. In a clinic I recently observed I heard the 'master' teacher recommend 'practicing conducting standing in a corner in order to find the proper angle of the elbows and arms to the body.' In my mind's eye I have difficulty trying to see Toscanini doing this.

Furthermore, I wonder if there is not a psychological block which prevents the student conductor from really paying attention to the suggestions of the master teacher. It has been my observation that when the student conductor receives his turn to stand before the ensemble to conduct that human nature takes over and the student is focused on his moment, he is the star, now is his opportunity to show what he can do, etc. It is distinctly not a moment to be receptive to comments intended to change what he is doing naturally and certainly not to be made to feel unnatural before an audience. In years of watching these kinds of clinics I have rarely

---

[19] Mark 10:15.

been convinced that anything in the student's technique actually changed. He may try something at the master teacher's suggestion, but he goes right back to doing what he did before because he is in every way put together physically and mentally different from the teacher.

I suppose it is important to have some review of basic baton technique in these clinics, but let's not make it more than it is. The basic time patterns are very elementary and no great conductor of the past ever worried about the patterns of his arms, but he gave a great deal of attention to what was in his mind.

The mind is the great teaching ground for conducting clinics. These clinics should offer an extraordinary opportunity for an inexperienced conductor to study important musical literature with a mature conductor. Such study should include stylistic principles of a technical nature, such as learning what Viennese idiom required Mozart to write, at the end of the first movement of his *Gran Partita*, K.361/370a, a half-note when all he really wanted in performance was a quarter-note, or for the chance to hear a master conductor explain what is German about a German masterpiece like the Hindemith *Symphony*?

Discussion of analysis should not be centered on grammar (analysis of chords, etc.) but on finding and projecting emotional elements. Milhaud said of his *Suite Francaise* that he was thinking of 'war, destruction, cruelty, torture and murder.' Should not a conducting clinic help an inexperienced conductor learn how such thoughts can be reflected in the performance, or do we simply treat this work as just another Vaughn Williams *Folk Song Suite*?

This last topic is one of two in which an inexperienced conductor really needs help and could really benefit from practical and candid discussion with an experienced conductor. Following the strong advice by Aristotle, let's begin with the most basic principles:

1. The only real purpose of music is to communicate feeling.
2. We have inherited from the late Middle Ages a notational system which does not have a single symbol dedicated to feeling or the emotions.

How, then, does the inexperienced conductor communicate the emotions of the music, of the composer?

The experienced conductor must help the younger conductor to understand that he is the surrogate for the composer. Mozart is dead. The conductor must employ his own emotions to represent Mozart's. This is appropriate and possible because of the universality of the emotions and because, given the enormous age of our species, we are actually so near to Mozart chronologically that we can learn, through score study, what he was feeling.

All good musicians understand this and want to do this. No good musician is content to play what is on the page. This, however, has always been a concern and it is why Mahler warned, 'The important things in music are not found in the notes.' For some reason, wind instrument musicians are not taught to understand this. The well-known composer formerly at the University of Michigan, Ross Lee Finney, once wrote to me, in 1967, of this problem.

Winds always embarrass me as a composer. Part of it is that wind players in ensembles don't know how to rehearse; they play a work over and over but they don't seem to have the ability that a string quartet has of understanding the MUSIC and creatively projecting it. They read much better than string players; in fact they are remarkable readers but that seems as far as they go. Is it that they expect a conductor to do the creative musical job for them? Let me illustrate: in a premiere the composer hopes to have the details of articulation and tempi crystallized. He has undoubtedly been very careful in his notation, but it is the first performance that clarifies his doubts and makes it possible for him to properly edit the score. Performers vary, of course, in the help they give. Menuhin was enormously contributive to me in the work I did for him. The Stanley Quartet gives endless help. John Kirkpatrick, the pianist, wrote me hundreds of letters as he worked out my piano sonatas. My experience has been that woodwind quintets give nothing. It never dawns on them in a premiere that they have a creative job. (There are, I feel sure, exceptions, but I have not been so fortunate as to meet them.) So the performance sounds OK in a kind of blah way but it doesn't sound as you thought it might and you don't know for sure whether it ever could.

Although not mentioned by Finney, singers do this best and most naturally. There has never been a singer who ever lived who sang what he or she saw on the page. The reason for this, of course, is because both the feelings and the instrument come from within the body of the musician. But hand a musician a wind instrument or a baton and the emotions seem to be blocked. A useful conducting clinic should focus on this.

The other area in which the inexperienced conductor needs help is with respect to time. Because the Church clerics who invented our ancient notational system were under orders from the Vatican to create an arithmetical system of notation the matter of time is exact and inflexible. The first problem, as was once pointed out by Carlo Maria Giulini, is that the entire time-rhythmic structure of the notational system is based on '1,' but no one knows what the value of '1' is.

An even more important problem is the fact that time itself does not exist. It is all man made, as evidenced by the fact that last December 31, 2009, the world added one second to all their clocks. The inexperienced conductor must learn that time is not bound by the page, but by feelings. Foremost among the topics which fall under this subject is what early music specialists call 'Placement,' basing entrance decisions on psychological time, not chronological time. A useful conducting clinic should focus on helping the inexperienced conductor understand this.

The student musician leaves his school experience having been given the impression that music is found on the page. A useful conducting clinic should unlock the doors for the inexperienced conductor and let him escape.

Since so much of conducting cannot be adequately described in language, any more than anything else which is experiential, the young band conductor and professor can gain much education by closely observing the most recognized men in the profession. Among my essays I included, as a fond memorial, some of my own impressions of my contacts with a few such men.

Some Band Conductors Remembered

My wind conducting career began in 1963 at the University of Montana. The great majority of wind conductors were still locked in the mold of the Sousa era and many sought and envied the popularity which Sousa enjoyed. The first College Band Directors National Association meeting I attended was a Western Division meeting during which the president asked everyone to stand for a moment of silence in honor of Sousa. Some university bands were still playing concerts which contained no original band music at all. The march form was the bridge to the past and band programs abounded with them. I once played a march under the baton of Edwin Franko Goldman, who must have been the very last man in New York City to wear spats daily. He brought all the percussion up by the podium and it was all show and a great noise, but hardly musical. If one programmed a march following, or before, some somber or profound composition it was called 'variety.' Aesthetics was never the question.

Sousa was an entertainer and this was their model. I saw a university band conductor come out to the podium during a concert walking on his hands and wearing a clown suit. I have seen university concerts where some players wore monkey masks. There is no point in giving more examples.

I thought wind conductors should be artists like string conductors. I thought wind conductors should wear tails when they conduct, and not band uniforms. And first and foremost I tried to make the point over and over again in speeches and in published articles that it should not be the responsibility of an educational institution to entertain the public. Therefore many of the old-time band conductors found my voice very alarming. Raymond Dvorak, then Director of Bands at the University of Wisconsin, once cornered me and attacked me for my views. He told me, 'The *only* criterion for judging a university band program is whether they have standing-room only audiences!' On his final concert he performed 'Flight of the Bumblebee' while he ran around the stage with a flyswatter while the band played on.

Mark Hindsley

Mark Hindsley, Director of Bands at the University of Illinois, was a member of the older generation and the first time I saw the University of Illinois Band it was a reminder of the history of the college band. Many college bands were once R.O.T.C. bands and the University of Illinois Band program still had many military hallmarks. The equipment manager, for example, was called the Quartermaster and military-type discipline was evident in many aspects of the program. During concerts both Hindsley and his assistant conductor would, upon the conclusion of a composition, turn sharply to face the audience, then make one measured bow to the center, one to the left and one to the right before an about face to begin the next composition or leave the stage.

The University of Illinois Band, by the way, was also not part of the Music Department. This was more characteristic than many today might believe. It has only been fairly recently that the university orchestra and band at the University of California have been taken into the music department. I myself, sometime in the 1960s, had a call from a student at Columbia University in New York City asking if I were interested in being the Director of Bands of a completely student-run organization. By the way, while I was an undergraduate student at the University of Michigan the new band building on the Illinois campus had its opening ceremonies. William D. Revelli was present, together with a large number of other college conductors. University of Illinois band members were standing everywhere, serving as guides, answering questions, giving directions, etc. The building was named for the legendary founder of the modern university band program, Austin Harding, and when Revelli asked a bandsman who Harding was, the student did not know. Even by the time of his return to Ann Arbor, when he told us about this, he was visibly shaken. *Sic transit gloria mundi.*

Mark Hindsley was a past president of the College Band Directors National Association at the time I was elected president-elect in 1973. At the banquet when it was announced that I had won the election, Hindsley approached me with tears in his eyes, begging me not to destroy the CBDNA. I had no such thought in mind, of course, but I was struck by this expression of the very human fear of change.

Hindsley was one of the last generations of college conductors whose training had not been in music. His undergraduate degree was in Chemistry, I believe. Men such as he must have had strong native instincts about music in order to leave one profession for another. Hindsley remained interested in science and once proudly invented a device which by colored lights would measure dynamics. The conductor, presumably, could point at it and say, 'you see, you're too loud.' He was never able to interest many other conductors in this invention, for the simple reason that dynamics is not a finite element of music. It is entirely personal.

During the 1970s I was frequently invited to the campus of the University of Illinois to lecture before the graduate music education classes of Charles Leonard and Richard Colwell and to conduct various summer bands which they hosted and in the course of these campus visits Hindsley and I became good friends. During these visits Hindsley would always invite me out to his house for a game of pool on a table he kept in his basement. You have to try to picture this very precise man, taking pool as a science, walking around the table for long periods studying the trajectory of his intended shot. Every shot was life or death! Then, it being my turn, I would immediately shoot, seemingly without thought or planning at all—fast and hard! Hindsley would never say a word, but I'm sure it drove him crazy since in the end our games always ended being close ones.

After he retired I invited him to Los Angeles to guest conduct my Wind Orchestra, as I then called it, in one of his transcriptions of Strauss' tone poems. He wrote a charming letter of thanks.

Mark H. Hindsley to David Whitwell
Clovis, CA, May 1, 1976

I do want to tell you again how very much I enjoyed being with you for the weekend festival last month.

It was a particular pleasure to rehearse and conduct your band–wind orchestra in *Don Juan*. The young musicians are truly a fine organization, and acquitted themselves extremely well, not only in *Don Juan* but also in the other fine numbers on the program.

Likewise I was impressed with Morrell Pfeifle's band [our second band] in its performances of the Hindemith *Symphony* and *El Salon Mexico* …

All in all it was an enjoyable weekend all around, and I came away with an even greater admiration for you and your work and your institution.

Clarence Sawhill

Clarence Sawhill had also been affiliated with the University of Illinois, as a young assistant conductor. Over the years I have met people in the Mid-West who remember him as a dynamic conductor with great leadership potential.

And then Sawhill moved to Southern California where he seemed to experience a personality change that I have frequently seen in men moving from the Mid-West or East Coast to California. Is it too much sun beating down on one's head? Is it the lazy general atmosphere of that area? I don't know. Sawhill spent most of his career at UCLA, where they didn't have a music education credential program and had very few music majors.

He was content that his UCLA Wind Ensemble rehearsed only one hour (fifty minutes, actually) per week. I thought Sawhill loved to conduct concerts, but did not enjoy rehearsals. I recall seeing him once at the first rehearsal of an All State Band in Kentucky. There were two hundred students eager to play, eager to hear the sound of the band, eager to test the abilities of the people around them, etc. Sawhill began by not playing a single note with the full band for one hour and twenty minutes of the scheduled two-hour rehearsal. During this time he was going around tuning individuals to a machine, which teaches students not to listen, and giving away little tidbits of information to individual students—Have you ever tried this fingering? Needless to say, the students who entered the room with such enthusiasm were bored to death. The only thing which bores students in rehearsal is talk, because talk has nothing to do with music. Talk can only be *about* music, and students want music. Curiously, music education in the United States is not based in music, it is based in talk about music. So, Sawhill was only doing what everyone did. I remember a rehearsal under Revelli when in the course of two hours the band only played five measures of one composition, a march at that. It is a very poor educational philosophy and its failure is measured by [1] the relatively few students in our music classes in spite of the fact that every child loves music, and [2] the great extent that young people are learning music on their own, completely apart of the educational institutions.

Sawhill's own concerts were an amazing thing to behold. There was a kind of single-sheet program, but it did not contain the repertoire one was to hear that evening. On the stage, to the right of the podium, was an empty chair. Just before the concert began, a stage hand came out with maybe fifty scores and laid them on the chair. After the band tuned, and Sawhill had made his entrance, he would go to this stack of scores and look through them. He would find one, he would show it to the band, who would seek their parts, and then they would perform it. When the performance was concluded, Sawhill placed the score on another chair on the left side of the podium and then returned to the first chair to look through the scores again. Sometimes he would find one, show it to the band but they would all vigorously shake their heads 'no!' So Sawhill would carry that score to the left chair and then return to look for another score on the right side. This continued until such time as Sawhill thought the concert had been long enough, at which time he thanked the audience and left. Such a concert, with no planning of repertoire, with no rehearsals to speak of, should have been a disaster, a humiliation for the university. The maddening thing was that it always sounded pretty good. Sawhill had some guardian angel who followed him throughout his life.

During his last semester at UCLA before he retired I engaged him to come to my campus to be the principal guest for a week-long band directors workshop. Clarence came every day with absolutely nothing prepared (one day he brought his son to give a trombone clinic). He would just sit down and ask if there were any questions. Long periods of silence ensued. I thought it was a waste of time, but the high school band directors present had no objections and seemed to enjoy the experience. One of them asked, 'Professor Sawhill, you are just finishing a long career during which you taught at the University of Illinois, USC and UCLA. As a result of all that experience, do you have any words of wisdom for those of us who are just beginning our career?' Sawhill thought for a moment, gave a little chuckle while placing a finger on the side of his nose—a characteristic gesture of his, and observed, 'The hardest thing about teaching is that you have to feel good every day!'

The following year I was considering another position and Sawhill wrote, mentioning this workshop,

Clarence Sawhill to David Whitwell
Los Angeles, CA, May 12, 1973

You have certainly made an admirable place for yourself in the band field in Southern California and all of us would really miss you. I know that the first few years in a place are usually the hardest, and too often the rest of us don't take time to tell a new man that he is appreciated, and that he is adding something fine to our region.

Whether you go or stay, I want to take this opportunity to tell you that I have heard nothing but compliments on your work at Northridge ...

Thank you for inviting me to take part in your workshop last summer. I appreciate it that we had that much work together.

Good luck in whatever you do!
Clarence

Some Noble Ones

Weston Noble, although he conducted the Luther College Band for twenty-five years, is a truly great choral conductor—a legend. Unlike all the rest of us, all conductors everywhere, Weston is saintly, quiet, completely spiritual and incapable of ever raising his voice above a modified whisper. I first met him when I was a member of the Oklahoma All State Band, in 1955. We high school students at that time thought you had to be a tyrant to be a good band director (mine threw steel batons at the students), so I'm afraid we did not appreciate Weston as much as we should have.

The next time I saw him I was with the US Air Force Band on tour in Iowa and I stopped to hear one of Weston's choral rehearsals. I was astonished at how musical it was. One day while I was living in Salzburg I found him wandering the streets, he having a few days between engagements. My family was preparing to take a ski trip so I brought him home and gave him a guest room for the duration of his visit in Salzburg.

I heard one of the concerts of his retirement choral tour recently in Austin, Texas, and it was remarkable to see a large Lutheran Church filled with former students and alumni of Luther College. The current president of the college was on the first row leading the applause. To see the singers' faces filled with love and devotion and to hear the exquisite soft sounds of purely spiritual music made one feel one was hearing something not of our world. And very recently I heard Weston as one of several choral conductors participating in a great choral festival in Austin. Present, of course, were the cheer-leader-style choral conductors raising the audience to a fever pitch. Then it was Weston's turn, creating his trademark soft and spiritual sounds with hand gestures so small you assumed his face must be doing the actual conducting. All those who knew him, knew we would not hear this again.

James Neilson was another noble one. He was the band world's Bruno Walter, always comparing what he heard with the great masterpieces of music. He was a quiet man, who projected sincere musical emotions when he conducted. He was very different from his colleagues and he was one person to whom I listened carefully when he spoke.

I want to mention two noble European conductors that I knew. *Giovanni Ligasacchi,* conductor of the civic band in Brescia, Italy, and founder of the civic music school there, was another noble man. When I first met Ligasacchi he took me to his home and showed me a manuscript translation of my book about French Revolution band music into Italian. He had done this himself, as an exercise to improve his English, which he had first learned in a prisoner of war camp. It is a small symbol of this man's constant desire to learn. He had found, and performed with his Brescia band, the one important French Revolution work I could not find in Paris, the *Cantata on the death of General Hoche* by Cherubini. He loved my own symphonies and was responsible for many performances of them in Rome and elsewhere. He was a special person.

Alfred Gross, conductor of the civic band in Wangen, Germany, is another noble person. To escape a future under Communism, he walked from his native Bohemia to Germany taking only the clothes on his back, and eventually found a job teaching brass instruments. His instinct for self-education converted him from being an ordinary civic band director into a real scholar of German music. I once attended the 175th anniversary concert of the Wangen band, where I sat in the audience next to the mayor. The mayor told me that Gross had more influence in the town than he did! I have on occasion driven one hundred miles out of my way to say 'hello' to Alfred Gross.

On one occasion I discovered that *Gerald Prescott*, CBDNA's second president, former Director of Bands at the University of Minnesota, and author of a book, *Getting Results with School Bands*, which once made a great contribution to the profession, was alive, alert and well at age 102. I recommended to the leadership of CBDNA that some form of recognition was due this man, perhaps a plaque or something. As far as I know, there was no response.

When I was president of CBDNA I appointed some distinguished men to a task force assigned the duty of considering whether we should establish a mentoring program for the general purpose of keeping track of our members as individuals. There was no interest as band directors in 1975 were not yet sharing much with each other.

THE YOUNG BAND CONDUCTOR must take every opportunity to hear and study the major professional conductors. Sometimes it is possible to gain access to a rehearsal, which can be very interesting. When I was young one could, if one waited long enough, be admitted into the 'green room' after a concert for a brief opportunity to visit with famous artists. This practice is rare today but there are occasions when a university or a cultural institution will sponsor an artist's visit when access is possible. I was fortunate in Los Angeles in that for a few years the Los Angeles Philharmonic ran a young conductors program which brought the orchestra, young conductors and each year a famous conductor into my rehearsal room, which, for example was how I was able to visit with Leonard Bernstein.

Following are some of my personal experiences and impressions of a few of our famous colleagues.[20]

OBSERVING THE GREAT ONES

LEONARD BERNSTEIN

Bernstein was, contrary to the impression one received from watching him on TV, quite short and the first time I saw him, passing him on a street in Vienna, I did not even recognize him. My wife pointed out, 'That's Bernstein.' Watching him conduct live, his short stature minimized his great gestures which, seen only on TV, caused some to call him too flamboyant. Indeed, in a wonderful concert in Vienna when he conducted the Beethoven *Missa Solemnis* I saw him at one point leap up in the air and it looked perfectly appropriate. A person larger, say

---

[20] Eugene Ormandy I give a more extensive discussion in my autobiography, *A Conductor's Diary*.

six feet, would probably look ridiculous. Let me not fail to say here that I, for one, never saw a conducting gesture made by Bernstein that I felt was not perfectly appropriate for the music at that moment.

This concert, by the way, ended with about fifteen minutes of applause, after which time Bernstein had to take the concertmaster by the hand and lead him off stage. But many people stayed in the audience and continued to applaud while Bernstein continued coming out to take bows on an empty stage. When the applause finally ended, it was possible to go down and talk with him. I told him I was in Vienna studying conducting and hoping to begin a career and he, very sincerely, wished me luck. During one of the rehearsals for the Beethoven my conducting teacher, Hans Swarowsky, who had married a younger woman, had a baby. The announcement came while the orchestra was rehearsing the 'Gloria,' whereupon Bernstein exclaimed to Swarowsky that he must name the girl, Gloria. And, I believe, so he did.

Some years later the Los Angeles Philharmonic was holding a summer orchestral institute for young persons on my campus at California State University, Northridge. One year Bernstein came for a few days and it was rather sad to see him. His health was declining rapidly and a young assistant followed him around everywhere with a canister of oxygen, from which he administered blasts to Bernstein from time to time. I had a chance to talk with him several times and one story remains in my mind, his tale about his own audition for the conducting class at Curtis Institute which was then being taught by Fritz Reiner. Reiner, by the way, he described as a much calmer and more friendly man than the Reiner we all came to know later when he was the conductor of the Chicago Symphony Orchestra.

The audition consisted of playing a score at sight on the piano with Reiner standing looking over one's shoulder. Bernstein, then quite young, told me that at the time he actually knew little orchestral repertoire and did not recognize the work in the open score before him. However, having been a student at the famous Latin School in Boston, he recognized on the page the famous European university tune, 'Gaudeamus igitur,' and so he knew the tempo to play that page and he attributed that for helping get him into the conducting program. He was surprised later to learn it was the *Academic Overture* by Brahms.

Georg Solti

I first saw Solti conduct in Vienna, in the old Sofiensaal, a former prostitution house which Decca bought and redesigned as a recording studio. The orchestra sat on what had been a large dance hall and I viewed the recording sessions from one of the opera house-like booths which ringed the floor. The Vienna Philharmonic had given him the entire month of September to record the *Rosenkavalier* by Strauss. In New York a conductor would probably get a week at most. Consequently it was a great recording and won the highest European award. It was while I was watching these sessions that it was announced that Solti would be the new conductor in Chicago. I remember how delighted I was for Chicago, after a long string of inadequate conductors, for I knew Solti was perfect for that historically 'German' orchestra. And, of course, he was.

I do not believe I ever saw a more energetic conductor in rehearsal than Solti. At the time I was first seeing Solti conduct I was not using a baton, but I could see that he could do things with the baton that I could not do and it convinced me to use one ever after. He had a score in front of him in concert, but he never looked at it much. A musician who knew him at the Frankfurt Opera just after the war told me that at that time Solti did all operas from memory.

My family and I lived for two years in Salzburg once and during that time I heard some remarkable Solti concerts. The tradition of the Salzburg Festival was that the Vienna Philharmonic was the host orchestra, but there was always an invited guest orchestra which played on alternating evenings. In the year in question, the Vienna Philharmonic had some conflict and the 'host' orchestra was the Berlin Philharmonic, due to Karajan's long association with the Salzburg Festival. The guest orchestra was the Chicago Symphony Orchestra. The European press immediately saw this for what it was—the great shoot-out, a competition between the two greatest orchestras of the world. And it was. Karajan had the first concert and he began with the *Rites of Spring* of Stravinsky. A flawless technical achievement by both conductor and orchestra. Karajan, by the way, as was his custom, did the Stravinsky with his eyes closed!

The second night it was Chicago's turn and Solti began with Mahler's *Fifth*, their great showpiece. And so it went, night after night, each conductor bringing out his most powerful warhorses. The final night was Chicago's and Solti performed the Tchaikovsky *Sixth Symphony*—with its great soft ending, here almost inaudible, serving as a kind of benediction to this battle. This soft ending caused the audience, consisting largely of wealthy German businessmen from Munich who drove down in their Mercedes, to leave the hall rather quickly as Solti offered no encore. Soon there were only a few of us, loyal believers in the great music we had heard, who continued to applaud. After an extended amount of applause by maybe two hundred of those of us remaining, Solti began to play encores, as if to reward the faithful. First, he did the 'Scherzo' from the Mendelssohn *Mid-Summer Night's Dream*, a pure display of technique. I never thought previously that any orchestra could play this movement so accurately. Next came an exquisite waltz or something, something so refined as to contrast to all the heavy artillery of the past week. And so it continued, three or four encores which left us all with only feelings of great musicality, and erased from our memory the whole idea of the previous 'contest.'

I talked with him briefly in Vienna, but a bit longer once in Chicago. On that occasion, after one of his concerts in Orchestra Hall, we were talking in the 'green room.' Solti, exhausted, was drinking what appeared to be tea and so I asked him what it was. He told me that after concerts he always drank tea with honey, to raise his energy level. Thereafter I always went to my own concerts carrying tea and honey.

Leopold Stokowski

Stokowski was a remarkably calm and friendly person to talk with, a man with no 'great conductor' persona. The first time I saw him conduct in person was a chamber concert at the Library of Congress. The most remarkable thing about Stokowski, from the perspective of conducting technique, was his hands, beautiful hands with very long fingers. He conducted without a baton, but his long fingers, used in great sweeping tenuto gestures, had the effect of drawing the most beautiful sounds from the strings. His music always sounded elegant.

During the year I spent studying with Ormandy in Philadelphia Stokowski returned to conduct. It was an historic occasion, his first return since he had resigned more than twenty-five years earlier. All the players were very excited to play for him and there were even a few members of the orchestra who had been members when Stokowski was the conductor. Stokowski was then eighty-six years of age and it was necessary to conduct sitting down. He conducted the *Second Symphony* of Mahler, a huge work of course, and he conducted using little more than his fingers. He was too frail to use his arms much. But with those long fingers, and of course the intense concentration of all the musicians because of the occasion, he had all the tools he needed. It was some of the most dramatic and emotional music-making I have ever heard.

Carlo Maria Giulini

Giulini was the most elegant man I have ever seen. His immaculate Italian tailoring, his hair style, his manner of walking, and his speech made you just sit back and admire the sight. He was also, of course, one of the most spiritual conductors in history. His concerts were like religious observations.

So it was that I was shocked when it was announced that he had agreed to come to Los Angeles to be the conductor of the Philharmonic. The Los Angeles Philharmonic Orchestra is greatly diminished by the presence of the film studios. Indeed, Giulini who once had an afternoon rehearsal of a Beethoven symphony was shocked to learn that a large number of the players had been recording cartoon music in a studio that morning. This hurt his feelings; he thought they should be at home meditating on the coming rehearsal. And, of course, he was right. But the fine players in Los Angeles really don't care what the music is, they just enjoy playing. Therefore, a great deal is missing in Los Angeles Philharmonic concerts compared to the great orchestras of the world.

The amount of rehearsal time given Giulini was also inadequate to overcome the spiritual and musical problems in this orchestra. Consequently one would hear a Mozart symphony, for example, in concert and one would hear one really beautiful, exquisite movement and the other three sounded like they were little more than just reading sessions. It was immediately clear that Giulini preferred to use his available time to at least make one movement truly musical. I had the feeling he was doing this to teach something about the importance of great music to the orchestra and the city. He misjudged the shallow aesthetically dead environment.

Of course, Giulini could not work like this for long and he must have been quite confused by much in Los Angeles. At the time of his final week he could not even get the Chandler Theater for his rehearsals as the hall was needed for rehearsals for the Academy Awards. So the Los Angeles Philharmonic rehearsed in my rehearsal room. There was Giulini spending his final week with the orchestra, making the most heart-felt comments about the Beethoven *Seventh Symphony*, while the players were reading *Playboy* Magazine, *Time* Magazine and the *Wall Street Journal*, all sitting on their music stands covering the Beethoven. No one was listening to him. The enormous, profound European musical wisdom in this man meant nothing to the Los Angeles Philharmonic. It was just another gig.

Herbert von Karajan

I met and had a conversation with 'the King,' as the European newspapers called him, in 1956. He was then aged forty-eight and was on tour with the London Philharmonic and it was an historic tour as it was the very first time he was permitted in the United States after his State Department ban based on his activities as a Nazi Party member before World War II. On this occasion I found him very friendly, very easy to talk with (he spoke excellent English) and willing to talk at length.

Every concert I attended when Karajan was conducting was a concert of very intense music-making. I remember in particular a concert I heard with the Berlin Philharmonic in their then new hall in Berlin. Aside from the musical impact, as a conductor I was always somewhat distracted by his preference of conducting an entire concert with his eyes closed. The reason for this, as he once explained to a critic, ran something like this, 'How can I think of beautiful music when I look out at the unhappy faces of the players.' That's not quite right, his description of the players was more negative but I can't recall his exact words. However, every conductor knows what he means—your concentration can easily be broken by visual things because our eyes are so much more dominant than our ears. Nevertheless, I always felt his conducting with his eyes closed gave a certain narcissistic quality to the performance; it made me concentrate on him more than on the music. Maybe I was wondering how he could keep from losing his balance and falling over? Since he also kept his eyes closed between movements, I remember I always wondered how he knew the orchestra was ready to begin the next movement? Of course, that sudden moment of silence which occurs when the audience finishes coughing, etc., would be a general signal to begin, but how did he know if the violinists had their instruments up ready to strike a down-bow?

The last time I heard Karajan was in a concert of Bruckner in Los Angeles. He was near the end of his life, he was infirm and forced to conduct seated in a chair. Nevertheless, all the old intensity and concentrated musicianship was fully present. It was a moving concert for we all knew we would never see him again.

Lorin Maazel

I met Maazel during the year I spent studying with Ormandy in Philadelphia. Ormandy had reached that point when he could foresee his work in Philadelphia coming to an end and he was generously bringing in a number of young conductors for extended visits to give the public and management a chance to get to know possible successors. In this year, consequently, Maazel was in town for six weeks.

Maazel, then thirty-eight years old, was generous in sitting down with me and having a long conversation on the routes to establishing a career. He, probably promoted by his parents like young Mozart, had had a brief conducting career when he was a child of eight years of age. It was a brief fad, fed by the newspapers, during which this little kid stood on the podium and conducted all the major orchestras. In retrospect this didn't seem to mean much to Maazel, but he did not hesitate to say that he used this in his initial efforts to get conducting engagements, for he could put in his resume that he had conducted a number of major orchestras.

His route to establishing a career, and one he recommended to me as the only reasonable way to begin, was in conducting radio recording in Europe. I followed his advice the following year and had some successful recording engagements. The problem was that even if you were very successful and the particular radio orchestra wanted you back, because they were always fully scheduled it might be three or four years before you were invited back. Thus, as he told me, it took him nearly ten years before these engagements added up to enough income to actually represent a career. By the time I met him he was well established with contracts at the Berlin Radio and the Deutsche Oper Berlin.

He frankly said that his early success was due primarily to the fact that he was the only young conductor who conducted rehearsals from memory. While his press praised the fact that he was 'born with an incredible photographic memory,' etc., in fact there was a lot of hard work involved. By the time his six weeks in Philadelphia ended he was looking very tired, with black rings under his eyes. I am sure he was spending many hours in his hotel studying scores. He gave me an illustration from early in his career. He was living in Italy and got a call from a radio station which had a conductor cancel due to health. The program director asked, 'By any chance is the Scriabin *Poem of Ecstasy* in your repertoire?' This was a Friday and the conductor was needed on Monday. 'Yes, of course,' replied Maazel, even though he didn't know the piece at all. He then described his frantic efforts to find a score, then to memorize it in time for the Monday recording session. I followed this example the following year when one of the Czech Radio Orchestras asked if by any chance the *Third Symphony* of Ives was in my repertoire? 'Yes, of course,' I assured them as I signed the contract before running back to Vienna and sending telegrams off to find who had the score and parts.

Returning to Maazel in Philadelphia, his work *was* very impressive. The first week included the *Rites of Spring* by Stravinsky and it was the first time I had ever seen anyone conduct it from memory. Actually, in this score there are, in my experience, only a couple of places which are difficult to conduct, one being the final sacrificial dance. I think an orchestra would always wonder if the guest conductor could do the hard spots. Therefore it was interesting to observe that Maazel, at the beginning of the very first rehearsal, did those spots, as if to prove 'OK, I can do it, now let's get down to work.' I might also add that watching him work was what convinced me to henceforth do rehearsals without scores. The greatest distinction is the speed with which you can work in rehearsal—it is a great time saver.

Maazel's career has had its ups and downs, as most careers do, but in my view he must be considered a great conductor.

Another recommendation which Maazel made to me, as a young conductor at the time, was to go to Europe and study with Sergiu Celibidache. I knew the name, but little else as the man did not believe in making recordings. Maazel thought him the greatest conducting teacher in Europe. Years later Celibidache made a very rare appearance with his Municipal Orchestra of Munich in Los Angeles. I, together with every conductor in Los Angeles, made sure I was there. I no longer recall the repertoire we heard, but it was standard repertoire. But the performance was so original, the music so transformed by non-traditional tempi, significant freedom in rubato, etc., as to make one think one had never heard these works before. The feeling I had, one shared by everyone I spoke with at intermission, was one of being completely unsure—were we hearing the greatest conductor of our time or a complete lunatic? There had been a long period in Europe in which the 'experts' said, 'just play what the composer wrote.' Celibidache, I believe, was thinking, 'No, just play what the composer was thinking.' A reporter during the week before this single concert asked him some question like, 'It must be wonderful to be surrounded by beautiful music all the time.' Celibidache immediately corrected the reporter, 'Anyone who talks about the "beauty" in music knows nothing about music. Music has beauty, but that is only the bait. Music is Truth.' He was a great musician.

Daniel Barenboim

During the year I was in Philadelphia, the great cellist, Jacqueline du Pre, came as a soloist with the orchestra. Accompanying her was her young husband, Daniel Barenboim, then aged twenty-five, although he looked much younger to me. He was, of course, the leading pianist of his generation. But when we were talking backstage he told me that he had become tired of playing recitals and aspired to become a conductor. He had a great advantage for he was in great demand as a pianist. He told me he simply told his agent, if you want me to do a recital, you must get me a conducting engagement. If you want me to do five recitals, you must get me five conducting engagements. So, he began his career that year and the rest is history.

The next time I saw him I was in Paris and he had a concert with the biggest orchestra there. He was doing a major Berlioz work which I wanted to hear, but the concert was so bad that I, for the only time in my life, walked out. He must have learned from his vast experience, for one of my close friends, a former member of the English Chamber Orchestra, tells me that in his view Barenboim 'is the only conductor who can do no wrong.'

Pierre Boulez

While I was living in Los Angeles Pierre Boulez was a frequent guest conductor. He was a famous composer of works that made no sense to me. As a conductor I found him cold and sometimes it seemed he had no respect for the works he was conducting.

Once, in a desperate attempt to build audiences, the Los Angeles Philharmonic instituted a new policy. At the conclusion of all concerts, if members of the audience wish to stay and come down to the front of the hall, they could ask questions of the conductor. So the next time Boulez conducted I stayed to hear what he had to say. He talked about the importance of twelve-tone music and went so far as to say that he believed it was impossible to communicate with anyone then alive except through twelve-tone music. This outrageous statement caused me to raise my hand and ask him, 'How do you explain the fact that Schönberg, towards the end of his life, began to compose more tonal music?' He answered, 'Well you must remember he had left his home in Europe, because of the war, leaving behind all his friends, etc. He moved to this alien and strange environment of Los Angeles. He was temporarily insane!'

Fritz Reiner

While a student at the University of Michigan friends and I would take the Saturday morning train into Chicago to hear the matinee performance by the Chicago Symphony Orchestra, which at that time many thought was the greatest orchestra in the world. It was always a strange experience to hear Reiner, because what you saw contrasted so dramatically with what you heard.

Both in his PR materials and on stage Reiner always had a severe scowl. He looked constantly angry and one of the men in the orchestra said to me, 'He's a great conductor, it's too bad he hates music!' The orchestra did not like him and once, when he called off a European tour ('Gentlemen, I am happy to tell you I have canceled that awful tour!') they hanged him in effigy—backstage in Orchestra Hall.

He used a long baton, but the men in the orchestra used to say that he could do the pattern for a 12/8 bar within the dimensions of a postage stamp. I think that might have been true, for the man stood there making infinitesimally small motions with the stick, while all around him the orchestra was producing the most voluptuous and full-bodied sounds! I can understand their playing technically well for him, but to this day I cannot understand how he produced such musical results, given his apparent participation.

It looked very disconcerting, but it was truly great music-making and some of his performances I have never heard equaled to this day.

George Szell

George Szell also looked rather unhappy most of the time. All of my colleagues during the 1960s thought the Cleveland Orchestra was the great orchestra of that decade, but I never agreed. To me Szell's music sounded cold and sterile. His head was always buried in the score and it always seemed to me that his listening response was quite delayed, as if he was reading music and listening to it. Once, in a performance of the Beethoven *Pastoral Symphony*, the principal horn was day-dreaming and failed to enter in the famous long horn solo. Szell seemed not to notice for a dozen bars and then looked up, looked around, sensing something was missing but not sure what. By the time he produced a serious scowl, the horn player had found his place already.

During the Spring of 1967, when I was casting my net out hoping to attach myself to some major conductor as an apprentice, I had a letter from Szell's manager inviting me to meet with the maestro on a certain day, for indeed the maestro was looking for such a person. Tempting as this sounded, I turned it down for I had heard from several people that Szell required outstanding piano skills, which I did not have.

He was right about this. In Europe there is a constant demand for young 'assistant conductors' in the opera houses. What is meant by the title is that one must sit in dark, ill-smelling practice rooms where one helps to teach the singers their parts and to help them memorize them. Several years of this and one day you are rewarded by getting to conduct a matinee performance. Even von Karajan had to put in a couple of years doing this when he was young.

While I was living in Vienna, in 1968–1969, the State Opera decided that the world was running out of opera conductors and they decided to host a training program for eight young conductors. I was invited to join this group, but once again my piano skills did not permit me to accept. I played in public when I was very young and I have a composition I played in public at age nine which I cannot play today.

Bruno Walter

A number of the concerts I attended in Chicago were conducted by Bruno Walter. Attending his concerts one felt one was worshipping in a great European cathedral, so spiritual was the atmosphere. The curious thing, in retrospect, was that one felt this descending from the train and walking down the street toward Orchestra Hall, like walking to some great religious shrine.

The man's great dedication to music was evident at every moment and his warm and emotional personality was fully reflected in the performance. When one left the hall one believed in the importance of music. Some of his concerts, especially the symphonies by Brahms I can still vividly remember fifty years later.

All this is communicated in his book, *On Music and Music-making* and in his autobiography. Both are necessary texts for all conducting students to read.

An office-mate of mine at California State University, Northridge one year was a German man who, when he had first come to this country, had worked as a gardener on Walter's estate in Los Angeles. Naturally I was eager to hear details of Walter's private life, but all my fellow colleague could remember was Walter sticking his head out a window and yelling, 'Shut up!' while he was mowing the lawn.

Sir John Barbirolli

I saw Barbirolli conduct only once, and he was completely drunk. Just recently I saw a letter written by Aaron Copland to Carlos Chavez on December 11, 1936, in which Copland writes, 'Barbirolli I heard once. Once was enough.'

While I was teaching at the University of Montana, the Houston Symphony came to perform as the first day of a Northwest US tour. We were all looking forward to this, as Missoula, Montana, was not, at that time, a place where one heard much quality performance.

The orchestra flew all day in a non-jet plane, in bad weather and most of them were rather sick upon arrival. Barbirolli, as I indicated, was so drunk he could not walk to the podium. An assistant helped walk him out, holding onto his arm. Once upon the podium Barbirolli conducted with his right arm while he held on for dear life to a metal bar behind the podium with his left arm. Occasionally, in giving a forte down-beat, the forceful motion of his right arm carried him down on his knees and he would have to stop conducting (the orchestra continued to play) while he struggled to his feet.

Consequently it was a very bad concert. This was a very significant event in my life, for all my music faculty colleagues thought it was a great concert. This frightened me, for I never want to be there so long that I forget what a good concert was! A few months later I resigned and left town!

Finally, a few of my observations and thoughts of some of the famous composers.

Alan Hovhaness

I had the opportunity to meet Hovhaness in 1966 when he was a guest at the University of Montana. What I recall most of him personally was a sense of frailty. Even when he walked he seemed fragile and when he was in my home I had the irrational fear that he was going to bump into a chair and kill himself. While visiting my home, I played a tape for him of my performance with the University of Montana Band of his *Symphony Nr. 7*. During the slow movement of this composition there is a long canon, a canon with an extremely long subject. I performed this slightly faster than the metronome marking he had indicated because it seemed to me to need a bit more sense of propulsion to work. As Hovhaness listened to the tape of the second movement he slowly began to move, his body swaying left and right. Given the Asian background of this music, I first thought he was going into a trance. But soon he began to moan, an ever increasingly painful moan. This pain, it turned out, was in reaction to my tempo. From this experience I did not conclude that one must always perform a tempo exactly as indicated by the composer, but I did conclude that it is a poor idea to play the recording while the composer is present!

Igor Stravinsky

I only saw Stravinsky once, in about 1962 I think. He was in Washington to conduct his *The Rake's Progress*, as I recall, with the members of the local opera. A close friend of mine in the Singing Sergeants also sang in the opera chorus and was able to sneak me into a rehearsal. As it turned out, Stravinsky's health had failed and his young friend, Robert Kraft, was conducting. Stravinsky sat watching the score, a small now somewhat shriveled up man, covered with coats and with his last wife hovering over him protecting him like some great bear. But from time to time he looked up and spoke and it did give me a sense of history just to see and hear him.

At this time also a small group of graduate students at Catholic University were invited to spend an afternoon with Nadia Boulanger, his great alter-ego (he composed, but did not teach; she taught, but did not compose), who was in town to give a speech on the role of Debussy in contemporary music. I found her to be a very sweet little lady, entirely devoted, of course, to everything Stravinsky. I said to her, 'For years in your classes in Paris you refused to even discuss the concept of twelve-tone music. But when Stravinsky surprised the world by suddenly becoming a twelve-tone composer, then immediately that is what you taught. How do you explain your sudden reversal?' She answered, simply and faithfully, 'Whatever the Master does, it must be right!'

I, myself, always regarded Stravinsky as somehow two people in one, perhaps one might say a left-brained Stravinsky and a right-brained Stravinsky. I always heard his music from the perspective of traditional music, by that I mean that, while it was certainly 'modern,' it seemed to me to express the kinds of emotions that traditional music did. But then, when he talked about music, or wrote about music, he would sometimes utter complete nonsense, as in his often quoted comment that music is capable of expressing nothing and can only be understood as B-flats and C-sharps. I have often wondered if this were some strange sense of humor, or if it was his way of bringing conversations with interviewers to an abrupt end. In any case, generations of young composers, instead of listening to his music, listened to his words and took off on a path writing music no one wanted to hear and music which has long since been utterly forgotten.

I conducted *The Rite of Spring* a number of times without scores and on the first occasion, simply as a personal challenge, I also did all the rehearsals without a score. In fact, it was my experience that this composition like many contemporary compositions was too difficult to conduct *with* a score. There is just too much detail for the eye to keep up with and at times the pages flow by so fast it is almost impossible to read them. The fact that students could now play this masterpiece is a testimonial to the great increase in instrumental technique in the twentieth century. I can remember in the 1950s hardly any major orchestra would risk playing *The Rite of Spring* in public.

Several of my colleagues at California State University, Northridge, in Los Angeles, had been members of the 'Columbia Symphony Orchestra,' which was actually a group of film studio players, who recorded a number of works with Stravinsky conducting. One of our clarinet teachers was the principal clarinet in these recordings and he told me that as he was preparing for one session, and I am sorry I cannot remember the name of the composition, he came upon an eight-bar clarinet passage which he could not play. He tried everything from his long experience, practicing slowly, practicing with different rhythms, etc., but he could not do it. Therefore, being also a very ethical man, he approached Stravinsky at the first rehearsal and said, 'Maestro, I am sorry to say that there is a passage I simply cannot play. I have tried everything, but I cannot play it up to speed. I wanted to tell you in case you have someone who you can replace me with who can play this passage.' Stravinsky answered, 'Oh, don't worry. I just did this work in Cleveland and the clarinetist had no problem. Here is a tape they made. Take this home and listen to it and just do whatever he did.' So he took the tape home and played it whereupon he found the principal clarinetist in Cleveland simply left the passage out!

This illustrates the fact that at some places there is so much going on, and going so fast, that it is almost impossible to hear everything. I know that in learning *The Rite of Spring* I found several mistakes, small ones in the form of accidentals, etc., but mistakes nevertheless, in a score that conductors and editors had been using for decades. It reminded me of a time when I did some freelance editing for Theodore Presser in Philadelphia. Among other projects I was given things to proof and I always found errors even though several professional proofreaders had gone through the material before me. When, being then young and innocent, I mentioned this to the editor-in-chief, he spoke to me with the dark, grave voice of wisdom, 'Nothing proves human frailty like proofreading!'

Heitor Villa-Lobos

I had a chance to meet and talk with Villa-Lobos in 1958, just months before his death, when he came to Pittsburgh where the American Wind Symphony, of which I was the associate first horn, was premiering one of his compositions. A very relaxed and happy man, with his big cigar he looked like one of those pictures of Brahms. I had a nice photo made with him by a local newspaper and while we were waiting for this to take place he drew a humorous picture for me on one of our programs.

In 1966 I was making a six-week recital of all the principal cities of South America in co-operation with the US State Department. The State officials always asked me if there were anyone I wanted to meet and so in Rio de Janeiro I asked if they could arrange a meeting with Mrs. Villa-Lobos. She invited us and at the appointed day and time we went to a large government building in which she had set up the fourth floor as a Villa-Lobos archive. It was a surprise, although should not have been given her husband's long identity with France, that we were met by a French maid. From the moment we left the hall, where like the rest of the city the language was Portuguese, and entered the door we had to converse in French. Fortunately, my wife, Giselle, was with me and her French skills were much more fluent than mine. Mme. Villa-Lobos told me that on this floor she had some 4,000 autograph scores by her late husband, but as I recall little progress had been made in cataloging.

As a parting gift, she gave me five recordings of her husband's music. Several of these recordings contained original music for band, but it appeared to be music intended for civic bands, thus rather in the popular style. These LPs, alas, did not survive the Northridge Earthquake of 1994.

Charles Koechlin

On one of my conducting engagements at a conservatory in The Netherlands, the great oboist, Evert van Traight, encouraged me to seek the wind orchestra works of Charles Koechlin. He supplied me with the address in L'Hay-les-Roses, France, of the composer's daughter, Mme Li-Koechlin. In our initial communication she agreed to meet me at the apartment of her brother, Yves Koechlin, in Paris in 1980. It was a wonderful apartment with artifacts of the composer and a huge oil painting of their father dressed as if in an aristocratic hunting scene.

I was particularly interested in asking Mme Koechlin about the location of her father's works for wind band. She replied that she had very little and she supposed the publishers of Paris had everything in their own archives. Most musicians today are not aware that the major publishers have quite extensive archives not only in Europe but also in the US. They vary, however, in their willingness to allow one to browse around in these archives. I once found some wonderful things in the Schott Archiv, in Mainz, which I was able to gain entrance only because a friend was one of the executives of this German publisher. And for years, whenever I was in Vienna, I would look in these private archives for the lost Mahler arrangement for band of part of Beethoven's *Ninth Symphony*. This only came to my attention when his wife's book, *Gustav Mahler: Memories and Letters*, was republished in 1969. Mahler made this arrangement and conducted it with members of the Vienna Philharmonic for a ceremony in honor of the *Sezession* artist, Max Klinger, in May 1902. Alma Mahler describes Mahler conducting the new arrangement, 'as stark as granite,' and Klinger who 'was so moved that tears ran slowly down his cheeks.' Klinger's statue of Beethoven was exhibited for the first time on this occasion, a striking, even startling work which I recently saw in the civic museum in Leipzig.

So, knowing how temperamental these publisher's can be about their archives, I asked Mme Kochelin if she could help me out in locating her father's works. First, she brought to my attention a number of works I did not know: The *Tu crois a beau soleil*, Op. 147, the *Sonneries pour trompes de chasse*, Op. 123, 142 and 153. The manuscripts for these works she felt were maintained by her brother, whom I did not meet.

She also mentioned the *Les Chorals pour les Fetes de Plain-air*, Op. 153, which had been recorded by Desire Dondeyne on an LP by Calypso in 1975, 'together with the *Dyonisiasque* de F. Schmitt et *la Chant funeraire* de G. Faure.' She later called Dondeyne and was told that the *Les Chorals pour les Fetes de Plain-air* was in the library of the *l'Orchestre des Gardiens de la Paix*. The *Eaux vives*, Op. 160, a work of twenty-two minutes duration she believed was held by the publisher, *Editions Max Eschig et Cie* in Paris. Finally she mentioned a *La Marche funèbre*, Op. 157, which exists in three versions, orchestra, wind orchestra and brass band. This was to be found in the archive Eschig.

In a later letter, of November 5, 1980, she reports that the publisher Eschig had informed her that the *Eaux Vives* was for large orchestra.

In a letter of April 30, 1981, she reported that the publisher *Chant de Monde* had performance materials for two additional *Chorales*. If I understood her correctly she also informed me that the publisher, *Salabert*, could not locate the performance material for the *Marche funèbre*, which was performed in 1977 in Drancy.

There are two more works which are now in the Whitwell Archiv in Trossingen, Germany, the *Jeux* and the *La Victoire*, both for band.

I sent Mme. Li-Koechlin a tape of my performance of the *Tu crois a beau soleil*, for which she thanked me in a letter of June 1, 1981, concluding, 'Je suis sur que la qualite de l'interpretation est excellente!'

Carl Orff

During the two years I lived in Salzburg I had the opportunity to meet Carl Orff. It was a tradition that he appeared each Christmas at a party given at the famous Orff Institute for music education there. His participation was in reading the libretto of one of his operas, which was very moving in spite of the absence of the music.

The entertainment followed and it consisted of folk-dances, which, naturally, found me standing against the wall, a wall flower, as they say. But then someone said the next dance was a two-step and would be done to a military march, Sousa's *Washington Post March*. This dance consisted of the people joining hands in a great circle, while running fast around the circle. It has been a very long time since the public associated military marches with a specific kind of social dance, but it was something I had to try. So I left my position of supporting the wall and joined in the circle. It was great fun and I am sure the experience forever changed my view of marches.

I conclude this section with a few stories of my own, intended to reflect the breadth of experiences one has in the university profession.

On University Life

Life as a university professor has its rewards, including working only a few hours per week, with this difficult schedule relieved by twenty-six weeks of annual vacation and sabbaticals. On the other hand, the pay is low when compared to other professions requiring a doctorate, much time is wasted in meetings and one learns to ignore mindless criticism of a level found in few similar professions. Let me give two examples of the latter. The composer, Karel Husa, and I once shared the stage with a number of other conductors in a concert before one of the educational associations. Karel and I shared a dressing room and Karel followed me as the concluding conductor of the concert. When I returned to the dressing room I found Karel in a panic for he had discovered that he had failed to pack his concert shirt. Immediately I removed mine, he put it on and went to conduct. It had been pre-arranged that all the conductors would appear together for the final bow and so there we stood, everyone in white tie and tails and me in a sweater and sports coat. There was much criticism, of course, for my apparent refusal to appear dressed like everyone else.

When I first went to Los Angeles the term 'wind ensemble' was unknown to the public and everyone always expected chamber music. Therefore, for several years I followed the example of several other Southern California institutions and renamed my ensemble, Wind Orchestra. It was a comfortable term for me, having lived in Europe where all serious wind ensembles are called 'wind orchestra.' Later, attending a conference on the East Coast, I was accosted by another university conductor for being 'ostentatious' in using the name, 'Wind Orchestra.' 'What,' I asked, 'do you call your ensemble?' 'Wind Symphony,' he replied.

My first job after leaving the military was teaching at the University of Montana. The position was advertised as a horn job, teaching horn and playing in a faculty woodwind quintet which they wished to form. As it turned out, the actual job was somewhat more busy: playing in the faculty quintet, teaching horn students; being the private teacher also for trombone, euphonium and tuba students; being the department percussion instructor; teaching a section of music theory, a vocal class and a music education class; and serving as director of bands, with the first marching band show required in the second week of classes. The annual salary for all this was $5,600.00.

This impossible load was improved after the first rehearsal of the new faculty quintet, when the ensemble ceased to exist due to the bassoonist blowing a hole in his esophagus! The first rehearsal, however, was remarkable. We read through the first movement of something and then put our instruments in our lap and sat, waiting. Being a new faculty member, just removed from a very busy and intense professional position, I thought it better to not to try to dominate this rehearsal so I elected to say nothing. The flautist was the dean of the school and he was careful not to use his position as dean to control the rehearsal, so he said nothing. The clarinetist was a meek and quiet fellow, who never said anything. The oboist, a fine player and musician, was part-time and since music departments always make part-timers feel less than 'real' faculty, he said nothing. The bassoonist was a graduate student, who felt unempowered to speak among the faculty. So, no one spoke a single word. We sat for several minutes until someone said, 'maybe we should play the next movement.' And so it went, driving me nuts, until the end of the period, when, as I have indicated above, the ensemble ceased to exist.

The greatest challenge, given my recent and uninformed arrival, was finding myself director of a marching band. I must say, the first year I found the marching band rather fun—diagramming things on paper and then standing on top of the press box and watching them unfold. In the second year as director of a marching band I became aware of the very disproportionate relationship between the hours of work necessary and the six minutes of fun watching the finished product. The third year it became a rut. The fourth year the marching band was rapidly becoming intolerable and added to my decision to leave this position. During this fourth year I had a call from the chair at Syracuse University begging me to come to be the director of bands. I was ready to go back east, but I told him I just had no interest in doing a marching band anymore. He moaned, 'Everyone is telling me the same thing!'

I tried to think of original things, even aleatoric things, for the marching band to do, such as spelling out the half-time score on the field at half-time. Everyone knew marching bands required much rehearsal to prepare these half-time shows, but the question on everyone's mind was, How did the band director know, in advance, what the half-time score would be? Not only was it the talk of the town, but I was once approached in my office by a shady character wanting my help in a betting syndicate.

When I returned to academic life in 1969 I was fortunate to find a position in Los Angeles which included no marching band duties. California State University, Northridge, founded in 1958, was at that time the fastest growing institution of learning in the United States. Within a short period of time I was able to develop four concert bands, three of them consisting of music majors. Serving an area with such a large population,[21] during most of my tenure there I never had to give a thought to recruiting. But, unfortunately, there was poison in the well. Just before my arrival the infamous Proposition 13, placing a cap on property tax, became law. The immediate financial cutbacks in education soon led to the elimination of elementary school music and, of course, this in time led to numerous junior high school band directors being laid off. We could all see that this tide would eventually hit the university music department and as it did the size of our music class rapidly fell.

Of course, the falling state budget, due to Proposition 13, also affected the university budget as well with things like cleaning the building, which became a once a week event. One day, standing in front of a marble wall behind the urinal in the men's room nearest my office, I noticed a rather bad smell and began to wonder just how often this wall was washed. As a test of the cleaning crew I made a very faint pencil mark on the wall, a mark which would easily be erased by any attempt to wash the wall. When I retired and left California, the mark had been on the wall for thirty-one years.

---

[21] The entire population of Montana, when I was there, was equal to 1/3 the population of the San Fernando Valley.

I used to teach a course in music appreciation to fill my load and I elected to do this as it was something I could do with no preparation thus giving me time for score study. Everyone who teaches this subject has a storehouse of stories and I will pass on two. Leaving a class devoted to Baroque music one day I overheard one student say to another, 'I didn't know they made records back then!' This demonstrates the reality today that you can never know how slow to pitch the ball. Once, driving to class to give an exam, I decided that one question on my multiple-choice test was one that, upon reflection, I decided I probably did not prepare adequately. Thus, upon entering the classroom, I wrote on the board, 'The correct answer to question Nr. 13 is "C".' I left this on the board and when the students arrived I announced this information orally and explained why I was giving them this answer in advance. Now, how many students would you guess missed that question on the exam? Twenty percent of the class missed question Nr. 13.

In the year following the abdication of the Shah of Iran we began to have many Iranian students. Most of these were from wealthy families who really would have rather have their children attending one of the more famous institutions in town, UCLA or USC. But a certain grade point was required for these schools and so on two separate occasions an Iranian father unsuccessfully offered me $50,000 to change a child's grade in music appreciation from a C to a B!

I would like to tell one story, in part as an illustration of the vast and diverse peoples one finds in a city like Los Angeles. In 1975 we were hosting the National Wind Ensemble Conference and I had programmed one concert of band music of the French Revolution. On this program were to be several of the works with chorus, including the historic *Te Deum*, the original composition of this revolutionary band repertoire.

I acquired a copy of the original manuscript of the *Te Deum* of Gossec from the National Library in Paris and found it to be a manuscript notated mostly in whole-notes and half-notes. Considering the 'alle breve' look of the notation, and considering the logic associated with the speed of the French language, I was 99% sure that this work must have been conducted with the half-note being the beat. But, confident as I was, the remaining 1% of my mind was reminding me that this work was performed in Paris by 300 winds and 1,200 singers, and that never before in music history had a performance with so large an ensemble ever been attempted. And, of course, the purpose of the occasion was a solemn observance connected to the revolution. So, just maybe, I was planning to conduct this work twice as fast as Gossec intended.

Sharing my concern with an older student, to my complete astonishment, the student said 'I know someone who has a recording of the Gossec!' 'No!' 'Yes, it is an organ salesman I was talking to in the mall.' I could not believe that anyone had performed this work after 1790, so I jumped in my car and drove to the mall. Sure enough, this fellow, a would-be film composer, had been a DJ on a classical music station on the East Coast. At some point the French government decided to make recordings (the old 15' size discs) of obscure French music and donate copies to radio stations. His particular station was closing, so my new acquaintance carried off a few of these recordings, he being a record collector himself. So I tell him I must hear this recording (to confirm my tempo conclusions) and he was delighted. But, he says, in return you must agree to hear some other recordings in my collection. No problem!

On a designated evening, the night before my first major rehearsal with the wind ensemble and the chorus, I made my way to his house in Topanga Canyon, a rather remote area north of Los Angeles populated with a collection of hippies, the unemployed and musicians. Driving, I soon left the freeway, and the subsequent road becoming smaller and smaller, ending in two unpaved ruts climbing up to his house. Dying to hear the performance of the Gossec, I first had to endure two hours of 'name the famous singer,' while drinking wine. Eventually he played the Gossec recording and although it was not the complete work it was enough to confirm that my tempi decisions were correct. So I made my goodbyes and asked him if he could please turn my car around and get it pointed down the hill. He gets in the car and drives the car over a little wall, knocking the entire muffler system to the ground. Much apologies. I tried calling AAA but found they do not serve Topanga Canyon at that time of night. So we decided to try to tie the muffler line up high enough to clear the rise between the two ruts going down to the paved road—but first he had to wait an hour for the muffler to cool. Being very dark in this wilderness, we had left on the lights of my car to be able to see to tie up the muffler. When completed, we found the car battery dead. Obviously, I could not go home unless we could get someone to come up with a jump cord. So, I called my grad assistant at perhaps 3:00 AM to have him get out of bed and come jump-start my car so I could make it to the morning rehearsal with the chorus. What are grad assistants for?

I should probably say a word about the famous Northridge earthquake of 1994, at that time the largest natural disaster in American history. It is impossible to describe an event so violent, but suffice to say there is pure fear and a feeling that man does not belong on the surface of this planet. My home required $85,000 in repairs and I must say that FEMA, unlike the FEMA of the Bush Period, was very helpful. The next morning a man walked down the street just handing out cash, in my case $1,300.00. No paperwork, no signature, no receipt, just cash to help you make the immediate repairs that allow you to live in the house.

The earthquake came just two weeks before the beginning of the Spring Semester at the university. With one hundred and fifty colleges and universities in Southern California we all were fearful of the legislature deciding that there were enough universities and why not just tear down CSUN instead of paying the enormous funds needed to repair it. So, to prevent this, we all understood that we must begin the semester on schedule, no matter what. To this end the university rented four hundred large size trailers in which to hold lecture classes. The offices were closed and guarded by the army, so you had to teach without your lecture notes, exams and teaching materials. There were those professors who read their lectures (all universities have them) and these people didn't know who Aristotle was anymore. Five months later we were informed that we would have fifteen minutes to enter our office to take out whatever we could carry in two suitcases. This was a wonderful and welcome announcement and in my case I made careful lists of the most needed teaching materials and valuable possessions (I lost a number of original eighteenth-century engravings) so I would know what to look for during my fifteen minutes. But, when the official accompanied me to open my office we found everything in a great pile on the floor. There was no possibility of finding anything on my list, so I just filled the suitcases with the first things available.

For rehearsals the immediate problem was no access to the library or to the instrument collection. The president asked for a list of our most pressing needs in order that she could rent instruments. Our wise chair presented her a list that began with '3 contrabassoons.' This resulted in the immediate removal of our instruments from the building by the officials. A tent was constructed with a cement floor. Of course traffic noise came right through the walls and the cement rendered even *piano* as a full *forte*. While this alone made any serious music making impossible, there were the students, each of whom had on-going personal problems of great magnitude. Looking at those faces I wondered why we were even trying to rehearse and give concerts, but of course it was important to do this for several reasons.

Fortunately we had a very special and capable chair, Jerry Luedders, who was able to get us back into our building before any other department, but it still took half a year. I lived through two of these great earthquakes in Los Angeles and one never quite gets over them. Small ones occur all the time and when a medium one happens, say one of 3.0 on the Richter scale, it brings back the damaged nerves from the big ones. One of the most pleasant aspects of my retirement in Texas has been going to sleep at night without worrying about being suddenly thrown from bed by a major earthquake.

On High School Band Activities

MAN CLEARLY HAS A RATIONAL SIDE OF HIS BEING, a collection of information he has absorbed from other sources and which for the most part are housed in the left hemisphere of the brain. It is equally clear that most of the knowledge housed there consists of agreed upon facts; there is only one way to spell 'cat' in English and everyone in the world learns that 2 + 2 = 4. Therefore, it follows that one can organize a competition in math or spelling and there will emerge an undisputed winner.

The other half of our person, and brain, is experiential knowledge, knowledge we have learned from our *own personal* experience. Hence while a concept like 'love' has a general agreed upon dictionary meaning, its *real* meaning for any person is a *personal* definition resulting from his life's experience with love. The experiential, emotional nature of music is analogous. Everything being based on personal experience, and not facts, one problem with the right hemisphere of the brain is that there are no 'correct answers' to be found there. That being the case, why would anyone ever want to hold a competition in love or music? What would be the point?

We might begin our look at music competition by considering the nature of the purpose that the ancient Greeks associated with their own music competitions. Often, it turns out, the purpose had nothing to do with music. For example, there were trumpet contests which began with the 96th Olympiad of 396 BC. But these contests seem to have been more physical than musical. Perhaps the modern Olympic motto, *citius, altius, fortius*, describes well what they were—who could play fastest, highest and loudest. Thus being essentially physical contests, and not musical contests, we are not particularly surprised to find that Heradorus of Megara, one of the winners of the Olympic trumpet playing competition, consumed, in a typical meal, six pints of wheat bread, twenty pounds of meat and six quarts of wine!

Antiphon, a famous fifth-century BC speaker and early interpreter of dreams, in a fragment of a speech[1] discussing the fact that pleasure often follows pain, suggests that the purpose of contests in general is to teach men the rewards of greater effort.

> For honors, prizes, the baits which God has given to mankind, bring them to the necessity of great toil and sweat.

Xenophon, 427–355 BC, an important early historian and, like Plato, a student of Socrates, also tells us that long periods of training and large sums of money were necessary to prepare a chorus for competition and he seems almost perplexed that they do this when the goal is only a 'paltry prize.' In a conversation with a political leader, Hiero, Xenophon speaking through the character of Simonides, one of the lyric poets, observes,

---

[1] Quoted in Rosamond Kent Sprague, *The Older Sophists* (Columbia: University of South Carolina Press, 1972), 228.

> Think of the large sums that men are induced to spend on horse races, gymnastic and choral competitions, and the long course of training and practice they undergo for the sake of a paltry prize.[2]

He preferred to regard the purpose of competition as being the essential catalyst which brings about the highest levels of performance. He credits Lycurgus, ninth century BC, as having instituted this philosophy.

> He saw that where the spirit of rivalry is the strongest among the people, there the choruses are most worth hearing and the athletic contests afford the finest spectacle.[3]

Xenophon finds a subordinate value in a model for civic discipline.

> There is nothing so convenient nor so good for human beings as order. Thus, a chorus is a combination of human beings; but when the members of it do as they choose, it becomes mere confusion, and there is no pleasure in watching it; but when they act and sing in an orderly fashion, then those same men at once seem worth seeing and worth hearing.[4]

Aside from such values as discipline and hard work, the important question remains, to what extent was musicality a value or purpose in the ancient Greek music competition? The extant references to this question are somewhat conflicting. Plutarch, 45–125 AD, was under the impression that musical skill was indeed the point of the earliest competitions. He writes of the active participation in organizing these festivals by Pericles, 495–429 BC,

> Pericles, also, eager for distinction, then first obtained the decree for a contest in musical skill to be held yearly at the Panathanaea, and he himself, being chosen judge, arranged the order and method in which the competitors should sing and play on the aulos and harp. And both at that time, and at other times also, they sat in this music room to see and hear all such trials of skill.[5]

But, musicality can be affected by the audience and in the case of competition attended by an audience there will always be the temptation to lower the quality of the music in order to gain the enthusiasm of the public. This seems to have been the point in an anecdote by Herodotus (ca. 440 BC) describing an instrumental contest in the context of some ancient Greek festival.

> In early times popularity with the masses was a sign of bad art; hence, when a certain flute player once received loud applause, Asopodorus of Phlius, who was himself still wating in the wings, said, 'What's this? Something awful must have happened!'[6]

---

2   'Hiero,' IX, in E. C. Marchant, *Scripta Minora* (Cambridge: Harvard University Press, 1956).

3   'The Lacedaemonians,' IV, Ibid.

4   'Oeconomicus,' VIII, trans. E. C. Marchant, *Memorabilia and Oeconomicus* (Cambridge: Harvard University Press, 1953).

5   *Lives*, 'Pericles.'

6   Athenaeus, in *Deipnosophistae*, XIV 631.

This was precisely the concern of Aristotle, 384–322 BC, who clearly rejected the introduction of music contests in education, because of the consequent impact on the quality of the music.

> Thus then we reject the professional instruments and also the professional mode of education in music (and by professional we mean that which is adopted in contests), for in this the performer practices the art, not for the sake of his own improvement, but in order to give pleasure, and that of a vulgar sort, to his hearers ... The result is that the performers are vulgarized, for the end at which they aim is bad. The vulgarity of the spectator tends to lower the character of the music and therefore of the performers.[7]

Polybius, 203–120 BC, found, in retrospect, that competition was a fundamental part of the educational use of music in ancient Greece.

> For it is a well-known fact, familiar to all, that it is hardly known except in Arcadia, that in the first place the boys from their earliest childhood are trained to sing in measure the hymns and paeans in which by traditional usage they celebrate the heroes and gods of each particular place; later they learn the measures of Philoxenus and Timotheus, and every year in the theater they compete keenly in choral singing to the accompaniment of professional aulos players, the boys in the contest proper to them and the young men in what is called the men's contest. And not only this, but through their whole life they entertain themselves at banquets not by listening to hired musicians but by their own efforts, calling for a song from each in turn. Whereas they are not ashamed of denying acquaintance with other studies, in the case of singing it is neither possible for them to deny a knowledge of it because they all are compelled to learn it, nor, if they confess to such knowledge can they excuse themselves, so great a disgrace is this considered in that country.[8]

The musical competitions of ancient Greece were designed for three mediums, the solo instrumentalist, the lyric singer accompanied by an instrumentalist, or by himself, and choral groups. Most of the poetry of the ancient Greek lyric poets which has survived was associated with the festivals held in connection with the Olympiad.

With regard to the choral competitions of ancient Greece, we have a great deal of information in Plato's book, *Laws*.[9] First, Plato addresses the importance of festivals to the state and the relationship of the contests to these values.

> As to rhapsodists and the like, and the contests of choruses which are to perform at feasts, all this shall be arranged when the months and days and years have been appointed for gods and demigods, whether every third year, or again every fifth year, or in whatever way or manner the gods may put into men's minds the distribution and order of them. At the same time, we may expect that the musical contests will be celebrated in their turn by the command of the judges and the director of education and the guardians of the law meeting together for this purpose, and themselves becoming legislators of the times and nature and conditions of the choral contests and of dancing in general. What they ought severally to be in language and song, and in the admixture of harmony with rhythm and the dance, has been often declared by the original legislator; and

---

7 *Politica*, 1341b.9.

8 Polybius, *The Histories*, IV.20.5ff, trans. W. R. Paton (Cambridge: Harvard University Press, 1954).

9 Regarding the dates of festivals, see 653d and following. For general information on the values of festivals, see 828 and following.

his successors ought to follow him, making the games and sacrifices duly to correspond at fitting times, and appointing public festivals. It is not difficult to determine how these and the like matters may have a regular order; nor, again, will the alteration of them do any great good or harm to the state.[10]

He notes that these festivals have a special value for older folk for 'it reminds them of our former selves; and gladly institute contests for those who are able to awaken in us the memory of our youth.'[11]

Next he discusses the concept of a mixed competition, but explains this never works well because people of different age groups will prefer different kinds of events. It is during this discussion that he pauses to define what he means by the highest kind of music.

> The fairest music is that which delights the best and best educated, and especially that which delights the one man who is preeminent in virtue and education.

Plato next discusses the qualifications of the judges for musical contests and explains why it is not appropriate to allow the public to judge these events.

> And therefore the judges must be men of character, for they will require wisdom and have still greater need of courage; the true judge must not draw his inspiration from the theatre, nor ought he to be unnerved by the clamor of the many and his own incapacity; nor again, knowing the truth, ought he through cowardice and unmanliness carelessly to deliver a lying judgment, with the very same lips which have just appealed to the gods before he judged. He is sitting not as the disciple of the theatre, but, in his proper place, as their instructor, and he ought to be the enemy of all pandering to the pleasure of the spectators. The ancient and common custom of Hellas was the reverse of that which now prevails in Italy and Sicily, where the judgment is left to the body of spectators, who determine the victor by show of hands. But this custom has been the destruction of the poets themselves; for they are now in the habit of composing with a view to please the bad taste of their judges, and the result is that the spectators instruct themselves;—and also it has been the ruin of the theater; they ought to be receiving a higher pleasure, but now by their own act the opposite result follows.[12]

Plato continues his discussion of judges and the wide span of knowledge they must have.

> AN ATHENIAN STRANGER. Surely then he who would judge correctly must know what each composition is; for if he does not know what is the character and meaning of the piece, and what it actually represents, he will never discern whether the intention is correct or mistaken.

After discussing some restrictions in musical idioms (men should not sing songs intended for women, one must not mix melodies of freemen and slaves, etc.), Plato makes some comments on the qualifications of the choral groups competing in these festivals.

---

[10] *Laws.*, 835.

[11] 657d.

[12] *Laws*, 657d.

> But we are considering now how our choristers, who are from thirty to fifty years of age, and may be over fifty, are not to use the Muses, but how they are to use them. And the considerations which we have urged seem to show that these fifty-years-old choristers who are to sing, will require something better than a mere choral training. For they need have a quick perception and knowledge of harmonies and rhythms; otherwise, how can they ever know whether a melody would be rightly sung to the Dorian mode, or the rhythm which the poet has assigned to it?
>
> CLEINIAS. Clearly they cannot.
>
> AN ATHENIAN STRANGER. The many are ridiculous in imagining that they know what is proper harmony and rhythm, and what is not, when they can only be made by force to sing to the flute and step in rhythm; it never occurs to them that they are ignorant of what they are doing.
>
> ......
>
> Then as now, as would appear, we are making the discovery that our newly appointed choristers, whom we hereby invite and, although they are their own masters, compel to sing, must be educated to such an extent as to be able to follow the steps of the rhythm and the notes of the song, that they may review the harmonies and rhythms, and be able to select what are suitable for men of their age and character to sing; and may sing them, and have innocent pleasure from their own performance, and also lead younger men to receive the virtues of character with the welcome which they deserve. Having such training, they will attain a more accurate knowledge than falls to the lot of the common people, or even of the poets themselves.[13]

Finally, Plato also provides some recommendations for the election of conductors for the choral groups.

> First of all, we must choose directors for the choruses of boys, and men, and maidens, whom they shall follow in the amusement of the dance, and for our other musical arrangements;—one director will be enough for the choruses, and he should be not less than forty years of age. One director will also be enough to introduce the solo singers, and to give judgment on the competitors, and he ought to be less than thirty years of age. The director and manager of the choruses shall be elected after the following manner:—Let any persons who commonly take an interest in such matters go to the meeting, and be fined if they do not go, but those who have no interest shall not be compelled. Any elector may propose as director someone who understands music, and he in the scrutiny may be challenged on the one part by those who say he has no skill, and defended on the other hand by those who say that he has. Ten are to be elected by vote, and he of the ten who is chosen by lot shall undergo a scrutiny, and lead the choruses for a year according to law. And in like manner the competitor who wins the lot shall be leader of the solo and concert music for that year; and he who is thus elected shall deliver the award to the judges.[14]

From ancient Rome we do not have nearly as many first-hand reports of music contests as we do from Greece. We have no doubt that music competition was going on in ancient Rome, but the writers had something much more vivid to report—the competitions of the coliseum. Thus the music contests now appear in fiction, and usually as mythology.

Perhaps the most notorious music competitor in history was the emperor Nero, who to aid his victories as both a singer and instrumentalist he bribed and even murdered his competitors. Of course the adjudicators, well aware of his reputation, always found him the winner. Not

---

[13] Ibid., 668c.

[14] Ibid., 764d.

content with a guaranteed victory, Nero rehearsed the audience in their applause and had the exits blocked so no one could leave when he performed. The historian, Suetonius, has left a few clues as to the rules of deportment for contestants.

> In competition he observed the rules most scrupulously, never daring to clear his throat and even wiping the sweat from his brow with his arm. Once indeed, during the performance of a tragedy, when he had dropped his scepter but quickly recovered it, he was terribly afraid that he might be excluded from the competition because of his slip, and his confidence was restored only when his accompanist swore that it had passed unnoticed amid the delight and applause of the people.[15]

We want to include a comment about winning made by the famous Spanish writer, Cervantes.

> If it's for a poetry competition, you ought to aim at the second prize, your grace, because the first prize is always awarded as an act of patronage or in recognition of social standing, but second prize strictly on merit, so that third prize really amounts to second, and what's called first prize, if you calculate matters this way, has to be truly the third—much in the fashion that universities award advanced degrees.[16]

The final question which should be raised is, did anyone ever object and declare that contests in music are bad?

The most enlightened of sixteenth-century Spanish philosophers was Juan Vives (1492–1540). In his *Introduction to Wisdom*, an early treatise on education, Vives discourages the spirit of competition, which he says leads to 'quarrels, wrangling and dissensions.'[17]

The great philosopher of the early Baroque in England, Roger North, accepted the importance of aristocratic money in supporting music, but he was much opposed to a current trend in London whereby nobles contribute money to a 'pot' to be given to the performer who pleases them best in a concert. Competition in music, he says, has largely negative results.

> Instead of encouraging the endeavors of all, the happy victor only was pleased, and all the rest were discontented and some who thought they deserved better, were almost ready to [give up music] … So much a mistake it is to force artists upon a competition, for all but one are sure to be malcontents.[18]

Of the great composers, the most outspoken against the idea of competition in music was Mendelssohn. In 1838 the English publisher, Novello, sent him some text asking him to join a competition among composers in setting this text to music. Mendelssohn answered,

---

[15] Suetonius, *Lives of the Caesars.*, VI, xx.

[16] Miguel de Cervantes, *Don Quijote*, trans. Burton Raffel (New York: Norton, 1995), II, xviii.

[17] Foster Watson, trans., *Vives: On Education* (Cambridge: University Press, 1913), II, i.

[18] Roger North, *Memoirs of Music*, ed. Edward Rimbault (London: Bell, 1846), 118ff. An advertisement in the London Gazette for March 21, 1699, reads,

> Several persons of quality having, for the encouragement of musick advanced 200 guineas, to be distributed in 4 prizes, the first of 100, the second of 50, the third of 30 and the four of 20 guineas shall be adjudged to compose the best …

> It is altogether impossible for me to do anything in the way of prize composition; I cannot do it … When I was compelled to do so, when a boy, in competition with my sister and fellow-students, my works were always wonders of stupidity … I think that is the reason why I felt afterwards such an antipathy to prize-fighting in music.[19]

In our introduction to this topic we pointed out that there are no 'correct answers' in the experiential side of our personality. As we also noted, this makes the very idea of competition in music (or love) questionable, for everyone's opinion is valid for them, but them only. Mendelssohn, in a letter to his mother, brings us full-circle by making this same point.

> I made a resolution … never again to participate in any way in the awarding of prizes at a musical competition … I should be the last person to set myself up as a criterion and my taste as incontrovertible, and, in an idle hour passing in review all the assembled competitors, criticizing them, and—God knows—possibly being guilty of the most glaring injustice towards them. So I have renounced such activity once and for all.[20]

༄༅༔

IN 2010 I WROTE AN ESSAY which recounted some of my own experiences in judging musical contests.

ON ADJUDICATING MUSIC COMPETITION

In 1991 I was invited to be the Chairman of the Jury for an international piano competition in Italy. This was a very interesting experience, especially during the first round when each pianist was required to perform two short compositions of their choice from among the works of either Liszt or Scribian. I heard more short piano works new to me, especially by Liszt, than I ever imagined existed.

There were eleven adjudicators, of whom ten were well-known European piano teachers.[21] I, as the eleventh, was to serve as an unbiased listener. We voted after each performance in the first round like so many Roman emperors—thumbs up or thumbs down; majority rules. I soon found the other adjudicators, the piano teachers, were judging on the basis of piano technique, without respect to the musicality of the performance. To my embarrassment, all too often when we stuck our hands out to vote with our thumbs the vote would be 10–1 in favor, or 1–10 in favor. And I was always the '1.' From time to time I got the evil eye from some famous teacher, but they had to be nice to me since I was the Chairman.

---

[19] Letter to Alfred Novello, April 7, 1838.

[20] Letter to his mother, March 30, 1840.

[21] One of these colleagues was a famous blind teacher from Switzerland. It was astonishing to me to hear him discuss topics like fingering and hand position purely from the basis of hearing.

I felt badly for some of the young pianists, kids who had traveled from all over the world and who had prepared for months only to be thrown out without comment after their performance in the first round. I felt even stronger in the cases of some of these who were eliminated, yet who gave really *musical* performances. Indeed, in several cases, after I had returned home, I wrote to young people and told them to please ignore the actions of the jury and just keep doing what they are doing because they are superb young musicians.

After several instances where some wonderful young musician performed, followed by our vote of 10–1 to throw them out, I consulted with one of the judges, an Argentine teaching in Italy, who spoke perfect English. 'I don't understand what is going on here,' I said. 'This last young lady (from Finland) was *very* musical, but all of you voted no!' He answered, 'But, a piano contest has nothing to do with music!'

I do not know why I was so shocked by his answer, because for decades I had been judging band contests which also had nothing to do with music. Band 'contests' (euphemistically called band 'festivals') are also judged on technical matters and no adjudication sheet asks, 'Was it musical?' This must certainly be one reason why some serious band conductors are so disgusted with these events.

But I do not mean to suggest that our high school contests are not taken seriously. Once during the 1960s I awarded a 'B' to a high school orchestra from Spokane and was subsequently threatened with a lawsuit by the conductor. 'You just don't understand,' he cried, 'we have never received a grade below A.' He was right, I did not understand. The organizing committee had failed to tell me in advance that he was supposed to get an 'A' no matter what.

The Texas band contests are especially serious and culminate in what in effect are state championships at each level of school population. Once I participated as an adjudicator in one of the final rounds of the top category in one of these. This was a tape round, with six or so of we adjudicators sitting in a class room facing speakers some five feet away. Immediately behind us were seated all the conductors of this category. Even if one of their tapes was not included, they were there to validate our judgment. Very serious stuff and you felt every movement you made, maybe like scratching one's ear, was being watched by a room full of conductors, sitting behind, for a clue to its meaning.

Each band in this top Texas category that year was playing large-scale compositions, works like Strauss's *Also sprach Zarathustra* or *Till Eulenspiegel*. Consequently we were sitting for hours with no break (breaks invite talking, consulting and other evil possibilities). At one point there came the tape of a band performing the Schönberg *Theme and Variations*, Op. 43a, conducted by a gentleman known to me as being, shall we say, 'very confident.' To be sure, his performance was virtually perfect with respect to intonation, accuracy, etc. Whether it was because I was becoming exhausted from these non-stop tape performances, or perhaps feeling some frustration over the process, I wrote on the adjudication sheet, after appropriate compliments, 'the only thing confusing to me in this performance was that I did not hear the third of the chord on the down-beat of bar 136.'[22] Of course, no one would ever hear this missing third,

---

[22] This is one of two genuine errors by the composer in his autograph short score. The unnamed individual who produced the full score we all know, published by G. Schirmer, made a large number of additional incorrect solutions, misreadings and just plain mistakes.

a genuine Schönberg mistake, and I would suspect that very few of my colleagues had ever discovered this missing note in the course of their study and analysis. But I mentioned I didn't hear it and after the event was concluded this conductor approached me in the hall apologizing that he did not hear this 'missing' note. Indeed, he was so humbled, so obsequious, that I really felt ashamed of myself for mentioning this. But this incident does illustrate the fact that in our band contests we are all too serious about the wrong things.

On the other side of the coin, there are, of course, some conductors who do not take these contests seriously. I recall once adjudicating the Western Massachusetts Band Contest in 1973. We, the adjudicators, had a program listing the name of the bands, the name of the conductor and the repertoire. The very first band which performed played the Morton Gould *Jericho*. Of course, being from Los Angeles, I did not know the high school bands of this area but the big letter 'A' on their uniform seemed to correspond with my program which listed a band from a town which began with the same letter. I was confused, however, by the fact that the conductor's name in my program was a man's name, whereas the actual conductor on this morning was a lady. So, when the performance was concluded, I called her over and said, 'I am confused because the conductor's name I have published here cannot be your name.' She responded, 'That's correct, I am a substitute because the conductor is on strike!'

I recall another instance when I called the conductor to the adjudication table. In this case he had performed someone's five-minute reduction and arrangement for band of the Beethoven *3rd Symphony*. The arrangement was so unbelievably bad, such an audacious sacrilege, such a sin against art and Beethoven, that I wanted to ask him what his reason was for performing this publication. So I asked, 'I suppose the reason you selected this publication was to be able to interest your students in wanting to get to know the original version for orchestra.' The reader must agree that that is a model of polite introduction to the subject, but the reader must also share my astonishment at the conductor's answer that he was unaware that the publication was arranged from a symphony of Beethoven.

The ignorance of this band conductor (in the Northwest) is insignificant when compared to the conductors I have listened to in band contests in the City of Los Angeles. I recall one poor fellow there whom we had to inform, after his performance, that generally conductors do not wear hats when they conduct indoors. To provide further examples would be too depressing for the reader.

So why do we have these band 'festivals'? Certainly they cannot be *music* festivals, for there is never an audience there to listen. Music makes no sense without a listener.

The answer is that these band festivals are said to be vehicles of validation of the band program. But can you have a reputable validation process if the judges are peers and friends? And what is the point of a validation vehicle if neither the school administration nor school board acts on the results?

With regard to the public school music competitions themselves, leaving aside the fact that they are ineffective in terms of validation, there are other fundamental problems. First, they are not music contests, they are grammar contests. Students are prepared and evaluated solely on the basis of how perfectly they reproduce the notational music grammar, everything which appears on the page. I have never seen an evaluation form which asked, 'Was it Musical?'

Second, it follows that music exists to be listened to, but there is almost never anyone listening other than the judges. Logic would stipulate that there would be an educational value in the other bands participating listening to each other. They do not.

Third, although it is the band which is given a grade, as all adjudicators know we are in fact judging the conductor. Few facts in human history have been so universally understood but never acknowledged. It was in recognition of this fact that William D. Revelli, in one of his most quoted observations, wrote on an adjudication sheet, 'the only thing that could make this band worse is one more rehearsal!'

Finally, generally speaking, the conductor pays little attention to the judges' comments. One reason for this, contrary to the fact discussed in Number Three, above, is that due to a typically human, psychological 'slight of hand' the conductor tells himself that the comments are about the band and not about him.

Another reason the conductor attributes little authority to the judges comments is because they have so little actual material value. Once, when I was judging bands all day and was waiting for a stage change for the next band, I divided the fee I was being paid by the number of bands and was astonished to see that I, at that time having some twenty-five years' experience in adjudicating bands, was being paid $11.00 per band. At that time one paid even a beginning plumber $65.00 for an evaluation. Why *would* anyone pay attention to an evaluation worth only $11.00?

In attempt to create a festival organization which made an attempt to begin to place some emphasis on music, and not grammar, in 1986 I published an essay describing a new format. Although generally it met that quiet death which tends to fall on anything requiring a change in the status quo, since that time I have had a few letters from educators who have tried this format and who report being more satisfied with this approach.

A Proposal for a new Festival Format

Philosophy and Purpose of the Festival

The purpose of a music festival is to listen to music. The purpose of a High School Band Festival should be for the band members to hear the music performed by other bands. The students should be prepared for the literature they will hear, and not prepared only for listening to who has the 'best' band. The conductor may rest assured that due to the genetic contributions to how we hear music his students will immediately correctly identify not only which band is 'best' but also which is the most musical. The general 'uneducated' public, for the same reasons, also knows whether a musical performance is good or bad. And there is no middle ground. The public never says, 'It was almost good.' The public never cares about what difficulties the band experienced—too few rehearsals, absent key players, music arrived too late, etc. The public only asks, 'Was it good?'

The above being a fact of life, there should be no necessity for numerical or letter ratings of any kind. Further, the festival should be divorced from any concept which holds that its primary purpose is as an instrument of accountability of the school band program (this will be discussed below). The festival might even serve to raise the quality of literature heard if the conductor were selecting literature to be listened to, and not for the purpose of confronting traditional adjudication.

A New Format

I would propose an invitational festival for six bands, performing approximately thirty minutes each during the morning hours. A rotating schedule should provide for each band to have one slot for warm-up, one slot to perform, one slot to put away instruments and three slots to listen as members of the audience. Three bands, together with accompanying adults and other audience members would provide each band with a reasonable audience to perform for. Each band member would only have to listen for an hour and a half of performance, a small enough amount of time that we should be able to expect quiet, concentrated listening.

The band director who wanted his students to profit even more from this experience might find out in advance what literature his students would be hearing and prepare them somewhat for this, as for example by perhaps using the repertoire of the other bands as sight-reading material.

After a noon break, the six bands would combine into three combined, larger bands to be rehearsed by the three adjudicators. The adjudicators should not discuss any literature heard during the morning, but rather use their own literature, selected for the teaching purposes they hold important.

On Adjudication

There should be no adjudication forms whatsoever.

The three adjudicators should have a rotating schedule, whereby they take turns going to a separate room to discuss with the conductor of the previous band his performance as a conductor. The format for this discussion would center on the viewing of a video made of the conductor from the back of the band, facing the conductor. Except for the first band (which would have three adjudicators present), all bands would then be heard by two adjudicators—the third always being out of the room with the previous conductor.

Regarding the two remaining adjudicators, one should make tape comments solely and privately for the conductor. These comments, except in an extraordinary circumstance, should not deal with technical problems, or the 'grammar' of music, such as 'in bar 129 the third clarinets were flat,' etc. The comments, rather, should deal with how to make the performance more musical or more effective in a general sense. If a director felt he needed a statement for the purpose of the accountability of his program for his administration, I would recommend that a confidential letter from this judge to the administration could be requested. I don't believe the present system, where often a rating is produced by three colleagues, carries much weight as an accountability document.

The second adjudicator should make a tape of his comments which could and should be played for the band members. These comments should center on compliments on musical achievement and musical suggestions.

One of the three adjudicators should be from out-of-state, someone highly respected by the six directors participating in the festival. It is a very great mistake not to do this, for it cuts these programs off from a connection with the rest of the band world and it very much limits their ability to evaluate how they compare with the best of the nation. This would be possible if each performing band paid a performance fee of $250 or so. This is not very much compared to what we raise for other purposes. It is not much for the school to pay for, given the value to so many students.

During the thirty years I was director of bands at California State University, Northridge I used to send out newsletters to high school band directors. Sometimes these discussed new repertoire I recommended, or various festivals I thought might be of interest and sometimes they were more philosophical. The latter were somewhat controversial, being of opinions which varied from the readers'. The following example was reprinted in the *Utah Music Educators Journal*, Winter 2010, at their request, twenty years later! Also I should add that these newsletters in general were cited with praise at the time I was inducted into the California Music Educators Hall of Fame.

A Letter to California High School Band Directors (1991)

On many occasions during the past twenty-three years I have addressed the subject of the concert band here in Southern California. Since our band programs are continuing to die, I hope you will allow me once again to ask you to think about the priorities of our school band programs.

Music is listened to by every person on earth. Music is one of the most universal of human experiences. Apart from biological things like eating, etc., music, like other basic experiences, such as love, seems to be shared by all people. And yet, in Southern California, we have not succeeded in making a secure place for music in the education of all students—even though it is a far more universal need than algebra, foreign languages or science. Why have we failed to do this?

The bottom line is that instead of using the band as a vehicle for music education, we have turned the band into an activity. Twenty-five years ago I wrote in an article that 'by emphasizing music education we might be able to save the band, but by emphasizing band we will not be able to save music education.' What I meant by this can perhaps be seen more clearly by considering the orchestra. There is nothing important about the orchestra, as a medium. There is nothing important about the LA Philharmonic. What is important is the music they play. That music, experienced by the listener, is where its value to the human race lies.

The same is true with bands. It is the nature of the experience in the literature which matters.

In the English language we unfortunately have only one word, 'music,' for everything from elevator music to Beethoven's Ninth Symphony. The Germans make a distinction between *Ernst Musik* (serious music) and *Unterhaltung Musik* (entertainment music), the German radio stations always placing these two branches under different administrations and often in different buildings. While this is only two words, as opposed to our one word, it does clearly serve to acknowledge the fact that not all music is equal in purpose. Because in the English language everything is included under one word, 'music,' some music educators make the mistaken conclusion that all music is therefore somehow equal. But in fact the various kinds of music throughout the world are *only* equal in the fact that they are notated with the same symbols. But to say this makes all music equal in significance is just as absurd as saying Shakespeare and comic books are equal in significance because they both use letters of the alphabet or words of the same language.

The reason great literature and great musical literature are more significant than their more popular cousins has to do not with the language (although, of course, Shakespeare and Mozart *did* use beautiful language), but with the importance of the experience that language communicates. Furthermore, on the experiential side of our being there are no 'equals.' On the rational side there are: 2 + 2 = 4 and everyone in the world shares that understanding. But on the experiential side we each are the product of our own different experiences. We arrive at music as listeners from the perspective of different experiences and the composer also composes from personal experience. Therefore, experiences to which we give commonly accepted names have uncommon definitions. For example, we have the word, 'love,' in the English language, but what each person understands by that word is the sum of his own personal experience and every 'love' experience is not of the same quality, significance nor of the same impact in one's life.

It is the same with music. With music notation a composer can, according to his purpose and ability, write music which communicates very superficial experiences or very profound experiences. I think the more profound the experience the composer wishes to communicate, the more inadequate the language is to express it. Therefore, in the great masterpieces of Western music, the notational language is only an incomplete shorthand offering clues to profound experiential truths which are incapable of notation in any symbolic language. This is what Mahler meant when he observed that, 'the important things in Music are not found in the notes.' I think the art of teaching music is the art of teaching the student to experience that which is beyond the written language of music.

Because it is the experiential aspect of music which communicates to the listener, and the player, we come to the real heart of the problem in music education. You cannot separate the quality of the experience (the music literature) from the quality of the education. The music we give our students *becomes* part of the experiential make-up of that student. The experience shapes the person and this cannot be avoided. If we want our students to have the best possible musical experience we must give them the best possible music. As Zoltan Kodaly stated it,

> Children should be taught with only the most musically valuable material. For the young, only the best is good enough. They should be led to masterpieces by means of masterpieces.

It is very difficult to relate parade bands and field show bands with the kind of musical experiences Mahler and Kodaly are talking about. These kinds of organizations are activities which serve other purposes. It is true one can teach the *grammar* of music, rhythm, pitch, etc., in these organizations, as indeed you must in order for them to function. But they are not vehicles for the kind of experiences discussed by Mahler and Kodaly and they cannot substitute for those experiences. It is the concert band which is the appropriate vehicle for presenting the student with quality experience in music and the concert band has a great literature available to us all for use in music education …

It is the secondary school music teacher who defines the secondary school music experience. It is simply not true that administrators or parents make us have the kind of programs we have. Quite to the contrary, it is because of the universal experience of music itself that administrators and parents will not fight to save music education. They cannot be fooled; they know the difference between an activity and music education. They will accept no argument which attempts to classify an activity as a core subject …

We must change what we are doing. Music education is blossoming in Europe and in other parts of the world, but dying in Southern California. I do not believe we can reverse this dismal trend by winning more trophies.

☙

THE OTHER ACTIVITY which universities often offer the public schools is to provide guest conductors for honor bands, generally composed of students from a number of schools. The following essay recounts some of my own experiences serving in this capacity.

ON HONOR BANDS AND ORCHESTRAS

Generally speaking, being the guest conductor of an honor band or orchestra is hard work. Usually there are many continuous hours of work each day of the engagement and often the pay for each of these hours is less than the hourly rate given without question to a plumber. Most hosts fail to understand that the guest conductor needs a private room at both the rehearsal and concert site. This is necessary for the purpose of rest, for changing clothes and for contemplation on the state of the progress toward the concert and reviewing scores. Some hosts forget to arrange prompt transportation to and from the airport to the motel. After a long flight, the guest is really not in the mood to run errands with you.

Common business courtesies are often overlooked by the host. Rarely, for example, are you informed in advance of when and how the fee will be paid. It is embarrassing for the guest to have to raise this question at the airport on the way out of town. Often you are not given an adequate introduction to the students and this can play a significant role in how things begin. Rarely does one find an adequate podium, a critical issue for the arms in the course of hours of rehearsal. It should not be the duty of the guest conductor to set up chairs and stands. Any plans for having the guest conductor join a meal or party with local teachers should be revealed to the guest even before his arrival in town.

Many hosts engage the least expensive hotel for the guest conductor and such places are usually not walking distances from good restaurants. At one very important All-State engagement I was put in a college dorm where I had to suffer the resultant noise and lack of privacy. Sometimes you will be asked, 'Of course we would like to have you stay with my family.' They mean well by this, but I learned early never to accept invitations to stay in private homes, for there even your daily schedule is not under your control. On one summer occasion I was engaged to work for a week as a guest conductor for a collegiate ensemble at Baylor University. A former student was then the trumpet professor at this university and he called me repeatedly trying to talk me into staying in his home. There are no motels walking distance from campus—there are no restaurants—you will have your own room, with separate entrance and key, etc., et. al. I broke my rule and agreed to stay with him and his family. As it turned out, the concert coincided with the end of the summer term and both my residence host and his wife were preparing to leave the state immediately thereafter. Consequently, each day there was less food as they were trying to clear out the refrigerator before closing the house for the rest of the summer. By the day of the concert, an occasion when I normally need full meals for energy, there was practically nothing to eat. After the concert I was approached by a well-dressed gentleman who introduced himself as the Controller of the University. He announced to me, 'I wanted to come in person to explain to you why your check is a bit smaller than the contract called for.' 'Oh?' said I. 'That's because we have deducted $40 because of the free food you received at Professor ***'s house!'

There was one other occasion when I was visited by the controller of a university and this was following my teaching a summer conducting course for band directors at the University of Texas in 1970. In this case the end of the two-week class coincided with the end of the university's fiscal year. The controller appeared after my last session and explained that my check would be somewhat *larger* than the contract called for. This was due, he explained, to the fact that they simply had some monies left over in the budget and having no other pressing requests they decided to 'dump it into' my check.

One of the unusual honor bands I was invited to conduct was one drawn from a league of Christian High Schools in California. They called me and I was free on those dates. I gave them the fee I expected and after a period of consultation within their committee they agreed. Then after two weeks, the original contact called me back, apologizing, 'Dr. Whitwell I am sorry to have to call back, but the committee has a question I forgot to ask and they demanded I call you back.' 'No problem, what is the question?' 'Well, we want to know if you are a Christian?' Upon hearing this I assumed that where this might be leading was to restrictions in repertoire, based on my memory of touring with the Air Force Band which, when performing on the campuses of certain Christian denominations, had its planned repertoire subjected to campus censors (no military marches allowed, no music from Broadway shows, etc.). So, very cautious, since I would not have anyone else select my repertoire for me, I asked, 'What, exactly, do you mean?' 'Well,' he answered, 'I don't really know!' 'In that case,' I answered, 'tell them, yes!'

This Christian honor band had a Friday evening rehearsal and rehearsals and a concert on Saturday. I had been housed in a motel quite far from the campus where the rehearsals were held, so when leaving Friday night I double-checked with the host to make sure the rehearsal the next morning was still scheduled for 9:00 AM. The next morning I arrived at the rehearsal site, a large chapel, a few moments before 9:00 AM. Normally, before an honor band's second rehearsal the students are conversing with their new found friends, getting out their instruments, etc. Therefore I was in a sudden panic to see no one outside before the doors and I assumed this rehearsal must be scheduled elsewhere and no one had told me. Then, going in through the double doors of the chapel I saw that the entire band was on stage in their places, whereupon I feared I was late. But I soon realized that they had obviously been obligated to come early and attend a devotional service before the rehearsal. At the very moment I opened the doors the pastor was praying, 'and dear Lord, please don't let Dr. Whitwell lose his patience again today!' The students, but not the pastor, saw me standing and listening to this. Very embarrassing. After the pastor and other adults had departed, I said to the students, 'I am rather confident that this morning's rehearsal will prove beyond a doubt that not all prayers are answered!'

Sometimes there used to be problems getting to the site of the honor band, something which has been made much easier today when one can make one's own arrangements on-line. On one occasion, back in the days of travel agents, I had been invited to guest conduct an All-State Band in Iowa City, Iowa. Everyone in the mid-west knows that to get to Iowa City one flies to Cedar Rapids, a large airport which can accommodate large jets. My Los Angeles travel agent, however, looked up Iowa City in some industry book of hers and found contrary instructions. She informed me that I could get a reservation only to Des Moines and from there I had to take a private plane owned by Iowa Air. This company issued no advance tickets and so I would have to be prepared to pay for the remaining leg of the flight in cash in Des Moines.

So I land in Des Moines and look for the Air Iowa counter. When I found it I discovered it was closed, dark and with a note to me lying on the counter. The note directed me to call a phone number in St. Louis, the home office of this airline. Moving to pay phones on an adjacent wall, I made the call and was informed that my plane was broken down but that their only other plane was making a freight run from Dallas to Minneapolis and would detour to pick me up and take me to Iowa City. Forget that! I went to the Hertz agency concluding it would be better to rent a car and drive. But due to a storm on its way, no rental agencies would rent cars which were leaving the city.

So I returned to the dark waiting room and soon, through a side door, I see a figure in jeans, beating his hands together trying to warm himself, staggering and falling in a seat. That's my pilot. 'I can't go on, I can't go on.' Apparently the heater in his small plane is broken and aloft it is something like thirty degrees below zero. I explain that I must get to Iowa City tonight for a rehearsal early in the morning. 'No! I can't go on.' I drag him to a bar and toss down a couple of shots to warm him up and eventually he decides to fly. 'OK, do you have a ticket?' 'No,' I say and explain that I was to buy it here in cash. 'How can we go without a ticket,' he asks, as he contemplates this insurmountable barrier. I recommend that he take the cash and that we make a manuscript ticket. Agreeing, he takes a blank piece of paper and writes,

1 trip to Iowa City
the pilot

I still have this document.

This was a fine group of students, but the host was somewhat upset because the repertoire I had selected did not keep the 'percussion busy enough!' This is a manifestation of the primary illness which permeates the band profession in the educational world. Few educators think as artists, which, of course, music is. Most educators only think of ensembles as activities. My host wanted to add a new educational composition of some sort with busy percussion parts. It did not occur to him that I had selected my repertoire only after a careful examination of the time available for rehearsal. So I recommended instead that the university percussion instructor take the percussion students out of some rehearsals to form a percussion ensemble which he would then conduct on the concert. This was a solution which pleased me, the host and the students. Only the university percussion instructor was upset, for he had to come in to work on Saturday.

This reminds me of another occasion when I had difficulty getting to the job. As a young man during the 1970s I was over extended with much guest conducting and vast amounts of CBDNA work added to my own conducting. The demands on my planning were such that once in order to be able to deliver a speech before a SW Division meeting of the CBDNA in Houston it was necessary to take a flight leaving Los Angeles late at night. Thus I had explained to my host that I would need a hotel close to the airport, for I would be dreadfully tired upon arrival. 'No problem! There is a Holiday Inn a few miles from the airport, right on the freeway. Just go out the door and take a cab.'

So, at perhaps 2:00 AM, I took a cab, gave the driver material regarding the name and address of the Holiday Inn and then immediately rested my head back on the seat and closed my eyes. At some point it occurred to me that we had been driving for a much longer period of time than that described by my host. I opened my eyes, looked out the window and even though it was very dark I could see cows and farm houses. Even though never having been in Houston, it seemed reasonable to conclude that the driver was lost. The driver, it turned out, was a foreign national new to both town and job. Polite inquires by myself of the driver having no effect, I was forced to demand that he call his supervisor. In those days before global satellite help, it took hours of trial and error before I arrived at my Holiday Inn. Upon arrival, the driver looked at his meter and announced, 'That will be $4,300.00.' I paid him somewhat less!

Another honor band that was complicated to travel to was one winter Wyoming All-State Band. Leaving aside any discussion of the various connections needed to get from LAX to Wyoming, the final part of the journey was a drive of more than one hundred miles over snow packed roads. I noticed the back of the car contained survival gear (for one person) in the event of car trouble in this vastly unpopulated area.

The other adjudicators and I arrived during a period of frantic activity by oil companies and the result was arriving at a hotel with no reservations for us. We were put on cots in a meeting room. This reminds me of an occasion one December when I ran into Frederick Fennell in Chicago at the Mid-West Conference. No one had arranged a room for him, so I had a roll-a-way bed brought to my room for him. I had a large room because I had in tow a young graduate student of mine[23] who had never been to Chicago. I made him go with me for the experience, of course, and on the morning we landed it was one of the worst of Chicago December days—temperature near zero, with blowing sleet. Naturally, for his experience, I immediately made him go on a walk with me around the then empty loop. We came to an intersection where an elderly lady was slowing making her way across the street, fighting wind and sleet. The light turned just before she made it across and a taxi waiting for the light honked loudly for her to get out of the way. She turned, raised her umbrella and began to pound on the hood of the taxi. 'Ah,' I remarked to my student, 'it's so great to be back in Chicago!'

Returning to this Wyoming All-State, the choral conductor was of the American cheerleader school of choral conducting, a display which he augmented by singing a solo, with high microphone volume, accompanied by the choir. The entire choral literature was pop-oriented and selected for the purpose of maximum, constant overflowing emotion on stage. Even the audience was emotionally drained by this performance. Back on our cots in the meeting room

---

[23] The student was Dr. Ronald Johnson, now Director of Bands at The University of Northern Iowa and today a guest conductor with vast experience in Europe.

he asked me what I thought of the students in Wyoming. 'Well,' I suggested, 'my students really tried hard to be musical.' And you? He moaned, 'My students had no emotion, no feeling at all!'

It is a tradition among honor groups for the students to take up a small collection for a gift for the conductor. This choral conductor, a frequent guest conductor of honor choirs, had a routine whereby he always left his wrist watch at home and then during rehearsal would constantly glance at his empty wrist and complain, 'Oh, I keep forgetting my watch broke this week!' Naturally the students always bought him a new watch, which he always immediately sold upon returning home.

The orchestra conductor on this occasion, a New York cellist new to guest conducting, was presented at the concert with a basket of fruit. Forgetting the audience, he exclaimed, 'What the Hell is this?' It was this cellist, by the way, who told me that once when he was the principal cello in the Houston Symphony one of the candidates for the conducting position of the orchestra was the young Leonard Bernstein, who did not get the job. The successful candidate was a man named Efrem Kurtz.

In a different year I was engaged as conductor of the Wyoming All-State Band, now meeting in Cody. When my host picked me up I asked how a certain California State University, Northridge student was doing, a question to which he registered no recognition of the name. 'Well,' I said, 'it is my understanding that he is the conductor of the Cody Civic Orchestra.' My host replied, 'Well I am Chairman of the Board for the orchestra and I assure you I have never heard of this person!' It turns out our student, a student of the orchestra conductor at CSUN, created a great lie for his resume. He went so far as to have sample programs of the Cody orchestra printed which he could send out with applications, etc. In one of the many desperate gestures of the Los Angeles Philharmonic, it once ran an auction for the privilege of conducting the National Anthem on a concert. This same student won with a bid of $500.

I also recall that on this occasion the All-State orchestra conductor was another cellist. He spent his evenings practicing in his room and one night, the choral conductor called the management complaining, 'I am really embarrassed to call you, but I think someone is strangling a cat in the next room!' Much chaos ensued.

Of my own involvement in this particular Wyoming All-State I recall that on the first day there were nine hours of rehearsal! The following morning in my motel I could not raise my arm to brush my teeth. I had to lay my arm on the plastic counter while I leaned over so I could rotate the brush with the wrist of the useless arm.

In terms of musical satisfaction, some honor band experiences have been more memorable than others. One challenge I recall was an all-city honor band in Pasadena in 1981. The California school instrumental programs have been in rapid decay since the 1960s when the famous 'Proposition 13' ending increases in residential real estate taxes was passed. Almost immediately the elementary programs were eliminated and then, of course, it was only a matter of time before the consequences spread upward. Pasadena is a typical illustration and the city director of music showed me a warehouse of string instruments, hundreds of them, no longer in use.

The all-city honor band had one rehearsal on Saturday afternoon, one on Sunday afternoon and then an evening concert. Knowing the level of the students there in 1981, and having only two rehearsals, I was careful to select literature with few challenges. You can imagine my concern when only half the students appeared for the Saturday rehearsal. It was explained to me that the other half would be there Sunday (but not the first half). Part-time jobs, family issues, etc. Only the timpanist appeared at both rehearsals, but when I thanked him the student replied, 'I wanted to come to both rehearsals because I cannot make the concert!'

So I faced a concert without ever having even a single run-through with the entire band. I told the organizer that I was very sorry but I believed the only composition we could have ready was a single march. That's OK! So Sunday evening we are in the Ambassador Theater, one of Los Angeles' two important concert halls, with this elegant hall was nearly filled and there I was with a program lasting three minutes! I made a long introduction, saying how important it was to the students for everyone to come, and then we performed the march. After I milked the applause by having the various sections of the band stand individually, I made another long speech about music education, making sure to give credit to the individual music teachers. 'Well, since these students worked so hard on this music, I am sure you won't mind if we perform it again!' Big applause. We played the march again, followed by a long speech about the importance of music in society, and then we performed the march again. I managed to stretch things out to nearly forty-five minutes and everyone was happy.

An All-State band that was stressful to me was one in Hawaii. My colleague, the orchestra conductor at CSUN, a talented but rather irresponsible person, had taken two engagements at the same time and came to me pleading to do the All-State for him. I was free that week-end and was happy to help him out, but the problem was the repertoire. In his careless way he had rattled off some titles to the committee months before, an impossibly long program for the amount of rehearsal. Since among these titles was the complete Hindemith *Symphony*, I called the host and asked if we might drop this work. No, he said, because a local music store had sold forty copies of the score to band directors on the island!

It didn't take much effort to brush up my memory of the Hindemith, but all the other scores, including one of the more difficult Rossini overtures, were works I had not previously memorized. I think I had four days to learn this material in addition to my already busy schedule. The program went well, but I was completely wet through and through at the end when I was told for the first time of an after concert dinner with the directors. I explained I simply had to, for health reasons, change clothes beforehand. A local graduate student drove me back to my hotel on Waikiki and we were caught in the infamous Saturday night traffic caused by small World War II era roads. It took an hour to get to the hotel, so by the time I changed the dinner was over. I told the young student I still needed some food and she joined me for a light meal. Meanwhile, of course (being the days before cell phones), the band directors had no idea what had happened to us.

There is one more poignant story I must tell about my colleague, referred to above, regarding an occasion when we were once doing a summer band together near San Jose. The band met on the campus of an exclusive private school which was otherwise closed for the summer.

One night he and I, to escape the camp for a few moments, were walking around in the very expensive residential neighborhood adjacent to the camp. After walking for a couple of blocks among million dollar homes, he says to me, 'Today I would be living in one of those homes were it not for the fact that when I was a little kid someone told my parents, *he has talent!*'

Especially difficult, for me, because I don't even know how to talk to Jr. High students much less know how to keep them in their chairs, were Jr. High honor bands and for that reason I only did two. One was a Jr. High All-State band in Hawaii, which I agreed to do because the conductor of the high school band was to be Karel Husa and this would give our families a week together there. The other instance was to help out a devoted friend in Marin County, CA (just above San Francisco).[24] In these rehearsals we were working a Nelhybel piece that contained a very loud single strike on the large bass drum. As we read through some of this work for the first time the student involved, a very large student, larger than the other students, did not play at all. When we stopped I explained to him that at Letter B this forte bass drum note is a solo so he should not be afraid to really hit it. The next time he stood there, making no attempt to hit the drum. So, I tell him, 'Look, when my arm goes across like this (I demonstrate) that is when you really hit the bass drum.' At this point I had him practice by himself, hitting a very loud forte stroke on the bass drum. Again, when we came to this passage, he did not play. Now I walked back to show him the place in his music and I then discovered he had no music! When I asked him about this, he responded that he did not read music. At this point, with the concert rapidly approaching, I told him to 'just do your thing, whatever you do with your own band.' So during the concert, in every composition, there were random forte bass drum explosions here and there throughout the concert!

No teacher had bothered to teach this student how to read music and I have wondered how many other percussion students have shared his fate since I once found another such instance in a college band in Georgia. It is a consequence of a national music education philosophy driven by activity and commerce and not by music education.

There was one guest engagement which everyone told me would be very challenging, but was not. This was the national honor band and the national honor orchestra of Israel. Colleagues told me it would be chaos, and that the students were so unruly that nothing could be achieved. Since I always work from memory I am capable of working very fast—much too fast, I suppose, for anyone to make trouble. Both ensembles played superb concerts. I have always had the impression that after several hours of rehearsal young people have most of the music memorized on some level. Often I will ask an ensemble to close the folders and then announce that we will now perform one of the compositions. I have even done this in concert. In Israel, in rehearsal, I managed to get the orchestra to play the third movement of the Dvorak *G Major Symphony* without music. The coaches, members of the Israeli Philharmonic, were quite amazed.

---

[24] Once, in 1975, I did a music camp sponsored by the City of Berkeley and, as a temporary employee, I was required to take an oath of allegiance to the city.

There are some things quite different in working in Israel, beginning with your host wearing a gun when he meets your plane.[25] And when you leave, the national airline, the most security conscious one in the world, does not give you a departure time. They will say only, 'Your flight departs between 2:00 and 5:00.' So you sit in the lobby and at some point an announcement is made that your flight is loading for immediate departure. All this, of course, is for security, so that no terrorist can plan in advance on shooting the plane on take off.

There are some honor band engagements which are a challenge. One was a district honor band in California, consisting of a Friday evening rehearsal, one Saturday morning and then following lunch a one-hour 'dress rehearsal' and a concert. After the last full rehearsal the host band director tells me that he thinks the program is too short and that we should add one more composition. I was quite taken back because we had remaining only one one-hour period to 'touch up' details and I already had more than enough to do in that one hour. How, I asked him, with the time remaining can we add a new work? He replied, 'Oh, I have something in the office we can pass out and they will be able to do it with ten minutes rehearsal.' 'Fine,' I said, 'I agree as long as you conduct it on the concert.' So after lunch he brings out a typical product of the educational publishing industry trash, a constructed work based on idioms familiar to the students (most of these educational works all sound pretty much the same). My philosophy in such honor bands was to play works and styles the students would *not* have played in their own bands. So I usually programmed Wagner and Strauss and artistic compositions which, as a consequence, were not all tutti but had thinly scored sections where one could actually hear instruments like oboe and bassoon. So, as the reader can foresee, in the following concert his conducting produced a perfect razzle-dazzle performance while my compositions retained flaws due to the lack of rehearsal time and the difficulty of the material. I'm sure the audience concluded that he was the better conductor!

I also recall that in the initial call regarding this engagement it was explained that there was no set fee. Rather I would be given the entire box-office receipts, which would probably be adequate if one multiplies perhaps two hundred parents by such and such a ticket price. I agreed. At the end of the concert an elder lady comes into my dressing room carrying a cash box, one of those gray steel boxes resembling fishing tackle boxes. I had a large brief case, made for large scores, and she took that cash box and dumped the contents into my brief case. I was spending quarters for a month!

I have always separated potential repertoire for school bands into two categories: 'constructed' music, such as the above, produced by music publishers, and 'inspired' music. On one occasion I was invited to be the guest conductor of a district honor band in Walnut Creek, California. In this case I was to spend an hour guest conducting each of six individual high school bands of the district in their individual rehearsal halls and then have a very short honor band rehearsal of a band made up of students in the six bands. We were to prepare only one brief composition, which would be the conclusion of a concert consisting of the performance of two compositions by each of the six bands.

---

[25] Two armed local conductors who admired my work followed me everywhere, day and night, armed to protect me.

I agreed to this format, providing all twelve of the individual scores were sent to me at least three weeks in advice so I could study them before visiting the six bands. All twelve scores sent me were of the 'constructed' category and I can still recall thinking as I look at them, 'how in the world will I fill an hour with music with these two scores [times six].' The concert was very interesting. The audience sat through twelve performances of 'constructed' music and rewarded the students with the normal parent-like, disinterested applause. My honor band, concluding the concert, consisted of six minutes of Wagner; six minutes of inspired music—real music. Although we did not perform this music very impressively due to the minimum amount of rehearsal time, the audience went crazy—it was like a rock audience. It was powerful testimony to the difference between real music and constructed music.

Some honor bands, of course, are pure pleasure and one of these for me was the 1973 Wisconsin All-State Band. This was a carefully organized event and carefully auditioned to produce an outstanding ensemble. The largest work I conducted with them was the Husa, *Apotheosis of this Earth*. Rehearsing without scores, as is my custom, these rehearsals drew wide attention, which in itself is unusual as usually the band directors go off and talk and never watch their guest conductors. One of the conductors who heard about this performance was William D. Revelli, who, at the following Mid-West Conference in Chicago, grabbed me and dragged me to his bedroom to find out my 'secret.' He was quite disappointed to learn the 'secret' was score study.

More than thirty of the students in this Wisconsin All-State Band wrote me letters after the event. Here is just a sampling of these comments, comments which I think any guest conductor would appreciate reading.

> Wow! I'll never forget your directing. Thank you. I loved *every* minute of rehearsal.
> Sue Eatough

> I started losing interest in music, but after this I don't think I'll ever forget it. Thanks.
> Becky Foster

> I know now what music is really like and must go out and try to create it myself.
> Dane White

> It was really an honor and a privilege playing under your direction. I've never seen any man so wrapped up in music. Dynamite!
> Ginger Wright

> Playing under your leadership abolished my preconceived idea about conductors' use of scare tactics to produce good music.
> Sally Wencel

> I really enjoyed having you as our conductor. You're really a great musician and this was truly a great musical experience for me and I shall remember it for the rest of my life.
> Cindy Falteisek

And finally, from a member of the audience, a member of the All-State Choir.

Thank you for the thrill you have given the tenors and me this afternoon. Your efforts in preparing the Husa are very commendable. The genius and skill of the composer's vision, as conveyed through your involvement, will stir the perceptions of listeners—as it did us.

    We had come from a very hot and sweaty rehearsal. As you began the second movement I became chilled with excitement and amazement. As the music became more compulsive and intense I could see 'goose bumps' on the bodies of others in the room. It was a most electrifying experience.

    Rodney Witte

PART IV
In Memory of Frederick Fennell

Fennell As I Knew Him

FREDERICK FENNELL, 1914–2004, was an institution before any of us knew him. He, as a student, had organized the first concert band at the Eastman School of Music in Rochester, NY, in addition to a marching band! Since its inception Eastman has been the most elite music school in the US, with no small credit due to the endowment left by George Eastman, the developer of the Kodak camera. Fennell told me once that when Howard Hanson, the director of the school, went to Eastman to ask for the money to build the school in his name, Eastman told him, 'I have just one request. Remember that every dollar of mine that you spend is a dollar that can only be spent one time, so please spend it on quality.'

Fennell had gone to Eastman as a percussionist, but that is where he learned and became inspired to conduct. Eventually, after he was added to the faculty, he was also assigned some conducting with the second orchestra at the school, generally beginning with pop concerts. He developed rapidly and soon was inspired to become a professional orchestra conductor. He was accepted into a special school for conducting at the Mozarteum, in Salzburg in 1938. But no sooner had he arrived than Hitler marched into Austria on March 12 which resulted in the closure of Fennell's program and his residence there. In reflecting about this in private with me he was deeply disappointed in this development as he was then age twenty-four and young enough that something might have developed for him in Europe.

Fennell and I had this in common. I too had lost out on a great opportunity, having been accepted for an intern program with the Vienna Philharmonic in the opera program but had to turn it down for lack of requisite piano skills. We both felt that we were drawn to professional conducting, but we both lacked the financial support to get us started and we both lacked the mentor to open the doors. We had many long private discussions on this subject, our remaining goals and, from time to time, our disappointments.

Fennell returned to Eastman where his founding of the Eastman Wind Ensemble in 1952 proved to be a great step in his career. He told me that this resulted from his despondency over the available repertoire for his concert band at Eastman, bands at that time playing mostly very low entertainment music. He began to walk the aisles of the Sibley Library, one of the great music collections in the US, where he first came upon some music of Gabrieli. He described himself to me as being astonished that this music existed and that he did not know it existed. It was finding, in the library, works such as this that was the true germ for the development of the wind ensemble. To play such works with the large concert band meant a very large number of students were not involved, causing additional administrative problems. Since even with a smaller 'wind ensemble' some students would not be used for the performance of a Renaissance work, it followed that the whole idea of the wind ensemble was one of flexible instrumentation. Fred was amused in later years, or so he told me, that the instrumentation he used for his first concert was taken by later conductors as an official part of the definition of the Wind Ensemble. In the same way the particular seating plan most conductors associate with the wind ensemble was a manifestation of what sounded best in the smaller concert hall at Eastman, not the result of a philosophical study.

During the Eastman years Fred generally attended the various band director organizations, including the ABA. But he told me he was rather ostracized in part because his involvement in the profession was so different and because of his youth. He told me that when he first became a member of the ABA the members would not even speak to him, with the sole exception of Albert Harding, of the University of Illinois, who Fred remembered as a very kind and candid person.

Beginning with his creation of his new wind ensemble and the almost immediate opportunity to begin making his many recordings with that group, Fred was enjoying a great, and in some ways the best, ten-year period of his career. But, lurking in the back of his mind was that ancient dream of becoming a professional conductor and it would now cause him to make a mistake, a mistake, however, that almost any of us would have probably made.

Major orchestras in the US are under the control of wealthy people, often well-intentioned people with just enough knowledge of music to give them the self-confidence to form personal preferences in music. They are very much like those aristocrats of old in Europe who would demand their servant—composers write the kind of music they liked. One such person became president of the board of the Minneapolis Symphony Orchestra and had seen Fred do a pops concert somewhere and with the best of intentions wanted to broaden the activities of his orchestra by hiring Fred to help reach a wider public.

The president of the board had the authority to hire Fred for a two-year period, the same period of his own tenure, and so he did, in 1962. This was a well-known orchestra, one which had made its own recordings and one which had launched the career of Eugene Ormandy, and so Fred, believing in himself, considered this a rare opportunity and took the job. He would later tell me that this was the most significant mistake of his life, that he did not stay at Eastman.

The first problem was that the president of the board had not told anyone about his new assistant conductor, not the board and not the conductor, an old world Polish man. The principal conductor, therefore, had nothing to do with Fred and I do not believe that in two-years time they ever had a single conversation. Since the principal conductor also held the position of director of music, and created the schedule for the orchestra, he planned nothing for Fred to do. Fred hung around, tried to do a bit of PR for the orchestra by visiting schools, etc., but did very little conducting. The president of the board regretted the problem he had created, apologized to Fred and reminded him that his two-year contract could not be renewed.

So, Fred had no choice but to begin to look for a job. He was not invited to return to Eastman so he wrote letters to the heads of the music departments of the ten best universities in the US and not one even answered his letter. When Fred was describing this to me, years later, he was still in pain and disbelief that with his great recording success and being only fifty years of age that not one person was interested. And, he told me, he had not specified a conducting position. He would have taught percussion or music appreciation or anything.

It was at this time, in 1963, that I first saw Fred. I was in my first year at the University of Montana and he came to town at the invitation of the Montana Band Directors Association to give a conducting clinic. He asked for an additional quantity of music stands and spreading them around the back of the hall in a great semi-circle he placed one of his recordings on each stand for the conductors to see. It was an ostentatious and, combined with his public plea that he was looking for a job, sad sight. I was not so interested in Fred at this time anyway because along with his recording of great literature there were an equal number of marches, etc., which to me gave the appearance of a man who did not really believe in playing fine original repertoire, something I was beginning to become very interested in. He mentioned later that that was part of the deal. Mercury Recording would only do an album of basic band repertoire if it were accompanied by an album of marches, which was the money-maker. While he was in Missoula, therefore, I do not recall even making the effort to meet him.

At this moment, in 1964, the dean of the school of music at the University of Miami called Fred and offered him the position of conducting the university band and orchestra and, of course, Fred accepted. This particular music school had bought into creating a jazz program, one of the few at this time, and this, with the general party-school reputation of the university and the town made this position a poor fit for Fennell. He had to take it, of course, but he was not only miserable but trapped. He would be there for twenty years without an offer to go elsewhere! A report back to me from one of my own students who went there to work on a DMA in 1977 comments on the sad scene at Miami.

> Fennell is sincerely and passionately committed to his position as an educator, as I'm sure you realize, but the students either don't know how, or don't want to try, to meet him halfway, so that the quality which I can see as intensity in him, impresses the students as fanaticism of the worst kind …
>
> As for the quality of the wind orchestra here, it is not what we are/were used to at Northridge. Many of the soloists are on or close to a par with the principals at CSUN (except the horns which are putrid beyond words), since graduate students play in all the ensembles, but the quality thins out somewhat more quickly after that in several sections. On the whole, their level is perhaps slightly above CSUN's second group, if the horns are tacet! Yuk!!

Although in time Frederick Fennell was to become a close confidant, the earliest letter I had from him, in January 1965, took me to task for not giving due credit to the Eastman Wind Ensemble and its recordings in an article I wrote called, 'Three 20th Century Crises in Band Repertoire.' Of course one must take into consideration his present situation, the failure of the Minneapolis job, his unsure future and his deep resentment that he had ever allowed himself to leave Eastman. In my own defense I could say that the subject of the article was focused on the years before the Eastman Wind Ensemble was founded, but he was right and in retrospect I realized I should have acknowledged him and the ensemble and I wrote him an apology to that effect.

If truth be told, by 1965 I did not know much about the Eastman Wind Ensemble. I recall it was a forbidden subject while I was a student at The University of Michigan in 1955–1959. In fact I recall a party at the horn professor's home (he had played horn in the initial Eastman

Wind Ensemble program) where he played some of the recordings for us and implied that we were doing this at his home as he was under some hesitation discussing the subject at school. Then, from 1959–1963 I was in the US Air Force Band, a period of very heavy concert and tour requirements and an environment far removed from the academic world. So, I was, in fact, 'behind the times' in 1965 with respect to putting the Eastman Wind Ensemble in perspective. As I reread his letter today, I find it very interesting and I have included some of his specific comments on my article as they contain fascinating observations.

Frederick Fennell to David Whitwell
Excelsior, MN, January 25, 1965

Dear Mr. Whitwell:
I have read and re-read with considerable interest your paper, 'Three 20th Century Crises in Band Repertoire …'

It is both an interesting and historically vivid approach—the crisis—and while I approached the subject as critical in my little book, *Time and the Winds*, it is obvious that we share the same concerns which we feel spring from the observations of history.

Perhaps you also know that I am convinced from that history that the name of the group has been a major deterrent to the 'acceptance' of the wind medium by composers of the first rank, and although you elect to ignore both the existence of the Eastman Wind Ensemble and its recordings as musical and educational factors which '… would enable those of *us* (italics mine) active today to take advantage of our present opportunity.' I wonder if you really mean to cut us out of your view of history?

In so doing, you have denied yourself a valid point and ignored the only guide to playing—as well as to what to play—that the wind band movement has really ever had in this country. It has been, and remains, a consistent commitment; in the discs is an undeniable commitment and I am amazed that it escapes you. Perhaps you'd like to tell me why—at least I should like to know.

Here are page and paragraph observations of 'Crises':

I/1. Don't let yourself and 'those of us' in for the blast that you deserve in 'relegating' Stravinsky's strings to percussive utterances. In doing so, you show your ignorance of the pedals at all layers upon and through which are hung 'the melodic duties' of the winds. I know what you mean, you just didn't say what you mean; further—you ignore the incredible and historically vital use of percussion instruments in the whole orchestral texture …

I/3. Are you positive it was a competition Goldman started? The out-right commissions are infinitely more important, and—as you also know, he never conducted them. I feel that on top of page 2 you must include a repertory blast at Harding, for it was his kind of concerts that set the whole pattern for A. R. McAllister & Company and thus for the school band movement in America. While you are calling spades, you may as well make them jet-black. 99% of your readers won't know what you're writing about in the areas 1920 to 1938 if you don't.

II/3. Why not lift your observations of the P. & C. Book and make it into a separate evaluation of that kind of influence. I wish Dick Goldman really liked the band, but he does not—and it shows.

III/top. Think you should mention that it was the service band that led this parade of transcribers into their way of life …

IV/2. Line 5: suggest you strike article 'the' from the sentence; the government means the Federal establishment to too many people. If you simply say—government, you are not only correct, but convincing. Perhaps the band is too free to perform the music of its choice—that is, the poor, uneducated, inexperienced-in-the-art-of-music bandmaster is too free to perform his own choices. Nothing ever progressed that was immune to criticism! That is the sad state of institutional music-making in schools and colleges.

IV/last. How can you fail to see what the Wind Ensemble's recording do every day in this direction? ...
If you do not have my book, please let me send you one.

Cordially yours,
Frederick Fennell

The first occasion we had to actually spend time together was at a meeting of the Eastern Division of the CBDNA which was held in Rochester, NY, in 1972. I recall that Bob Wojciak, of USC, and I flew to meet Bob Reynolds at the home of his mother and then the three of us drove together to Rochester. At this conference I conducted the Eastman Wind Ensemble in a performance of the Wagner, *Trauermusik*, and I recall Fred, who was seeing me conduct for the first time, enthusiastically exclaiming, 'Don't change a thing!' This carried over three weeks later when Fennell was visiting with James T. Matthews at the University of Houston, who wrote me, 'I was visiting with Frederick Fennell the other evening and he spoke of you very highly.' Husa was also present at my rehearsal in Rochester and wrote,

> And above all, I was most impressed by your tremendous conducting technique, when I saw you rehearse at Eastman ... I was looking at your very economical gestures, simple and exact way of explaining problems to the band; I thought it was most effective.

On this conference program at Rochester I also did a clinic introducing some representative Harmoniemusik works which I had found in Vienna. Fred, in a letter of May 3, 1972, mentioned, 'I was very taken with the Salieri things which you did so convincingly in Rochester.' Another conductor present, Prof. Willis Traphaghan of Lowell State College in Massachusetts wrote of this clinic,

> I thought that your workshop was by far the highlight of the convention! You have opened up a whole new area of literature for me. I will start rehearsals on the Krommer *Partita* next week and I'm anxious to get at it.

When I became vice-president of the CBDNA in 1974 I appointed Fennell and four other past presidents to a task force to study and make recommendations on the question of Ethics. The chair was William D. Revelli, and nothing ever came of this task force with the exception of some views by James Neilson, which have been quoted earlier in this book.

In February 1975 the CBDNA had its national conference in Berkeley, CA. Fennell turned up at the last moment and could not get a room in the motel we were using some distance from the campus. But I had an extra bed in my room and immediately offered to him. He refers to this in a note which is very characteristic of his expression at this time.

Dear David,
Thanks for taking me in and for such pleasant hospitality beyond that! Things look up for your biennium [as president], and—I hope for all and especially for you professionally. We had no chance to explore so many by-ways, including where you might go should you get and choose to accept an invitation among those open. Again, if my recommendation be not the kiss of death, please call. Anticipating May and Mozart and with love to the family from Lynne and
FF
PS. Many thanks, safe journey, a warm bed, endless drumbeats—magnificent releases!

The reference to May and Mozart was a reference to my invitation for Fred to guest conduct the Mozart, *Gran Partita*, K.361, on my campus as part of my hosting the National Wind Ensemble Conference at California State University, Northridge. Immediately after this conference I wrote a letter to Fred which I should like to quote as it documents the inspiration I always had for his work from the time I became acquainted with him.

Dear Fred,
I want to thank you for your contribution to the Wind Ensemble Conference. Needless to say, the various groups who had an opportunity to perform with you were thrilled beyond description. I want to say, personally, that I not only learn something every time I see you but I am filled with desperation to do my work better and to try and reach some day the musical standards which you have set for all of us. I am always astonished at the musical results whenever you conduct.

A couple of days later Fred, in turn, wrote a note of thanks which included some very interesting information associated with the forming of the Eastman Wind Ensemble.

Dear David:
In the mad rush of getting back and picking up activity on this end I have neglected writing you my thanks for your many courtesies during the Conference. It is too bad we didn't have more time to be with each other but yours was a great responsibility and a mire of details without which obviously an affair like that doesn't work. You certainly made it work and we all very much admired your Planning *and* execution.[1]

Your particular interest in and devotion to the repertory which you elected to conduct afforded everybody there the chance to really hear some things that were totally new out of a distant past. Your groups were considerate and patient with all of the visiting firemen and it must have been quite a weekend for them.

I'm sure you have had a report from Reynolds about our visit to the desert [to visit with Ernst Krenek] which was very worth it to us all.

I am sorry that summer plans do not include the possibility of seeing you and all of the family, for they both [my wife, Giselle and son, Stefan] looked just great. I don't know how much I can in any way contribute to the CBDNA Biennium, but what I am able to do I will.

The 25th Anniversary of the Wind Ensemble concurring with the CBDNA National Meeting is something I suppose you will want to work out with Hunsberger. That first rehearsal, incidentally, was on the 20th of September, 1952. The debut concert (our first activity was to record six one-hour broadcasts for the rural radio network and the New York State School Music Association) consisted of the Bb Mozart *Serenade*, the Wallingford Riegger *Nonet for Brass* and the Hindemith *Symphony*; the concert was played on Sunday afternoon, 8 February, 1953.

---

[1] In a letter to James Neilson, in June, 1975, Fennell referred to 'some brilliant conducting by Dave.'

Again, thanks for your imaginative hosting of the Sixth National Wind Ensemble Conference.
Best Wishes,
FF

During 1975, in addition to organizing the National Wind Ensemble Conference in Northridge and as president of CBDNA and beginning to organize their 1977 conference, I was also doing much guest conducting. Among these was the Illinois Summer Youth Music band at the University of Illinois. I received some remarkable letters from the student members and the following one from the director of the camp.

> Dear David
> On behalf of the Illinois Summer Youth Music of 1975, may I extend thanks and appreciation for the musical inspiration and leadership you brought to the Senior Concert Band. Your impeccable musicianship, devotion to high musical standards, and brilliant conducting endeared yourself to the students and the staff. It was refreshing to see the students so 'high' on music culminating in a superb final concert.
>
> If my compliments sound profuse, it is because I meant them to be. It was our pleasure having you on the U of I campus
>
> Sincerely,
> Dale Kimpton

William D. Revelli had been hearing reports of my guest conducting and in Chicago that winter he dragged me to his hotel room and demanded I tell him the secret of my learning these difficult scores from memory. He refused to believe it was the product of study, so I instead talked to him about the new clinical research then coming out on left and right brain hemispheres of the brain and the importance of learning the music in the right hemisphere as well. When I left he was wearing his usual frown but several weeks later sent a note referring to this discussion.

> Dear Dave,
> I shall never forget our 'visit' in Chicago—It was a most interesting and stimulating discussion.
>
> I am trying to develop the left side and right side. Hopefully not *versus* each other.
>
> Your assistance is very much appreciated. I regret often that we are so far apart. There are so many things to discuss and to learn about.
> Bill

I have included the above Revelli note primarily because a letter from Fennell at the same time also mentions the same conference in Chicago and gives a hint that Fennell was still not regarded as one of the Old Guard of the band profession.

> Dear David,
> Frank Battisti and I were together last week-end and he told me about the Chicago scene, and I would have liked the chance to reaffirm beliefs with you in person. Nobody is likely to know you any other way than the wonderful way in which we behold you—so hang in there all the way!

As soon as I get back from San Antonio where Revelli and I have the two groups, I'll call. We possibly won't see each other until the concert, and since it is always difficult to converse, I'll not pursue him in any case! Since the lines have been clearly drawn, I'll once again have to let my work and its thought speak for me.
FF

In April 1976, a few months later, there were two letters from Lynne Fennell regarding trying to find time to come by and visit me in Los Angeles. I place these letters here because they indicate the busy life Fred was living at this time, references to his passion for sailing and mention of his displeasure with the final concerts of the year at the University of Miami.

Lynne and Frederick Fennell to David Whitwell
Miami, FL, April 14, 1976

Dear Giselle, Dave & Stefan,
It was great hearing from you Dave—but we're so sorry to hear that you were back in the hospital. I hope your leg problem has cleared up and you're all well by now.

We're writing to let you know that we'll be stopping off in LA on our way home and would love to take you up on your offer if it is still good. And Fred would love to come work with your group. But most of all we'd like to be with you three. It's been too long since we've all been together …

We're sorry we can't come see you before we go to Hawaii—but Fred's schedule is terribly busy. He is leaving for Madison this Sunday—Easter. He'll be there one week and home for a few days till we go to Hawaii. The Minnesota Orchestra will be here on Monday the 26th so we'll be taking some of them out sailing on Tuesday. Then Wednesday Fred is putting on a professional Wind Ensemble concert, with Trust Fund money.

I've been doing a little professional playing lately—I also had a church gig on Palm Sunday—at a church on Key Biscayne. We sailed over there and docked at the Yacht Club—where Will Ludwig keeps his boat. He was there that day and took us out for a spin on his 63 foot power yacht. We had a lovely afternoon out on the ocean …

Fred gave his last Wind Ensemble concert on Monday—and today he gave his last orchestra concert for the year … He wasn't too pleased with the Wind Ensemble concert—felt they forgot too much he had taught them. But the orchestra went real well.

We leave for Hawaii on Thursday, April 29 and fly into LA that night with only a two hour lay-over. We'll give you a call then … We're sure anxious to see those beautiful islands … How was your last trip over there? Have you any suggestions for things to see—please let us know …

Here are the details for our return trip from Hawaii … I hope your schedule isn't too busy that day so we can see you all. Please let us know if these plans can coincide with yours? We have to leave LA on Saturday the 15th …

Fred has a new assistant [Fred adds in his hand, 'who is very good, indeed, and a great help]—Bill Nicholls from Cal State at Fullerton. He's working out so well—Fred's really pleased with him. He's a good friend of Gene Corporon and the Reynolds …

We'll be seeing Bob Reynolds and Margie this summer in Ann Arbor—for his conducting symposium. We'll be at Interlochen again and in Madison for the conducting clinic.

We've been sailing as much as we can this year. The weather has been weird—much colder than ever …

[In Fred's hand] Lovely people, we *need* your address at the new digs and home phone number—and we hope you have found something out about that unspecified illness/whatever it is you have. Be looking for a call from a guy named Anderson from Seattle who sounds like he's made for study with you.

The Williamsville Wind Ensemble Conference drew *no* conductors, but those that brought their groups (good) had a good week-end.

Things finished here today with *Leonore III,* Brahms *Schicksalslied*, M-R *Pictures*—pretty good for a mostly no talent group and small number of upper strings.
FF

And a few days later.

Lynne Fennell to David Whitwell
Rockville Centre, LI, NY, April 19, 1976

Dear Giselle, Dave and Stefan,
It was so nice talking with you Dave on Easter Sunday. Right after you called, Fred called me to say he was still in Miami—his plane had a fuel leak …

Well, when he called I told him about your idea of having him conduct the Krenek *Symphony*. Well he was very excited about that, but he said he hadn't conducted it in many years and would have to study the score again. But he thought that would be a great idea and he told me to find him a flight that would get him into Madison … so it's all settled—you don't have to worry about conductng that piece—he'll do it.

I'm really anxious to see you three … It would be terrific to take a camping trip up to Sequoia and see the redwoods … It's a beautiful state—you're so lucky to be living there. I'd move in a second if Fred got job offer (so would he) …

We're sure looking forward to being with you and seeing Krenek. I've never met him—it will be an exciting concert. Anxious to see your new house.

Much love,
Lynne

The reference above was to a special concert we gave at California State University Northridge, performing all the wind ensemble works of Ernst Krenek to celebrate his seventy-fifth birthday. As it turned out, Fred's schedule did not permit him to prepare the *Symphony*, so I conducted that and Fred did the Krenek marches. Lynne wrote the following letter after this concert and of particular interest are the comments about the creation of a dinner theater in Miami, for which Fred would be the person in charge of entertainment. Fred at this time felt his career was over and this dinner theater was going to be the center piece of his retirement. Fennell invested heavily in this project which folded soon after it opened, leaving Fred in financial difficulty. All this well before any thought of Japan.

Lynne Fennell to David Whitwell
Miami, FL, ca. May 20, 1976

Dear Giselle Dave & Stefan,
We had such a marvelous time with you both last weekend. I'm looking forward to seeing you all again in August. I hope you're feeling better by now, Giselle. This year is not the year for you to be sick—with another baby on the way.

I sure enjoyed being with Stefan—he is so adorable. It must be a real pleasure to have him around. He is so well behaved and so smart. He's a real jewel.

Fred really enjoyed conducting the *3 Merry Marches*. He especially enjoyed hearing your groups, Dave. They are excellent musicians—and it looks like you are definitely on your way to be the most outstanding California school …

And now that you've reached that high standard of quality—you can be very choosy and only take the top notch students. It must be a thrill to watch a school grow and evolve, and to know you have helped it do that. That is quite a reward in itself.

I enjoyed meeting the Kreneks. They seem like lovely people and am sorry we couldn't spend more time with them.

We just got together with our partner in this 'Dinner theater' adventure, and I'm going to be very busy it seems. I'm looking forward to doing whatever I can to make this thing go. We're well on our way thanks to Larry, or lawyer partner. He has found a lot of money and people to help back it, and he has done all of the detail work. We're hoping to break ground by August—so we can possible open the doors by Xmas ... that's really very soon. But this is quite an exciting project and we all feel strongly that it will make it OK. And then once we get this one going and well established—then we have big plans to build one in Honolulu ... and go retire there. Aren't those lovely dreams? ...

I wish there were some tiny college that would ask Fred to come teach ...

Frederick Fennell to David Whitwell
Miami, FL, May 26, 1976

Dear David,
We are home safely after a long journey, which had the happy addition of our visit with you.

I was genuinely impressed with the rapid strides which have been made on all sides at Northridge, beginning with recruiting and the inevitable final evidence of that in the extremely high standard of performance which is emerging there. I was impressed with their handling of styles, and pleased with their reaction to Krenek. It was great to see him again and to find him not missing a thing at age 76, in spite of the absence of vision in one eye and hearing in one ear. His pieces stand as positive contributions, not alone to the neo-classical inspiration of the Stravinsky time—which of course they are, but as positive reflections of a musical conviction that is still present in what he's doing today. Your simply masterful memorization of the symphony was a plus in its performance, and I hope that you will have put that on some sort of tape and disc for us all to have.

I urged his wife to urge Boonin to make *Kleine Blasmusik* available for sale, and I hope you will urge Boonin to do the same.

My brief opportunities to peruse *Dream Sequence* convinces me, as it does you, that this is a very successful commission [of the CBDNA].

In the Fall of 1976 I asked Fred to write a Foreword for a publication by MENC of papers from previous CBDNA conferences. Excerpts from his letter, and an addition by Lynne, follow.

Frederick and Lynne Fennell to David Whitwell
Miami, FL, November 22, 1976

Dear W's,
I've found the perfect somnolence: reading that CBDNA Source material. I'm up to page 117—those endless dumb papers on instrumentation and Revelli's Junior High prose will one day be just plain embarrassing to many ...

[In Lynne's hand]
Congratulations!!! That's so exciting—your new boy sounds very healthy (7.7 lbs. Wow) ...

I played some tennis this morning … Fred and I get out about once a week. Dave are you playing much tennis now? Or is school too busy this year. Glad to know this is your best group so far. Fred hasn't been pleased with his wind ensemble. But he has some hope for the orchestra …

The closing for the property for our dinner theater will take place this Monday—so then they can start building soon—it's getting exciting now. Larry (our partner) says after we make our million on this one, we'll build one in Los Angeles. Then one in Hawaii …

In 1977 we had the national conference of the CBDNA at the University of Maryland, a conference I designed as president. For years there was observed a rule that no school could perform at a national CBDNA unless their group was called a 'band.' Many older members were frightened by the new Wind Ensemble movement. I broke that barrier in 1975 when I selected performing organizations for the conference in Berkeley and again in 1977 which I built an evening around a performance by the Eastman Wind Ensemble, then celebrating their twenty-fifth anniversary. Fred was very grateful.

Dear David:
I trust that you already know from what little but pleasant time we had together there, that the Maryland Conference was one in which you honored us all, and greatly. The fact that you could and did initiate a quarter-century observance of my old group within the CBDNA is the sort of purely artistic judgment not always present in such Associations. Thank you.
FF

With the failure of the dinner theater, and Fennell's subsequent significant financial loss, he was reduced to taking every conducting offer which came along, even Junior High School honor bands. One can easily sense his depression in the following letter.

Frederick Fennell to David Whitwell
Coral Gables, FL, Feb. 14, 1978

Dear David:
I have had three weekends of the past four that really bother me, David. All of them involve junior high players that were assembled for 'Honor' Bands, and in all three instances the musicianship of every group was *nil, zilch, niente*, nothing! I could not achieve a thing! Last weekend in Enid at Phillips University's Northwest Honor Bands, a junior high band could not get started at the concert with *Totem Pole*, Osterling's easy march, and after we did get started, they played in the most miserable, non musical, non articulate fashion to the end. A second junior high band was no better, being unable to play the 'O Sacred Head' Chorale Prelude of Latham's *Three*. In a Region IX Honor Junior Band in Spring, Texas they had a good sound, but that was all. I had to teach them to play crescendo, diminuendo, play forte, piano—closed doors to them! At an 'Honor' band in McNeese State, Louisiana, it was the same scene with high school kids.

So, I am beginning to withdraw from this scene, to leave the field to the young men who need to find out what 'honor' bands really have become …

School is better than in some years. Sorry my 'retirement' scene is what it is; in two years I'll be ready for anything.
Best wishes,
FF

In a letter of April 26, 1978, Fennell mentions the successful completion of the DMA work by one of my former students. Speaking of his situation at the University of Miami he recalls, 'I warned them both that there was nothing here, but they had to come to find that out.'

He speaks more of his retirement and then mentions his historic recording with the wind players of the Cleveland Orchestra in making the very first digital recording.

> When I do retire, I'm not so sure there will be much still left here for anybody to pick up, but at least we can see our way to 1980. I've warned everybody that I'm going out with Beethoven IX even if I have to do it with a chamber orchestra and mini chorus!
>
> My new recording with the Cleveland Symphonic Winds (all of the orchestra, plus) will be the first Digital tape record for symphonic repertory in the US. Did it there April 4–5. Bach G Major *Fantasia*, Handel *Fireworks*, the two Holst *Suites*. Due out in the Fall in the $15.00 version and around Christmas at Bb analog prices.
>
> The recording for TESARC, a Cleveland group called Advent Recording Co. of Ohio … Direct disc is now passé—its time of the digit—all 50,000 of them every 36 per second on 16 tracks!

In a letter threes later, Fred speaks again of his coming retirement.

> I do not plan to live anyplace but here, David, unless something is offered. And I do not expect that offers will come.

But an offer did come, out of the blue, in an occurrence reminiscent of Wagner, when at his last resources, was rescued by Ludwig II, the period of Fennell's long suffering at Miami suddenly and unexpectedly came to an end with his invitation to become conductor of the Kosei Wind Orchestra in Tokyo. I can still recall how happy I was when he informed me of this, for I knew this invitation would result in his rejuvenation. And so it did.

I was in Tokyo and heard his second concert with this new ensemble. It was a rough performance, but I could see he had the player's attention and I knew it was just a matter of time before he built another fine Wind Ensemble.

Fred maintained his Siesta Key residence for use when he returned from Japan visits. A letter of April 5, 1991, includes interesting comments on competitions.

> Dear David:
> I have accepted the recent suggestion of the John Philip Sousa Foundation to sponsor what will be called the 'Frederick Fennell International Young Conductors Competition.' That's kind of high-sounding for me, but much consideration of a viable alternative leads to its acceptance, too. And although I have not completely abandoned a long-held belief that competition is for race horses, it has become apparent in recent years that the validity of purpose and the critical factor of thrust make me join the force that both discovers and promotes young people destined for worthy and oh-so-elusive podiums.
>
> Wishing to do this through the winds medium we will need the service toward decision of people who may wish to join me in a jury selection, and I hope that you may find it possible to do so.
> Sincerely yours,
> FF

In 1992 I began a trial effort at an autobiography and sent it to Fred to look to get a first impression. He said 'Don't change a thing,' but at the same time I appeared I hit a sensitive topic with him.

Dear David:
Please know how much your confidence in me does mean to me. I devoured both parts of your autobiographical beginnings. First—you transported me to times & places that I knew of but second-hand, having felt that the University of Michigan's so-in-need-of-the-past-of-the-profession 'Director of Bands' should solely represent the institution! Sadly, [Revelli] never meant very much to almost anybody ... You have been kind to Revelli; wait until you read some sort of memoir by one of those kids he really crucified!

When back in Florida much of his time was now spent in creating new editions of wind ensemble music, one of which was the Mozart, *Gran Partita*, K. 361.

Frederick Fennell to David Whitwell
Miami, FL, January 10, 1993.

I've just finished proofing the part for Oboe II in the new edition. It has been the most marvelous excursion into the 'process' of a great mind. The music goes only where we now know it has to go—and I'm especially writing about the *Adagio* where every note is so charged with emotion, is *so absolutely Right!*—and so hauntingly beautiful. I'm sure you know that this had to be *the real* reason why I had to start the Eastman Wind Ensemble for Eastman players—and now for so many others. The edition will have 19 parts including Bb's for Bassets, F's for Bb horns, contra, string contra, contra clarinet, that's 956 bars times 19, and there goes my January, 1993, and no better possible place for it. Engraving already has us close to $10,000, which we'll never see returned, of course. This is *my* piece!

After re-recording many of the familiar band works with the Kosei Wind Orchestra in Tokyo, Fred got the urge to record some chamber works, especially works from the *Harmoniemusik* repertoire. The following is a very interesting letter regarding one of these efforts.

Frederick Fennell to David Whitwell
Tokyo, April 24, 1993

Hello David,
I need your help with information I can quote about Beethoven's Symphony VII and its authorized version for 9 instruments (which we record today), and about Joseph Triebensee who did the Haydn Nr. 92; that and the 1st mvt of Mozart #39. Those two are recorded tomorrow.

I need page numbers from your books if you can spare time. KOR wants my liners *yesterday*, of course, and with all of the editing for those three pieces, writing-conducting-narrating 4 scripts for a video, rehearsing for 2 CDs of 32 marches has kept me without sleep for days. I recall much that you wrote of the early 19th century.

I felt I *had* to do a lot of [?] restoration of the Beethoven original without destroying what got published by Edition Compusic/Amsterdam—a terrible computer job. The players preferred it over the mss one I bought from you.

I will be critically interested in your reaction to this CD. The Haydn works well, too and so does the Mozart when I got the intro back in his full-scales-way.

It is a great reverse ... instead of transcripting the Beethoven 7th for the 108 piece Michigan Symphony Band—here we are reducing Beethoven's great and extensive orchestral masterpiece—to 10 player chamber music!

Just to give you an idea how tough that is, with player and mike placement it has taken 2 1/2 hours to record the 1st movement! At players' request, after this 15 minute break we will begin and record that impossible 4th movement. Wagner may have called it 'the Apotheosis of the Dance,' but with our terrific clarinet players hurting from the hundreds (it seems) of [measures quotation of passage work] we will spot record IV and make the engineer and editor cover for us, something I've never done until this; But I still have the great Scherzo and Allegretto to get in the can. It is now past 16:00 and I just listened to the final takes. MY GOD! such uncompromising music—the expression 'No Place to Hide' was meant for this glorious music, and all 10 players (I added our magnificent strong contrabass player with his gorgeous Josef Gagliano Italian instrument—and I'm very glad I did—all insisted on the most minute retakes.

Now comes the Allegretto and we have only 47 minutes to get it and the Scherzo. E-gad m'lad.

Our principal clarinetist has a good C instrument which he used for the above music example—then switched to the Bb. It is the toughest piece for all. This session goes until 8:00 so we still have 1 hr & 20 minutes left for the incredible Scherzo. Everybody listening well and players have been picky, picky ... guaranteeing a good Beethoven.

I can't get over this switch from large orchestra to chamber players. One liability very difficult to handle: contrasts. It is difficult to get dynamic spread as with the regular players of the wind orchestra—of course, the symphony where the large body of strings can deliver that unison or octave pianissimo *just not possible* with 10 players. As it is I moved the horns some 18 feet back from the rest to let them produce with the intensity that you—as a horn player know just *comes* with the horn sound. It worked so that they still had presence, without inundating the rest.

Ima [illegible] Hall where we're doing this is a fine small hall where we also did Mozart. It has a [illegible] stage allowing me to move the oboes, clarinets & bassoons farther out into the hall. I can't wait to hear the final result.

And not only the horns need to play at intensity—so do the rest. [After a comment on the clarinets having to play without rest in these arrangements] I'm surprised that they had *anything* left for the Scherzo, but they were stronger than ever at the end of the session, as is very common with all TOKWO players.

And, David, there are *no problems* in this group. No prima donnas, just very serious and 2,000% professionals.

We have our new oboe player, finally after 1 1/2 years of search and audition. What a baptism of fire—Beethoven, Haydn, Mozart! He's equal to it all and he is very young, graduating from gai dai in June. Our old player with the wide vibrato must have been guilty of many breaches of TOKWO conduct, including divorcing his wife for a young pupil, being late for rehearsal, losing his instrument in restaurants, trains—whatever. As you may know from me, this like the L.S.O. is a very democratically operated ensemble—all is 100% by vote. And the oboe player Maekawa, fellow student at gai dai, buddy to all first chair players—they just voted him *out*.

Our new player is a Tabuteau 'descendent,' and his tone more accepted by everybody.

I am here and asked back only because the players think so. I have had your name in as a guest ever since they asked Craig. You & Reynolds are the ones I want to see come. Obviously Alfred Reed has his way paid by his publisher and Southern Music obviously paid for Jim Barnes ...

And—there just are *not* the men available in the States you would think can make it with this group! Huns doesn't seem to have much sympathy for it and Paynter's been here; I think they'd find Battisti OK.

We've just finished Haydn 92, I, II—such a world of difference from the Beethoven of 1812/13 and the Haydn of 1788—a quarter century for such a change in the writing of a symphony—even the demands on players—certainly the presence of a leader of some sort—and the time span for the listener.

When Beethoven approved the 9 player version he cut the development of Mvt IV, and there some others. All 450 bars of I are here, and all 278 bars of II are in our CD. III got slashed by 232 bars mostly repeats, absence of the second assai meno presto. The original 653, this in 421 with the development of IV gone there are 354 of the original 467.

All the Mozart is here and the Haydn has some strange cuts, but it is simply wonderful to hear in this chamber music version. We've just finished Haydn and are on a 40 minute break. Next: Mozart. I just couldn't [keep] the scales that weren't Mozart's and I added the [two thirty-second notes] before the contra [cadence notes]—as an old kettledrummer, I could not do without them!

Mozart finished at 5:50, and all happy with what was played. Me too! One of the best things about our non-union recording here is the time factor. Unlike the States where the old 2 hour symphonic session at the EWE, the LA Phil, etc. was 40 minutes of recording, 20 rest each hour, here we arrived at time for the session to begin at noon and end at 7:00. 7 hours—and this affords the playback, time that the EWE never had, and doesn't have. It is our plan in a tough piece like Beethoven VII to make all the stop and rest and listen places. They learn so much in the playbacks of course—who doesn't?

Like Fred I had also grown tired of flying to remote places to do honor bands, for it always seemed to me that one gives so much more than one gets on these occasions. In my case I began to use the resulting time to write more and I always sent my things to Fred to proof read. Responding to one of these projects he wrote,

Frederick Fennell to David Whitwell
Sarasota, FL, Nov. 19, 1993

Dear Sir David,
Before the rest of this year slips away, as it is so certain to do before I can do half of what I'd like to, these words of thanks for your sharing with me all those incredible life experiences! These, together with whatever you choose to pursue, make you one of the most facile writers—with something to say that all of us need to read ... I can't imagine the 2nd half of the 20th century—without you and what you have given to all of the rest of us. No changes, please.
Affectionally,
FF

My university gave me a sixtieth birthday concert, after which I sent the program to Fred.

Dear Sir David,
Thanks for sending that great 60th Birthday-type concert ... Your great career is incredibly drawn out on those pages—beneath your two portraits. Don't stop anything!
All good thoughts for you.
FF

In 1998 I sent Fennell a copy of my new conducting book which resulted in several letters from him commenting on discussions which he particularly liked, among them the following:

Frederick Fennell to David Whitwell
Saratoga, FL, May 19, 1998

Leafing thru Chapter 17, on programming, it exposed exactly in Plato's words, pp 210–211, the scene with Rock—more than exposed—it explodes! Allowing the society of them—Lord knows *who* today would speak it with the power to have it received? I'm so glad it is in your book.

And again a week later.

Frederick Fennell to David Whitwell
Saratosa, FL, May 25, 1998

Again I found myself reading your great conducting book. It is, of course, unique and extraordinary in the way that this expression was generated to be. Among those, stating this as purpose, there is none like this one known to me.

During his final years we began to communicate by phone as it had become more difficult for Fred to write letters. I recall one occasion when he called me when he was in a state of panic for he found himself, in walking through his apartment, running into things, sofas and chairs and it frightened him greatly.

On his final day he requested to be moved from a medical care facility back to his apartment because he wanted to see the sun setting over the ocean one more time. His daughter told me that she heard him ask, 'Where is a drummer? I can't go without a drummer.' And then, 'There he is! Now I can go.' And so he did.

About the Author

Dr. David Whitwell is a graduate ('with distinction') of the University of Michigan and the Catholic University of America, Washington DC (PhD, Musicology, Distinguished Alumni Award, 2000) and has studied conducting with Eugene Ormandy and at the Akademie für Musik, Vienna. Prior to coming to Northridge, Dr. Whitwell participated in concerts throughout the United States and Asia as Associate First Horn in the USAF Band and Orchestra in Washington DC, and in recitals throughout South America in cooperation with the United States State Department.

At the California State University, Northridge, which is in Los Angeles, Dr. Whitwell developed the CSUN Wind Ensemble into an ensemble of international reputation, with international tours to Europe in 1981 and 1989 and to Japan in 1984. The CSUN Wind Ensemble has made professional studio recordings for BBC (London), the Köln Westdeutscher Rundfunk (Germany), NOS National Radio (The Netherlands), Zürich Radio (Switzerland), the Television Broadcasting System (Japan) as well as for the United States State Department for broadcast on its 'Voice of America' program. The CSUN Wind Ensemble's recording with the Mirecourt Trio in 1982 was named the 'Record of the Year' by The Village Voice. Composers who have guest conducted Whitwell's ensembles include Aaron Copland, Ernest Krenek, Alan Hovhaness, Morton Gould, Karel Husa, Frank Erickson and Vaclav Nelhybel.

Dr. Whitwell has been a guest professor in 100 different universities and conservatories throughout the United States and in 23 foreign countries (most recently in China, in an elite school housed in the Forbidden City). Guest conducting experiences have included the Philadelphia Orchestra, Seattle Symphony Orchestra, the Czech Radio Orchestras of Brno and Bratislava, The National Youth Orchestra of Israel, as well as resident wind ensembles in Russia, Israel, Austria, Switzerland, Germany, England, Wales, The Netherlands, Portugal, Peru, Korea, Japan, Taiwan, Canada and the United States.

He is a past president of the College Band Directors National Association, a member of the Prasidium of the International Society for the Promotion of Band Music, and was a member of the founding board of directors of the World Association for Symphonic Bands and Ensembles (WASBE). In 1964 he was made an honorary life member of Kappa Kappa Psi, a national professional music fraternity. In September, 2001, he was a delegate to the UNESCO Conference on Global Music in Tokyo. He has been knighted by sovereign organizations in France, Portugal and Scotland and has been awarded the gold medal of Kerkrade, The Netherlands, and the silver medal of Wangen, Germany, the highest honor given wind conductors in the United States, the medal of the Academy of Wind and Percussion Arts (National Band Association) and the highest honor given wind conductors in Austria, the gold medal of the Austrian Band Association. He is a member of the Hall of Fame of the California Music Educators Association.

Dr. Whitwell's publications include more than 127 articles on wind literature including publications in Music and Letters (London), the London Musical Times, the Mozart-Jahrbuch (Salzburg), and 39 books, among which is his 13-volume *History and Literature of the Wind Band and Wind Ensemble* and an 8-volume series on *Aesthetics in Music*. In addition to numerous modern editions of early wind band music his original compositions include 5 symphonies.

David Whitwell was named as one of six men who have determined the course of American bands during the second half of the 20th century, in the definitive history, *The Twentieth Century American Wind Band* (Meredith Music).

A doctoral dissertation by German Gonzales (2007, Arizona State University) is dedicated to the life and conducting career of David Whitwell through the year 1977. David Whitwell is one of nine men described by Paula A. Crider in *The Conductor's Legacy* (Chicago: GIA, 2010) as 'the legendary conductors' of the 20th century.

> 'I can't imagine the 2nd half of the 20th century—without David Whitwell and what he has given to all of the rest of us.' Frederick Fennell (1993)

About the Editor

CRAIG DABELSTEIN began studying the piano at age seven and took up the saxophone at age twelve. Mr Dabelstein has Bachelor of Arts (Music) and Bachelor of Music degrees from the Queensland Conservatorium of Music, where he majored in the performance of classical saxophone repertoire. He also has a Graduate Diploma of Learning and Teaching and a Graduate Certificate in Editing and Publishing from the University of Southern Queensland.

He has held the principal alto and tenor saxophone chairs in the Australian Wind Orchestra and has been an augmenting member of the Queensland Philharmonic Orchestra, the Queensland Symphony Orchestra, and the Queensland Pops Orchestra. For many years he was also a member of the Queensland Saxophone Quartet.

He has been a casual conductor of the Young Conservatorium Symphonic Winds, and has previously been a saxophone teacher at the Queensland Conservatorium of Music. He is a regular conductor of the Queensland Wind Orchestra, having served as their artistic director and chief conductor from 2004 to 2009.

Craig Dabelstein is a research associate for the *Teaching Music Through Performance in Band* series of books, contributing analyses to volumes 7, 8, 1 (rev. edn), and the *Solos with Wind Band Accompaniment* volume. He served as the copyeditor and layout designer of the *Australian Clarinet and Saxophone Magazine* from 2007 to 2009 and he has written many CD and book reviews for *Music Forum* magazine. He is the editor of the second editions of the books by Dr. David Whitwell including *A Concise History of the Wind Band*, *Foundations of Music Education*, *Music Education of the Future*, *The Sousa Oral History Project*, *Wagner on Bands*, *Berlioz on Bands*, *The Art of Musical Conducting*, and the *Aesthetics of Music* series (8 volumes) and *The History and Literature of the Wind Band and Wind Ensemble* series (13 volumes). From 1994 to 2012 he was a staff member at Brisbane Girls Grammar School. He now teaches woodwinds and conducts bands at St. Joseph's College, Gregory Terrace, Brisbane, Australia.

www.ingramcontent.com/pod-product-compliance
Lightning Source LLC
Chambersburg PA
CBHW081354230426
43667CB00017B/2827